VISITING
THE MIDWEST'S
HISTORIC PRESERVATION SITES

To Pann — good tripping

Rosemary

MARJORY & URI GRANNIS
AND ROSEMARY & GEORGE HALE
Foreword by Nancy Stevenson

Visiting
The Midwest's
Historic Preservation
Sites

JAMESON BOOKS, INC.

Ottawa, Illinois

Contents

Foreword

THIS is an invitation to adventure and discovery. For residents in or near the Chicago area, it is a challenge to "know thyself." Based on the premise that we need not go elsewhere to find history, the authors have created a guidebook to lure people into looking at an area of the midwest, a region often ignored, certainly underappreciated, for travel, study, beauty, architectural treasures, and a sense of our past and our future.

Within these pages there are hints of great sagas, clues to the mystery of community evolution, stories of family settlement and separation, indications of the bravery of lone pioneers with hopes, fears, or a new idea. We who live in the great center of our country often forget that many of our highways retrace Indian paths, or that a supermarket may sit on what was once a vast, empty prairie. The early settlers brought their roots and their values with them, so that Mineral Point, Wisconsin, has miners' cottages reminiscent of Cornwall, and Galena, Illinois, shows traces of New Orleans. Carpenters copied Doric columns, Gothic arches, and Italianate brackets out of books to create beautiful houses in these settlements on the edge of the wilderness in this region of the new Republic. Yet new concerns created change. The balloon frame house and the prairie plow grew out of the midwest experience. They too shaped our cities and our landscape. And the newcomers kept coming, carrying the signs of their past, their work, and their dreams.

This book is a useful beginning for exploring the rich midwestern heritage. The authors have limited the range to roughly 250 driving miles from Chicago. They have focused on designated historic districts, both official and unofficial. They give introductory information about each area with explicit suggestions for places to stay and eat, and they even include sources to call for further information. There is, of course, much more for you to see than they have been able to cover in this book. In Illinois, for instance, there are Marengo, Pontiac, Oregon, and Quincy, to mention just a few, and the sixteen-sided barn on the way to Rockford, and the three experimental round barns just beyond Freeport, and much more.

Remember, as you go, that history is everywhere. It doesn't stop or start at a magic date. It can be found in the small house as well as the mansion; in the fence, or lack of it, along the highway; in the way the furrows are tilled and the factories are built. This is a tool for delight and discovery.

Nancy Stevenson

Introduction

America is young no longer; we have a past. The Constitution was signed more than two hundred years ago, and many of the states are even older. Middle America is middle-aged, vital, strong, independent, and proud. How did these virtues develop? To answer this question, we began exploring the history of towns around Chicago: in Indiana, where canals carried early settlers; in Illinois, the cradle of the Republican party; in Michigan, the great lumber region; and in Wisconsin, home of the early trappers. In all these states we found towns that have preserved the labors of the past. History shows in the stores, homes, churches, and courthouses, cared for and restored by people who take pride in the past and in where they live and whose towns have prospered through renovation.

The area covered in this book falls roughly within 250 miles of Chicago but does not include the metropolis itself,Milwaukee,or Springfield, both of which are the subject of many good studies. All directions assume a Chicago starting point. All the districts described either are on the National Register of Historic Places or have been carefully studied by a community group that has not sought outside direction.

In an effort to make trip planning easier, towns that are close to one another are grouped together. To ensure that we cover the same information for each historic district, a standard format is used. The architectural tour is to be taken primarily on foot, for we think that this is the best way to view the environs. You can approach the area from any point, but the guide is organized to start and end at the same place—one where parking is available. Each district has a map as well as descriptions of the most notable buildings from an architectural standpoint.

When you are walking through a commercial downtown, look up. The first floors have usually been remodeled many times. The upper floors, however, are often original and include highly varied bay windows and turrets. Watch for elaborate window trim, brackets, and cornices. Many of the facades are fanciful cast-iron panels which show the changing commercial tastes during the last half of the nineteenth century. In the residential areas the earliest remaining buildings are of Federal style. Greek Revival architecture was very popular in the mid-nineteenth century, followed by the grander Italianate and the highly ornamental Queen Anne styles, which may range from small to very large with porches, balconies, turrets, and bay windows. By the beginning of the twentieth century the variety of styles had increased, with many revivals from Romanesque to Colonial, as well as the American prairie style of the Chicago school.

Our tours are self-directed. Many of the areas have house tours or festivals that may be of interest to those who want to see the interiors of the private dwellings. Most of the buildings are private residences, and the interiors can be seen, if at all, only as part of a tour. Dates of tours and festivals are included when available, but it is wise to contact the organization listed to be sure that there have been no changes.

Although much information about the historic districts is summarized, in some cases there is considerably more available. In the next section of each tour we have included the names, addresses, and telephone numbers from which further information may be obtained.

The last section of each tour is a selective list of lodging and restaurants in the various areas, with addresses and telephone numbers.

This guide was written because we could not find information about historic midwestern architecture in one book. Our discoveries opened our eyes to the history and beauty of a region that many wrongly believe to be a flat plain with little of architectural or historical interest. After visiting these towns we hope that you, like us, will feel enriched by your journeys.

PART ONE

Day Trips

Cedarburg

OZAUKEE COUNTY
Wisconsin

CEDARBURG was on an Indian trail that ran from the south end of Lake Michigan to Green Bay. In 1634, the French Jesuit missionary Jean Nicolet passed through the area; he was followed by French traders and trappers for the next 150 years. Indians pushed westward from the original English colonies supplanted native Indians in the region, and after the Blackhawk War ended in 1832, both the Menominee and the Potawatomi Indians ceded their lands to the Federal government. In the 1830s and 1840s, English, Irish, and German pioneers started to settle in the region, and German tradition in particular persists to this day. Cedarburg recently celebrated its 100th birthday with a month-long demonstration of its carefully restored mills, inns, shops, and houses. The centerpiece is the Cedarburg Settlement's Old Wittenberg Woolen Mill, now housing shops and restaurants.

Directions

Cedarburg is a pleasant one-day trip from Chicago. Take Interstate 94 north from Chicago to Milwaukee. Then take Interstate 43 north fifteen miles to the Cedarburg exit, which is also County Route C. Drive west four miles to State Route 57. Turn right, or north, and you will enter Cedarburg on its main north-south street, Washington Avenue. The historic district begins south of Hamilton.

ARCHITECTURAL TOURS

Cedarburg's Washington Avenue is a multipurpose area containing residential, commercial, religious, and industrial buildings. Park on Hanover Street at its junction either with Turner or with Center and proceed by foot. The town's novel numbering system was imposed by the fire department to facilitate the location of fires.

NORTH TOUR

The five blocks from Columbia to Elm will take less than an hour to cover on foot. 1. The Hilgen-Schroeder mill store is a three-story

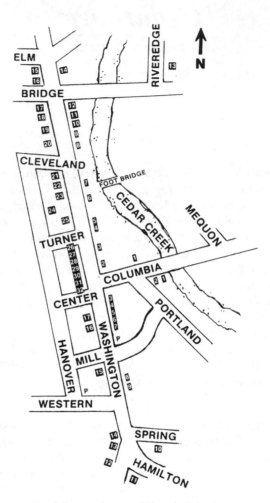

Washington Avenue Historic District,
Cedarburg

Greek Revival brick building erected in 1856. This structure, at W58 N6194 Columbia Road, was one of the first commercial buildings in the town. 2. The original Hoehn furniture store and residence, located at W62 N582 Washington Avenue, is a cream-colored brick building with gables, a bracketed cornice, and stone windowsills. 3. The handsome Italianate limestone three-story commercial building at W62 N588 Washington Avenue was erected by the Lehmann brothers in 1874. 4. E.G. Wurthmann's building at W62 N592–94 Washington Avenue was erected in 1888. This rather modest Queen Anne commercial building features a decorated pediment. 5. The Armbruster jewelry store at W62 N620 Washington Avenue was built in 1906; it is one of the three oldest in the state. Its white terracotta veneer facade is divided by pilasters, and it has a central entrance. The second story has a garland frieze band. Although an ornamental pediment has been removed, the facade and interior of this building are little changed. The cast-iron sidewalk clock is a Cedarburg landmark. 6. The Greek Revival single-story-plus-attic limestone house at W62 N628 Washington Avenue was built by Henry Roth. A one-story brick L-shaped addition is covered by a gable roof which extends over the porch and runs the length of the wing. Before the next stop, take a detour east to the Milwaukee Northern interurban iron bridge spanning Cedar Creek. It offers a good view of the creek and its mills and dams. 7. At W63 N642 Washington Avenue is the Advent Lutheran Church. This limestone building, a combination of Romanesque Revival and English Gothic, was built in 1909. 8. At W63 N664–66 Washington Avenue is a house built by John Roth in 1870. The style is Greek Revival with Italianate window treatment. 9. The Friederich cobbler shop and residence at W63 N670–72 Washington Avenue is a cream brick two-story building. Erected in 1873, it is distinguished by its arched windows. 10. The Italianate building at W63 N676–78 Washington Avenue was built for August Weber. This 1860 L-shaped Italianate stone house has a corner porch and bracketed roof. 11. The combination Greek Revival and Italianate stone building at W63 N684 Washington Avenue has its original windows and bracketed eaves. 12. The Groth building at W63 N692–98 Washington Avenue was constructed in 1876. The two parts of the building are differentiated by two original cast-iron fronts complete with cast-iron columns. One of the earliest commercial buildings, this is a fine example of vernacular Italianate architecture. 13. The Cedarburg brewery, across the river one block east on Riveredge Drive, is one of the oldest breweries in southeast Wisconsin. The three buildings date from 1848. Across the street west of the brewery is Boy Scout Park, with a seating area overlooking the dam on Cedar Creek. 14. The old Hilgen-Wittenberg-Trottman woolen mill at W63 N700 Washington

Avenue has been renovated. Its seven Greek Revival buildings face Washington or Bridge Streets and were built between 1864 and 1873. Next, cross Washington Avenue and walk south. **15.** The Boehme residence, W64 N717–19 Washington Avenue, is an 1864 Greek Revival stone house. **16.** Diedrich Wittenberg's residence at W64 N707 Washington Avenue is a fine example of vernacular Italianate style. The bracketed eaves are original, but the windows and the one-story wraparound addition on the north and west are recent. **17.** The Queen Anne Roth Hotel, constructed in 1888 at W63 N697–99 Washington Avenue, has a fine facade with a central entrance topped by a pediment and divided by pilasters. The second story has a corner bay window, and the first floor has arched windows reminiscent of the Romanesque Revival. Most of the facade is original. **18.** The simple cream brick Queen Anne house at W63 N681 Washington Avenue was built in 1860 by Godfried Bruss. **19.** A far grander house of the same style, built in 1898, is the Leopold Jochem residence at W63 N675 Washington Avenue. This house has a bracketed roof, a two-story bay, another two-story bay with a turreted and gabled roof, a large third-floor gable, and a wraparound porch. The materials are also varied, as is common with this style, and include shingle siding, wooden moldings, terracotta, and various window materials. **20.** The Maronde residence at W63 N667 Washington Avenue was built in 1880. This cream brick structure is Greek Revival but with Italianate windows. **21.** Herziger's meat market, W63 N653–55 Washington Avenue, was built in 1904. Its architecture is Eclectic with an Italianate cornice, second-story Queen Anne bay, and Classical corner entrance. **22.** The cream brick Queen Anne residence at W63 N647 Washington Avenue was built in 1907 for Fred Schuette. This L-shaped house has an entrance porch, windowed gables, and a two-story bay. Many of the windows are cut glass. **23.** The 1908 high school at W63 N645 Washington Avenue is much like the adjacent public school. Known locally as the Washington Building, it has a tower and is constructed of stone with Classical touches in the form of pilasters, brackets, and arches decorating its facade. **24.** The Cedarburg Public School at W63 N643 Washington Avenue was designed by architect William Hilgen in 1894. Its dominant feature is a five-story tower flanked by two-story-plus-attic gabled wings decorated with bargeboard. This massive limestone building, one of the town's landmarks, is called the Lincoln Building. **25.** The George Fischer house at W63 N627 Washington Avenue was built in 1848. The Greek Revival two-story section is original; the one-story stone addition was built in 1864. **26.** Hoffman's meat market at W62 N599–601 Washington Avenue is a two-story commercial building constructed of brick and stone. **27.** The German Free School was built by Conrad

Horneffer in 1855. This Greek Revival limestone building at W62 N593–95 Washington Avenue has had its original windows enlarged. **28.** William Schroeder built the Queen Anne house at W62 N591 Washington Avenue in 1885. As is typical of this style, the first-floor facade is clapboard, the second floor and attic shingled. A projecting window with decorative canopy distinguishes the latter. A graceful corner porch decorated with carpenter's lace protects the entrance. **29.** The Juergen Schroeder residence at W62 N589 Washington Avenue was built in 1870. This plain cream brick house has an ornate front porch decorated with scroll-cut gingerbread and cast-iron cresting. **30.** The Juergen Schroeder building at W62 N583 Washington Avenue has a facade similar to the Henschel-Jochem building (31). It is an Italianate structure made of brick. **31.** The Hendschel-Jochem building at W62 N577 Washington Avenue is an Italianate-style building with bracketed cornice and lunette (eyebrow) windows in the attic. Its storefronts have been much altered. **32.** Washington house, at W62 N573 Washington Avenue, was built in 1886. Its facade is embellished by a central bay, parapets, and cornices.

SOUTH TOUR

This walking tour takes less than an hour. It begins at the corner of Columbia and Cedar Creek and proceeds south about five blocks. Start on the east side of Washington and return on the west side. **1.** The Cedarburg mill, N58 W6181 Columbia Road, built in 1855, is a limestone five-story structure built by Frederick Hilgen and William Schroeder. It is remarkable as an example of nineteenth-century industrial design. The Cedarburg Landmark Preservation Society restored this Wisconsin landmark, the oldest functioning mill in the state. It is listed on the Historic American Buildings Survey as well as the National Register of Historic Places. **2.** Wadham's at N58 W6189 Columbia Road is a unique structure. Designed by architect Alexander Eschweiler in 1926, it has a distinctive brown pagoda roof and Japanese lanterns suspended from the cupola roof. **3.** Built on the site of Market Square at W62 N572–78 Washington Avenue is a commercial building erected in 1904. It has a rock-faced stone facade and a simple entablature crowning the top. **4.** The State Bank building, erected in 1908 at W62 N570 Washington Avenue, has a Romanesque Revival facade divided by pilasters into three units, topped by a smooth stone entablature. **5.** The Grundke residence, located at W62 N562 Washington Avenue, is a Greek Revival brick house with five windows on the second story and two on each side of the center entrance. This 1853 house has been enlarged and remodeled. **6.** The Queen Anne house at W62 N560 Washington Avenue has a three-story chimney, decorative wood trim on the front gable, and beading accenting the arched front porch. **7.** At W62 N550 Washington Avenue, smooth stone lintels, entrance, and quoins contrast with the heavy stone walls. **8.** The Central House Hotel at W61 N520 Washington Avenue was constructed before 1855. The dormer of this Greek Revival limestone building was added in the 1880s. **9.** The Immanuel Evangelical Lutheran Church, erected in 1882 at W61 N498 Washington Avenue, replaced an earlier building. This limestone Gothic church has a prominent steeple with two bells. The stained-glass windows are particularly fine. **10.** One block east in the next block south at N47 W6033 Spring Street is Frederick Hilgen's frame Greek Revival house. This fine house has a two-story front porch resembling those found in South Carolina. **11.** Returning to Washington Avenue, St. Francis Borgia Catholic Church stands at the intersection of Hamilton Road and Washington Avenue, dominating the streets' view. A fine Gothic church, it has Romanesque windows and doors and was built in 1870. **12.** Frederick Hilgen's earlier house, built about 1850, is at W61 N439 Washington Avenue. Originally frame, it was later covered with brick in front and limestone rubble on the sides. Because it was built before the street was laid out, it slants at an odd angle. **13.** John Nieman built the Queen Anne house at W61 N469 Washington Avenue in 1907. Not only is the house outstanding, but the lot is well landscaped. **14.** Another Queen Anne-style building is the commercial structure at W61 N493 Washington Avenue. Built in 1885 as the Conrad Wiesler Hotel, it is made of cream brick with a frame third floor. **15.** The Wirth building was constructed in 1871. This Italianate limestone building at W61 N513 Washington Avenue has a fine triangular pediment and protruding cornice. Although it has been painted, its stone texture is apparent. **16.** The Lauterbach building was constructed as a clothing store in 1865. This Italianate structure is located at W62 N553 Washington Avenue. **17.** The Kuhefuss Union House Hotel at W62 N555–59 Washington Avenue was built in 1883. Its facade is decorated by a pediment, pilasters, and carved floral motifs on its arched windows.

Festivals, Tours, and Other Places of Interest

The Chamber of Commerce sponsors the Stone and Century house tour in early June, 414–377–1317. Historic Cedarburg Area Tours are provided for groups on a half- or full-day schedule. Contact Mary Denis, Landmark Communications, W62 N591 Washington Avenue, Cedarburg, WI 53012, 414–377–4113. Ozaukee County Pioneer Village is a collection of fifteen buildings dating from 1840 to 1907, completely refurbished including barns and outbuildings, open to the public, noon–5:00 P.M. Wednesdays, Saturdays, and Sundays, from the first Sunday in June to the second Sunday in October

(Sundays only after Labor Day), and located on the north edge of Hawthorne Hills Park, ten miles north of Cedarburg on Highway 43 and County Route I, 414–692–9658. Cedarburg Antique Show, end of October at the Cedar Creek Settlement, 414–377–8020. David C. Uihlein Racing Car Museum, a collection of antique racing cars dating from the 1920s, open Wednesday–Saturday, Memorial Day–Labor Day, 10:00 A.M.–5:00 P.M., and Sunday 1:00 P.M.–5:00 P.M., is housed in Turn Halle one mile southeast of downtown on Hamilton Road, 414–352–2100. Cedarburg Cultural Center, Dr. Robert Teske, director, W63 N643 Washington Avenue, P.O. Box 84, Cedarburg, WI 53012, 414–375–3676.

Historical Information

A Walk Through Yesterday in Cedarburg, Wisconsin by the Cedarburg Landmark Commission. *Washington Avenue Historic District, Cedarburg, Wisconsin* by Edward A. Rappold. Ozaukee County Tourism Council, P.O. Box 801, Cedarburg, WI 53012. Cedarburg Chamber of Commerce, P.O. Box 204, Cedarburg, WI 53012, 414–377–9620. Ozaukee Historical Society, P.O. Box 206, Cedarburg, WI 53012. Cedarburg City Hall, Cedarburg, WI 53012, 414–377–4500. Cedarburg Public Library, Cedarburg, WI 53012, 414–377–1730.

Lodging

Stagecoach Inn, W61 N573 Washington Avenue, 414–375–0208 or 414–375–3035.

Washington House Inn, W62 N573 Washington Avenue, 414–374–3550.

Restaurants

Barth's at the Bridge, N58 W6194 Columbia Road and Cedar Creek, 414–377–0660, handicapped accessible.

Creme and Crepe Cafe, Cedar Creek Settlement, 414–377–0900.

Finks' Public House Restaurant, W61 N497 Washington Avenue, 414–375–2212.

Neville's on Washington, Columbia Road, 414–375–4850, handicapped accessible.

Tomaso's Italian and American Restaurant, Cedar Creek Settlement and Bridge Road, 414–377–7630, handicapped accessible.

Woolen Mill Inn, Cedar Creek Settlement and Bridge Road, 414–377–7111, handicapped accessible.

I:2
Beloit

ROCK COUNTY
Wisconsin

THE Rock River, running north and south, splits the city of Beloit in two. Originally known as the Winnebago's Turtle Village, Beloit's first white settlers arrived in the mid-1830s. A French Canadian trapper and trader named Joseph Thiebault, or Tebo, depending on sources, built a cabin at the junction of the Rock River and Turtle Creek in 1835, followed by Caleb Blodgett, who arrived in 1836. He and other industrious New Englanders largely shaped the town's physical and social character. It received its name in 1837. Beloit College, the town's chief landmark, was chartered in 1846.

Directions
One of the south-central Wisconsin historic towns, Beloit is an easy one-day outing from Chicago. Or, it can be combined with other towns in the area for a weekend tour. Take Interstate 90 northwest from Chicago to the South Beloit exit, State Route 75. Go west to U.S. 51, Dearborn Street; turn right, or north, onto it, and continue along 51 to Park Street. Turn north, or right, onto Park to Bushnell and turn left. Across from the First Congregational Church you will find limited parking.

ARCHITECTURAL TOUR
The Near East Side Historic District is the main attraction, although you may also want to drive through the Bluff Street district on the west side of the Rock River. The Near East Side is a quiet, tree-lined area anchored by Beloit College on the west and the First Congregational Church on the southeast. The earliest buildings date from the 1840s. Italianate and Queen Anne styles predominate, but there are also early Colonial Revival and Prairie School buildings. You can walk through the district in about an hour. 1. Horace White Park is named for physician Horace White, leader of the New England Emigrating Company, who promoted emigration from New Hamp-

shire, and whose religious fervor led him to have his patients pay their fees by building the Congregational Church. The village green was part of the original 1837 plat. In 1898 O.C. Simonds, a well-known landscape architect, designed it as a park. 2. At 822 East Grand Street, facing the park on the south, is the Church of St. Thomas the Apostle. It is a fine example of late Victorian Gothic Revival. 3. Across the park is the First Congregational Church. This structure dates from 1859. Cream brick, called Milwaukee brick, was used in the construction of this Greek and Romanesque Revival church whose central square tower now ends in a wooden cupola. 4. At the northeast corner of Park and Bushnell, number 905, is the fine white clapboard Italianate Newcomb house, built in 1869. It has a porch across the front, which is topped by a balustrade. 5. On the northwest corner of Bushnell and Harrison is the Queen Anne Reitler house, built in 1892. It is rather plain for a Queen Anne house, but it does have a three-story porch on the south and a tower as well as two other porches. 6. At 703 Park is an Italianate white clapboard house built in 1869 for Sereno T. Merrill. It features a tower, entrance portico, and fine cornice. 7. Across the street at 746 Park is the C.A. Dazy house, which reflects the Eclectic architectural taste of the period during and after World War I and is reminiscent of the Prairie School. This house is a combination of modern brick masonry on the first floor and Tudor-esque paneling on the second. 8. In the next block north at 802 Park is a glorious example of the Queen Anne style. Its massive gables, conical tower, bay windows, and elaborate porch are distinctive. 9. Next door at 808 is an example of Eclectic and Prairie styles in a house built in 1906 by E.L. Philhower. The most remarkable features are the six piers, four in front and two in the rear. The cornice shows Egyptian influence. 10. Across the street, the Noble Ross house at 819 is another fine example of the Queen Anne style. It was built in 1896. A long pillared porch stretches across the front; above it is a massive bay window; on the third floor another bay forms a tower with a conical roof. There are also gables, dormers, and a side porch. 11. A block north and west on Church is number 905, built in 1893. Although it shows traces of Queen Anne and Colonial Revival, it is best described as Eclectic. 12. A block south on the other side of the street at 824 is a simpler Gothic Revival cottage, built in 1858 by Thomas D. Bailey. Notice the carpenter's lace, or bargeboard, outlining the front gable. 13. The more opulent Elijah J. Kendall house at 818 Church was built in 1860. The Italianate house features an ornate bracketed roof, window trim, and entry porch. 14. William Hamilton built 805 Church in 1905. The dominant features of this late Queen Anne are the massive three-story tower and the sweeping front porch, but it also boasts a two-tiered back porch and gables. 15. In the next block south on the

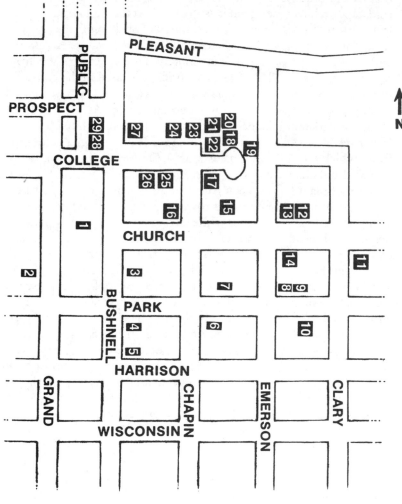

Near East Side Historic District,
Beloit

west side is 732 Church Street, another Queen Anne house that was built in 1894 for Charles Emerson. Prominent architectural features are the fanlike siding accenting all three gables and the columned front porch. **16.** Half a block south at 722–24 Chapin Street is a two-story frame Italianate house built by John B. Pfeffer. The house was obviously added to over the years. It has nice carpenter's lacework decorating the porch and bay windows. **17.** A block west and a bit north is 709 College Street, the residence of Aaron Lucius Chapin, Beloit College's first president. The architect was the well-known Racine, Wisconsin, designer, Lucas Bradley. Built in 1851, it was originally a Greek Revival house with some Italianate features. It was extensively remodeled in 1937, removing most of the embellishments and leaving only the bay windows, roof line, and chimneys of the original. **18.** Cross the street and enter the college campus where you find the Richardsonian Romanesque chapel named for the second college president, Edward Dwight Eaton. **19.** Slightly northwest is the early Classical Revival brick Campbell Hall, built in 1854 and also designed by Racine architect Lucas Bradley. Despite numerous remodelings, including the addition of a portico in 1940–41, it retains its original classical lines. **20.** Pearsons Hall, built in 1891–92, is a monumental Romanesque Revival structure, the only work in Rock County of the Chicago architect Daniel Burnham. Its facade has not been altered. **21.** Further south is Middle College, the original college building, which was constructed in 1847–48. In 1939 its Second Empire embellishments, added in 1879–80, were removed, and it was returned to its original Greek Revival style, except for the addition of a massive portico, which seems to dwarf the facade. The building is best seen from Chapin Street. **22.** Just to the east are effigy mounds dating from 500 to 1300. They are not burial grounds, but some contain artifacts. **23.** South College, originally constructed in 1858, was a building adapted from designs by Racine architect Lucas Bradley. The recessed windows and the blind arches are original, but the roof, pediment, and upper center window are later additions. **24.** South on College is the stately Pettibone World Affairs Center, built in 1904. Designed by the Chicago architectural firm of Patton and Miller, it is a fine example of a Classical Revival public building. Its entry, supported by large Corinthian columns, is impressive. **25.** Across the street at 647 College is the Brimsmade-Blaisdell house, built as a one-story vernacular cottage in the mid-1850s. This much-altered building is actually three houses joined together. **26.** Next door at 635 College is the Jesse McQuigg house, built before 1857. This Greek Revival house is the finest example of this style in Beloit. **27.** Across the street is Memorial Hall, a fine Victorian Gothic structure, built in 1869. **28.** A. Gillespie built the house at 516 College in

1870–71. This massive house has a large, gracious front porch and is truly an Eclectic structure. **29.** Around the block at 517 Prospect Street is the Rasey house, built in 1850. It is important as an example of a cobblestone house, popular in New England, New York State, and Ontario, Canada.

Festivals, Tours, and Other Places of Interest

The Beloit *Daily News*, has tours at noon and 12:30 Monday–Friday, 149 State Street, Beloit, WI 53511, 608–365–8811.

Historical Information

Beloit Historical Society, publishes *Pioneer Beloit* by Arthur Luebke, $16.50, Lincoln Center, Beloit, WI 53511, 608–365–7835. Beloit Historical Museum, open Wednesday–Sunday, 1:00 P.M.–4:00 P.M., April 1–October 31, 2149 St. Lawrence Avenue, Beloit, WI 53511, 608–365–3811. Michael Gerecki, Planning Department, City Hall, Beloit, WI 53511, 608–364–6700. Beloit Chamber of Commerce, 126 West Grand Avenue, Beloit, WI 53511, 608–365–8835. Richard P. Hartung, Rock County Historical Society, 10 South High Street, Janesville, WI 53547, 608–756–4509.

Lodging

Dillon Inn, 2790 Milwaukee Road, 608–365–6000.
Holiday Inn, U.S. 51, Rockton, IL 61072, 815–389–3481.
Ike's Motel, 114 Dearborn Avenue, 608–362–3423.
Plantation Motor Inn, 2956 Milwaukee Road, 608–365–2501.
Wagon Wheel Lodge, Rockton, IL 61072, 815–624–8711.

Restaurants

Capital Restaurant, 444 East Grand Avenue, Hilton Hotel, 608–365–6979.
Lucille's Restaurant, 325 State Street, 608–362–9889, handicapped accessible.
615 Club, 615 Broad Street, 608–362–9722, handicapped accessible.
Trumps, 328 State Street, 608–364–1984, handicapped accessible.

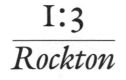

I:3

Rockton

WINNEBAGO COUNTY
Illinois

LIFE was rugged in the Rock River valley. The Indians were not unfriendly, but they were frightening, especially to the women who were often alone with their children when foraging Indians came into the cabin to clean their game or to demand whiskey. The cabins were crude with sod chimneys which collapsed when it rained. Winters were fierce. In 1842–43 the thirty-inch snow had an icy crust strong enough for the cattle and horses that had survived to walk across. In addition, "claim jumpers" or "land sharks" were always eager to grab the land of a settler who had failed to register his claim. To make matters worse, "prairie pirates," horse thieves, counterfeiters, and robbers infested the Rock River from 1837 to 1845, at which time the settlers formed and fought back with the "Regulators." Using lynch law, they bested the pirates.

The first white settler was Indian trader Stephen Mack, whose 1830s town Macktown was united with Rockton. Rockton's history is a tale of the thrifty, hard-working Yankees who came here first for fur and lumber and then to establish industries tied to water power and transportation. The plain, sturdy Greek Revival limestone houses they built still serve their descendants.

Directions

Since it is just across the state line from the south-central Wisconsin towns, it is easy to stop in Rockton and see this nineteenth-century village en route to Beloit or its neighbors. Take Interstate 90 northwest to the South Beloit exit. Proceed west to U.S. 251, then south to State Routes 2 and 75 to Rockton.

ARCHITECTURAL TOUR

Route 75 takes you to Blackhawk Boulevard, the principal north-south street. Parking is no problem in Rockton. Most of the buildings on the tour were built between 1838 and 1855, and the majority are Greek Revival in style, made of local limestone. Almost all the houses

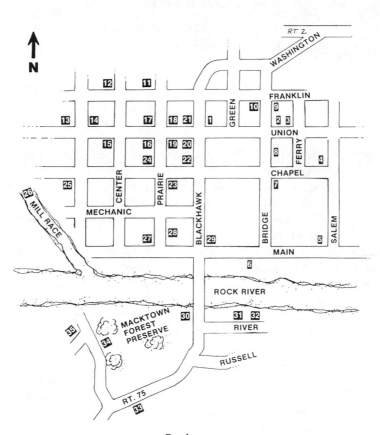

Rockton

of note are labeled with a bright marker giving the house's name and date of construction. You can cover the area north of the Rock River in about an hour on foot. We also recommend that you drive across the Rock River to view the area on the south side. Blackhawk Boulevard becomes State Route 75 here. **1.** Old Stone Church, 101 East Union, was built in 1849–50 of local limestone and lumber. The original tower of this Greek Revival structure, destroyed in a 1913 windstorm, was replaced in 1958. **2.** Proceed two blocks east to the handsome Greek Revival Matson house at 309 East Union, probably built in the 1850s. The house is a simple two-story structure with a one-story wing. The entry porch and front door are obviously recent additions. **3.** Still farther east in the same block is another Greek Revival limestone house, built earlier in 1848. It has a recessed entry and eyebrow windows to ventilate the attic. **4.** South one block and east another is the Talcott-Ballard house at 202 Salem Street. In 1966 this Greek Revival house was moved to its current location and a roof similar to the original one installed. **5.** One long block south at the northwest corner of Salem and Main is another limestone house, this one built in 1852 by Leonard Osgood. **6.** A long block west on the south side of Main is the Adams-Grossen house at 212, which was built in 1838. It was originally a Greek Revival house, but it was later altered by adding Victorian bay windows designed by architect Frank Packard. The rear addition and front porch are not compatible features. **7.** Retrace your steps east to Bridge and turn left, or north, one block to the southeast corner of Chapel and Bridge. Here at 221 North Bridge is the Greek Revival Weld-Lundgren house, built in 1851. Although it is partially obscured by evergreens, you can see the eyebrow windows in the cornice, the Victorian porch added by a later owner, and the clapboard addition to the rear. **8.** In the next block north at 309 North Bridge is the red brick Reed-Oberst Greek Revival house, built in 1851. The cream brick addition, constructed around 1900, contrasts with the original. **9.** A block north at the southeast corner of Franklin and Bridge is the Richardson-Grant house at 431 Bridge, built in 1853. **10.** Across the street on the southwest corner at 430 Bridge is the Nelson-Henry house. **11.** Three blocks west on the northwest corner of Franklin and Prairie is 203 West Franklin. Known as the Veness-Nelson house, it was built around 1840 and is a fine example of Greek Revival architecture. **12.** A block west, at the northwest corner of Center and Franklin, is 305 West Franklin, the Mack-Wingert house. Built by Stephen Mack in 1839, it was moved from Macktown to its present location after Mack's death in 1850. **13.** A block south and a block west on Union at 403 is the Shaw-White house, built around 1840. It is unusual in that it was made of "grout," a mixture of mortar and pebbles that was a popular building material in the mid-nineteenth century. A number of "grout" houses are to be found in nearby Milton, Wisconsin. **14.** Across the street to the east at 319 is the simple Greek Revival limestone Lyman-Hicks house, built in 1852. Three years later the one-story east wing was added. The two-story house with a one-story wing is prevalent in Rockton. **15.** On the south side of Union at the corner of Center and Union is 302, the Gibson-Scott house, built in 1858. It features a hip roof and bracketed eaves. **16.** One block farther east on the southwest corner of Prairie and Union is number 320 Prairie, the Fairchild-Warriner house. The original was a brick Greek Revival house built in the 1840s. The clapboard section is an addition. **17.** Across the street on the northwest corner is the Stearns-Bigelow house at 203 West Union. This small brick Greek Revival house was built in 1849. It has a new small entry porch. **18.** Across Prairie on the northeast corner, at 119 West Union, is the Comstock-Staub house. The original brick house, built in 1847, was mostly destroyed by fire in 1895. It was rebuilt as a simple Queen Anne house. An elaborate carpenter's lacework front half-porch and detail over the large front window are its distinctive features. **19.** On the southeast corner of Union and Prairie is 120, the Adams-Weldon house. This Greek Revival house was built in 1854. **20.** Slightly east and on the same side of the street is 110 West Union, the Farmer-Sockness house. It was built in the 1850s. **21.** On the northwest corner of Blackhawk Boulevard and Union is 103 Union, the Peterson house, built in 1847. Although it appears to be made of stone, it was constructed of brick with a plaster surface marked to simulate stone. **22.** A block south on the northwest corner of Chapel and Blackhawk Boulevard is a limestone house built in 1843 by Walter Henry Talcott. The house has handsome detail around the entrance door. **23.** A block west on the south side of Chapel at 122 is the Coons-Jecklin house, built in 1869. **24.** On the northwest corner of Prairie and Chapel is the Greek Revival Veness-Fiorenza house at 203 West Chapel. The stonemason was Thomas Farmer, who built both the Old Stone Church and the Talcott Free Library. The house was built in 1841. **25.** A block and a half west at 402 Chapel is Rockton's first stone building, constructed by Martin Ormsby. **26.** Go south one block to Mechanic Street, from which you can see the millrace, which looks now as it did when it was dug by William Talcott in 1838. **27.** At 201 West Main is the Coons-Hopkins 1868 commercial building. **28.** A half-block north on Prairie is the rear wing of the 1841 Sylvester Talcott Greek Revival house, which was moved from Main and Prairie in the 1940s. The main part of the house was moved to 202 Salem Street in 1966. **29.** At the northeast corner of Blackhawk Boulevard and Main is the Talcott Free Library, built by Wait Talcott in 1854. **30.** After crossing the bridge over the

Rock River, look sharply to your right; there is the Hollister-Balsley house at 226 South Blackhawk Boulevard. This fine Italianate house was built in the mid-1850s and remodeled in 1862 by architect Frank Packard. **31.** Just south of the Hollister-Balsley house on the left is River Street. Turn left to see 141 East River Street, the Bowker-Marzano house. This handsome Greek Revival house, built in 1847, has Ionic columns. **32.** Farther east is 203 River Street, a two-storied stucco Greek Revival house built in 1855. **33.** West on State Route 75 you will find the Wagon Wheel Resort, begun in 1936. **34.** Turn off State Route 75 into the Macktown Forest Preserve to see all that is left of the original settlement. On the right look for the remains of the Whitman Trading Post, a series of limestone buildings. **35.** Continue on the road west to the Stephen Mack house, a Greek Revival house with attic fanlight, built in 1839.

Historical Information
Rockton Township Historical Society publishes a *Driving Tour of Rockton*, P.O. Box 2, Rockton, IL 61072. Talcott Free Library contains a rare copy of E.I. Carr's *History of Rockton*, 101 East Main Street, Rockton, IL 61072, 815–624–7511.

Lodging
Wagon Wheel, Rockton, IL 61072, 815–624–8711.

Restaurants
China Palace, State Route 75, 815–624–2636.
Twin's Rockton Drive-In, State Route 75, 815–624–2532.
Wagon Wheel has three restaurants, Rockton, IL 61072, 815–624–8711, handicapped accessible.

I:4

Janesville

ROCK COUNTY
Wisconsin

ITH the coming of peace with the Indians after the Blackhawk War ended in 1832, the Federal government surveyed the west bank of the Rock River in 1833. The first settlers came in 1835 to this fertile and beautiful countryside in the persons of John Inman of Philadelphia and William Holmes of Ohio. They built a log cabin on the banks of the Rock River where nine hardy souls spent the winter. In 1836 Henry Janes built a cabin and the county seat was established here. Janes applied for a post office to be called Blackhawk and recommended himself as postmaster. Postmaster general Amos Kendall granted the request, but named the town Janesville.

Present day Janesville seems to be filled with art. The former Parker Pen building, "Caligraph," and a statue representing a field trip by General Motors' executives in River's Edge Park are two of the many sculptures and handsome buildings worth seeing.

Directions

No trip to south-central Wisconsin would be complete without a tour of Janesville. You can combine it with a trip to Beloit or to Milton, or on a weekend add both for a leisurely sojourn. From Chicago take Interstate 90 northwest to State Route 11, which is also Racine Street. Turn right, or north, onto Main Street and drive to Milwaukee Street. There is plenty of downtown parking.

ARCHITECTURAL TOUR

Through the efforts of the Rock County Historical Society and the Janesville Historic Commission, there are a number of sites listed on the National Register, which are not discussed here, as well as several historic districts in the process of being listed on the National Register. The latter include the Look West Historic District, which includes the Tallman Restorations, located just northwest of the downtown; and the Old Fourth Ward, located just southwest of the downtown. For this tour we have combined the North Main, East Milwaukee, and Courthouse Hill Historic Districts. We have extended the former to include the blocks of South Main to East St. Lawrence Street. The historic center of Janesville is the intersection of Milwaukee and Main and the adjoining streets. On foot the tour will take about an hour. **1.** The simple brick two-story building with a stepped parapet at 23 North Main was built in the mid-nineteenth century. Unfortunately, the first story is covered with wood paneling except for the Classical doorway. **2.** At 21 ½ North Main is a two-story twelve-foot-wide brick vernacular Greek Revival commercial building dating from the mid-1850s. **3.** After the 1865 fire destroyed the east side of North Main and several blocks to the east, 20–24 and 18–20 North Main were rebuilt between 1866 and 1868. Although the structures were rebuilt by three different persons, there is a unifying element in the cream brick, the continuous bracketed cornice, and the cast-iron Corinthian pilasters. Note the second-story three-sided metal bay window, added later. **4.** Turn-of-the-century commercial buildings at 19 and 21 North Main have metal bay windows protruding from their second stories. This was a favorite nineteenth-century decoration and also a practical way of gaining more light. **5.** Allan C. Bates built 15 North Main between 1865 and 1868. It boasts a metal cornice, three second-story windows with brick arches and keystones, and cast-iron columns and pilasters. **6.** Allan C. Bates also built 13 North Main in 1853. Originally a three-story structure, it was remodeled around 1900 into a two-story commercial Queen Anne with a decorative metal cornice and bay window. **7.** The building at 11 North Main was erected by Otto Frederick Meyer between 1865 and 1870. This three-story brick building has brick arches and keystones, which decorate the upper-story windows. **8.** Cross Milwaukee and on the southwest corner, at 20 East Milwaukee, is the Lappin-Hayes block, listed on the National Register of Historic Places, built in 1855. Thomas Lappin, whose fine house is at 404 St. Lawrence, moved his frame structure from the site to make room for his four-story commercial Italianate building. Throughout there are stone windowsills and the ornate cast-iron window hoods differ on each floor. **9.** On the east side of the street is 33–39 South Main, really four contiguous storefronts or two buildings constructed in the mid-nineteenth century for John C. Fredendall and Hiram J. Baker. The architect was George Schulze. The building has elaborate window hoods and a cornice. **10.** On the west side of South Main at the corner of Court is 36, the Court Street Methodist Church, built in 1869. This three-story Second Empire structure is listed on the National Register of Historic Places. **11.** At 50 South Main is the Kent block, built in 1895. This Queen Anne commercial structure has an ornately decorated

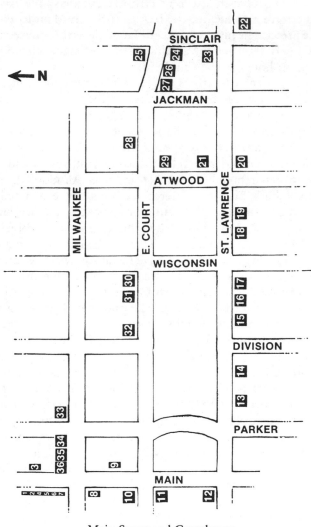

Main Street and Courthouse
Historic District,
Janesville

corner bay, with the second and third stories ending in an elaborate tower. **12.** The Neoclassical former Janesville public library at 64 South Main was built in 1902 and listed on the National Register of Historic Places. Its facade is dominated by a two-story portico with Ionic columns and decorated pediment. Turn left on St. Lawrence. You are now entering the Courthouse Hill Historic District. One of the important features of this district is that houses numbered 13–21 all front on the Courthouse and Upper Courthouse parks, as do numbers 28–32. While the houses are nicely spaced, the view of the parks gives a feeling of even greater spaciousness. **13.** At 202 St. Lawrence is the Merrill-Nowlan house, remodeled in the Neoclassical style in 1904. **14.** The glorious cream brick Queen Anne Allen-Lovejoy house at 220 St. Lawrence was designed in 1881 by Milwaukee architect James Douglas. This massive two-and-one-half-story house has a wealth of detail, including two front porches, gables, and a facade that features brick, wood, and shingles. **15.** In the next block east is the George Barker house, designed by Chicago architect Hugh M. Garden and built in 1904. This Prairie School house has a low-pitched roof, overhanging eaves, and enclosed front porch details often seen in houses of this design. **16.** At 314 St. Lawrence is the Shingle-style Julia Brittan house. Built in 1890, it has a wide gable roof with a long slope, shingle siding, and a front gable with a Palladian window over a one-story gabled front porch. **17.** The Romanesque Revival house at 320 St. Lawrence was built in 1900 by Archie Reid. It is a rare Janesville example of a residential building in this style. **18.** In the next block east is the fine Italianate Thomas Lappin home, built in 1864. This house, designed by Janesville architect Garry Nettleton, has a gabled roof with pediment, which is held up by prominent brackets and a columned porch across the front. **19.** The Second Empire house built by Wadworth G. Wheellock in 1867 is located at 418 St. Lawrence. This fine three-story brick house has a mansard roof with protruding paired dormers with decorative hoods. Its central pavilion projects, and its fine interior is replete with imported marble and glass as well as fine black-walnut woodwork. This house is probably the sole remaining residential example of this style in the city. The Court Street Methodist Church (10) is the only extant example of this style of a public building. **20.** In the next block east is 502 St. Lawrence, the Prairie-style house built in 1906 by Malcolm G. Jeffris. The two-and-one-half-story red Galesburg-brick house has a central portico supported by brick piers and columns and the leaded windows characteristic of the style. **21.** At 69 Atwood is the Queen Anne Claremont Jackman house. This fine house, built in 1884, has a conical tower, projecting bay windows, and a veranda with spool and spindle balusters as well as scalloped shingles, projecting dormers, and a massive chimney with four pots. **22.** On the southeast corner of St. Lawrence and Sinclair is 700, a Georgian Revival two-story red brick house built in 1929–30 for William G. Wheeler. The architect was A.P. Clark of Washington, D.C. This house has a central doorway and prominent portico with supporting columns and a pediment. **23.** On the northwest corner of the same intersection is 625, a massive Colonial Revival house built in 1899 for David K. Jeffris. Its most prominent feature is a massive porch across the front. **24.** Proceed on Sinclair one block north to Court; on the southwest corner is 622, the Queen Anne house built by William P. Sayles in 1897. This three-story house has steep gables and a wraparound porch. **25.** Across the street, 623 East Court was built by David W. Wilson in 1863. In 1937 this Italianate-style house was the first in Janesville to be restored. In recent years it has been upgraded to include a Victorian color scheme. **26.** At 606 Court is the Mark Ripley house, built in 1898. It also is a three-story Queen Anne with steep roof, front gable, and entrance off the wide front porch. **27.** At the end of the block, 602, is the vernacular Italianate Platt Ecyishimer house, built in 1862. A clapboard house, it has a bracketed roof and a porch across its front, which is supported by four groups of double columns. **28.** Across the street in the next block is 509 Court, a house built in 1892 by Frank C. Cook. This Queen Anne house has a corner tower, veranda, and bay windows. **29.** At the next intersection turn left on Atwood. At 55 is the handsome Italianate Timothy Jackman house, built in 1858. The house has an enclosed cupola, bracketed eaves, and a central entrance portico with two sets of paired columns. It is similar to the much grander William Tallman house on the west side of town, which is now operated as a restored house museum. **30.** Return to Court Street, turn left, or north, and note 14, 18, and 22 South Wisconsin on the west side of the street. These identical vernacular Queen Anne houses were built between 1888 and 1890 by C. W. Hodson. **31.** Parker Pen "Caligraph." **32.** On the north side of Court Street is 303, an Italianate double house constructed by George Barnes. Built in 1858, it has carved window hoods and decorative bracketed eaves. **33.** Turn right, or north, on Parker Place; proceed one block to Milwaukee Street; and turn left. At the northeast corner of Parker Drive at 201–3 Milwaukee you will find the Janesville Carriage Company building. In 1888 the three-story Italianate building with cornice and brackets was constructed. **34.** Across the street at 121 East Milwaukee is the London Hotel, which opened its doors in 1893. Its corner entrance evolves into bay windows on the second and third floors and ends in a conical tower. **35.** At 113–17 East Milwaukee is the Peters block, built in the mid-1850s. The 1915 renovation reduced the number of floors from five to four and produced the new Tudor

Revival-Prairie School facade. **36.** The building at 109–11 East Milwaukee was erected about the same time as its 113 neighbor. In 1892 it was remodeled by removing the cornice and adding the bay windows. You are now approaching the intersection of Main and Milwaukee, one short block from where you began the tour.

Festivals, Tours, and Other Places of Interest

Tallman Restorations, operated by the Rock County Historical Society for the City of Janesville, is a house-museum complex furnished in period pieces at 440 North Jackson. It is open Saturdays and Sundays, 11:00 A.M.–4:00 P.M., the first Sunday in May to the last in October, and Tuesdays–Sundays, June–August. The tour takes one and one-half hours and includes not only the mansion but also the 1842 stone house nearby. To arrange a group visit or to obtain more information contact Tallman Restorations, P.O. Box 896, Janesville, WI 53547, 608–756–4509. William M. Tallman's remarkable Italianate house, listed on the National Register of Historic Places, was built between 1855 and 1857. The house is probably the grandest ever built in this area. It has 26 rooms, 17 closets, 14-foot ornate plaster ceilings, and such 1850 novelties as a water system, provision for gas lighting, and two indoor privies. The Italianate house had a solid main section with bracketed cornice, eyebrow attic windows, ornate window hoods (different for the first and the second stories), an enclosed cupola, and a fine entrance portico in addition to a conservatory and an L-shaped piazza. There is a Janesville historic house tour the third Sunday in May, conducted by the Historical Society, which also sponsors the annual Tallman Arts festival at the Tallman site on the second Sunday in August. For information contact P.O. Box 896, Janesville, WI 53547, 608–752–4509.

Historical Information

Historic Janesville: An Architectural History of Janesville, Wisconsin (1982) by the City of Janesville. The Rock County Historical Society operates a large museum and archives in the former Armory building at 10 South High, which is listed on the National Register of Historic Places. The museum is open Tuesday–Saturday, 1:00 P.M.-4:30 P.M. year round, except for major holidays. The archives are open only by appointment. For more information contact P.O. Box 896, 10 South High Street, Janesville, WI 53547, 608–756–4509. Chamber of Commerce, 60 South River Street, Janesville, WI 53545, 608–752–7459.

Lodging

American Inn, 2723 Milton Avenue, 608–752–9411.
Janesville Motor Lodge, 3900 Milton Avenue, 608–756–4511.

Monterey Hotel, 5 South High Street, 608–754–4451.
Ramada Inn, 3431 Milton Avenue, 608–756–2341.
Sessler's Guest House, 210 South Jackson, 608–754–7250.

Restaurants

Orleans Restaurant, 5 South High Street, 608–756–1226, handicapped accessible.

Riverside, 208 South Main, 608–754–9006, handicapped accessible.

Town and Country Restaurant, 22 South River, 608–752–4491, handicapped accessible.

I:5

Milton

ROCK COUNTY
Wisconsin

A MARKER near the Storrs Lake Wildlife area tells the story of the pursuit of Chief Blackhawk up the east side of the Rock River near Milton by General Henry Atkinson. With Atkinson was a twenty-three-year-old scout doing his third thirty-day enlistment. On July 10, 1832, the scout, Abraham Lincoln, was mustered out, and the story continues, "His horse was stolen so he returned to New Salem by foot."

In 1837 the scout Peter McEwan came by way of Philadelphia and Canada to settle in the "Little Prairie." Joseph Goodrich of New York, arriving in 1837 to explore the rich timber and farm lands of Michigan and Wisconsin, discovered this point halfway between Chicago and Madison. He built a log cabin and became a trader and farmer. It was the abolitionist Goodrich family that established an underground railway stop in Milton for escaping slaves; that helped to underwrite the arrival of the railroad which ran right through the center of town, with the station on Goodrich land; and that paid for Milton College.

Directions

A trip to see Milton could easily be combined with a day trip to Janesville. In a weekend you could take in Rockton, Illinois; Beloit, Janesville, and Milton, Wisconsin. From Chicago take Interstate 90 northwest across the Wisconsin line to State Route 26, north of Janesville. It leads straight to the town of Milton and to your destination, Milton House.

ARCHITECTURAL TOUR

Milton has two unique characteristics. One is the prevalence of "grout" buildings which are poured-concrete structures that incorporate gravel, stone, sand, and slacked lime; all are native materials. "Grout" buildings were cheaper to build and withstood the elements better than those made of other materials. The second unique charac-

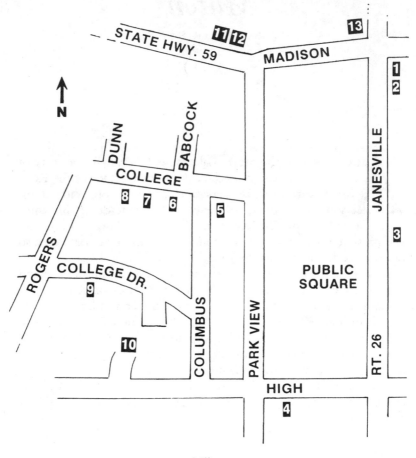

Milton

teristic is Milton College, now closed, which marked the town's high point both geographically and intellectually. Our tour includes both walking and driving. Park at Milton House and tour this complex, then drive along State Route 26 to the "grout" warehouse; 711 High Street, the McEwan-Johnson house; and then to Milton College. Proceed to Madison Avenue and complete the tour on foot. The entire tour should take about two hours. 1. Milton House is a "grout" building constructed in 1844 by Joseph Goodrich, founder of the town and the college. It is a three-story hexagonal structure; the third story, added in 1867, opens off a spiral staircase that is wrapped around a central pillar rising from the limestone basement. It contains stovepipes for the individual rooms and conveys rainwater to the basement cistern, a highly developed system for its time. In its heyday, this busy inn accommodated twenty-five stagecoaches a day. Not only did it serve ordinary travelers, but escaping slaves were provided with shelter and protection in a tunnel connecting the inn with Goodrich's cabin when federal marshals came prowling. On the northeast side of Milton House is the pioneer cabin moved by Joseph Goodrich from Lima township in 1839. The third building in the Milton House complex is the country store. 2. Moving south, at 28 Janesville Road, is the Goodrich "grout" blacksmith shop, dating from 1844. 3. The Alexander-Sunnyview "grout" warehouse farther south on Janesville Road was built in 1850 by John Alexander. The foot-thick two-story walls are pierced by one central window in the front gable. 4. Turn right, or west, on High Street. At 711 you will find the McEwan-Johnson house, platted in 1843 by Peter McEwan. This "grout" building was remodeled in 1858, and in the twentieth century an enclosed front porch was added. 5. Drive to the Milton College campus and park. At 605 is a fine Italianate cream brick house built in 1867. The columned porch on the north and west sides is original. 6. Whitford Memorial Hall, built in 1904–6, is an Eclectic building designed by New York architect C.C. Chipman. 7. Next door is the Italianate Main Hall, the first college building, constructed in 1854–55. In 1867–68 a front pavilion topped by a tower and a south wing were added. 8. Goodrich Hall next door is an 1857 simple cream brick Italianate building. It is unaltered except for a one-and-one-half-story pedimented entrance which detracts from the original design. 9. Daland Fine Arts Center on College Drive was built in 1911. It is a reinforced-concrete stuccoed building. 10. Fraser House, built around 1850–56, is a two-story Italianate cream-rose brick house with an observatory on the roof. The front has a delicate portico and six-over-six windows. 11. Proceed north to Madison, where you will find 528, the Buten-Nottingham house, built in 1850. This one-and-one-half-story "grout" house has a sash window in the front gable and eyebrow windows under the side eaves. A frame wing was added on the rear in 1870, and the pillared front porch and rough cedar exterior siding in the twentieth century. **12.** At 602 East Madison is the Polly Goodrich house. The two-story Greek Revival house was built of Whitewater brick. The nineteenth-century porch was removed and two small porches added later. **13.** At the northwest corner of Madison and Janesville Streets is the Ezra Goodrich house. The two-and-one-half-story cream brick house was built in the Italianate style in 1867.

Festivals, Tours, and Other Places of Interest

Guided tours of the Milton House complex are available and include the house itself, its surroundings, and the tunnel used by the underground railway. These tours are available May–October, 11:00 A.M.–4:00 P.M. In May, September, and October the house is open only on weekends, but June–Labor Day it is open daily. Write to P.O. Box 245, Milton, WI 53563, or call 608–868–7772. The Milton Historical Society sponsors a bi-annual house tour. For information write to P.O. Box 245, Milton, WI 53563, or call 608–868–7772.

Historical Information

Juliette H. Lukas, curator of Milton House and administrator of the Milton Historical Society, can be contacted at her office, P.O. Box 245, Milton, WI 53563, 608–868–7772. Rock County publishes a *Resource and Tourism Guide* annually. It is available from Diane Everson at the *Edgerton Reporter*, 21 North Henry Street, Edgerton, WI 53534, 608–884–3367.

Lodging

Bed and breakfast, Peggy Stromer, 1172 West County Trunk M, Route 2, Milton, WI 53563.

I:6
Evansville
ROCK COUNTY
Wisconsin

THE northwest corner of Rock County was first surveyed in 1835, and the Wisconsin Territory was created in 1836. The first settlers arrived in 1839, a small group of New Englanders who were searching for prime agricultural land. The early town was called The Grove; later it was renamed Evansville. Today Evansville remains a small, handsome place with a good collection of mid-nineteenth- and early twentieth-century homes and commercial buildings.

In the heart of this small town lies a quiet shady section of old dignified houses where the visitor can picture the ice cream social on one columned porch, the gathering of parasols marking Miss Allen's outdoor sewing circle, or Dr. Evans' knickered children playing one-o-cat on the wide lawn. The essence of that ambling pace and graceful way of life remains in Evansville.

Directions

Evansville is one of several cities in south-central Wisconsin that are well worth a visit. If you have a long weekend in mind, you could visit Evansville, Cooksville, Janesville, Milton, Beloit, and Rockton. Different combinations could be toured on a weekend. From Chicago the fast route is north via Interstate 294 to Interstate 90 and then to U.S. 14 north of Janesville. Go west on U.S. 14 about seventeen miles to Evansville. It will take a little over two hours. A slower and more scenic route is via Interstate 294 to Des Plaines, and then to U.S. 14, which meanders in a northwesterly direction into Evansville.

ARCHITECTURAL TOUR

The tour, which will take less than an hour, includes Main and Church Streets west of Madison to Fourth Street. The easternmost block of Main is commercial. As in many other small cities, the upper floors of the commercial buildings have retained their original facades with elaborate cornices, sometimes including the building date, cast-

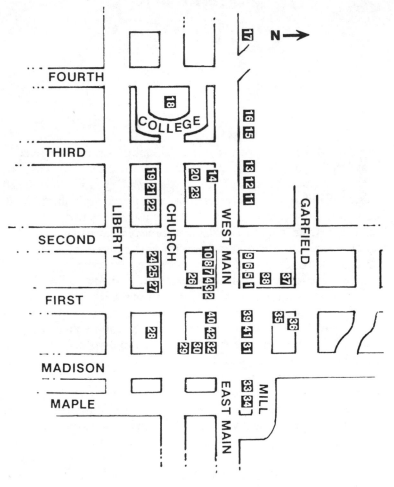

Evansville

iron bay windows, and interesting window detail. Parking does not pose a problem as there are several lots in the immediate vicinity. The tour starts at Main and First Streets. **1.** At 104 West Main, the high Victorian house with Italianate hooded windows is one of only two Gothic Revival buildings in town. The house was built after 1873 for John M. Evans of red brick with ornate white hoods over the windows and a pointed gable roof. **2.** Across the street at 103 West Main is a fine Greek Revival house built before 1858 for William Quivery. It has the distinction of being the only house of this style in the county that has a fine Doric portico across the front. **3.** Next door at 111 West Main is a Neoclassical Revival house built in 1910 for J.T. Baker. The facade is of cream-colored brick with a tiled hip and porch roof. The porch across the front is supported by Ionic columns. **4.** The next house is 117 West Main, a Queen Anne house built in 1896 for T.C. Richardson. It has a massive corner porch with a smaller second-story porch and a variety of window treatments. **5.** Across the street at 120 West Main is the 1880s Late Picturesque or Queen Anne four-story Porter-Fish-Wilson house. The clapboard facade is decorated with entrance and second-story porches and many gables, all with small windows. **6.** Next door is an Italianate white clapboard house built for John Evans about 1850. It has the heavily bracketed roof, wraparound porch, and corner pilasters common to the Italianate style. **7.** Across Main on the south side is 129, another Italianate house built in 1858 by William Quivery. This white structure has typical Italianate features, including scroll brackets supporting its fine cornice and a bay window. A unique feature was a gas generating system that provided light. **8.** Next door at 137 is the 1886 Stick-style George Pullen house. Currently painted green with white trim, the house is noticeable for its elaborately decorated porches. **9.** On the north side of Main at 138 is the Greek Revival Levi Leonard house. **10.** On the south side of Main at 143 is another white clapboard Italianate house, built about 1875 by C.H. Wilder. The house has an elaborate cornice with brackets, highly decorated windows, and a fine bracketed entrance portico. **11.** On the north side of West Main between Second and Third Streets is 228, an Italianate home built in 1874 by Almeron Eager. The handsome arched windows and doors, the bracketed and columned veranda, and the equally elegant eastern bay window are notable architectural features. **12.** Next door is another Italianate house, built in 1879 for William Smith. **13.** The Greek Revival house at 250 West Main was built about 1855 by Moses Vervalin. The cream-colored Watertown brick is found in a number of Evansville houses. **14.** Across the street is a Greek Revival house built around 1860 by E.M.S. Hawley. It prefigures the arrival of the Italianate style, as its windows and entrance door are decorated. **15.** West of Third Street

on the north side of Main at 318 is a Greek Revivial double house built
in 1855 by John Winston. The middle of the house is two-story with
three bays. A one-and-one-half-story wing extends from each side.
The side-lighted entrance is thought to be original. **16.** Another fine
Greek Revival house is 340 West Main, built around 1855 by Elijah
Robinson, whose son Theodore was an early American Impressionist
painter. **17.** Where Fourth and Main Streets meet is a fine Italianate
house built in the 1860s. It is notable for its long veranda, supported
by columns, which wraps around two sides of the house, and for its
bracketed roof. **18.** By far the most imposing of the town's buildings
is the Evansville Seminary at the western end of Church Street. This
three-story late-Federal structure was built in 1855. It has an Italianate
bracketed roof, a columned portico entrance, and evenly spaced
white-trimmed windows on its red brick facade. **19.** At 263 Church is
another Greek Revival house. It embodies some Italianate elements,
such as a wide frieze and eyebrow windows to ventilate the attic.
20. Across the street, the home at 262 Church was built in 1864 by
Jacob West. The house has scroll roof brackets, pilastered corners,
and a corner-columned first-floor porch that becomes an open
second-story porch. **21.** On the south side of the street is 233 Church,
a typical Rock County, Wisconsin, Greek Revival house. Its six-over-
six windows, modest cornice, and pilastered door with side lights are
common features of this style. **22.** The Stick-style house next door,
built in 1885 by C.J. Pearsall, is unfortunately in sorry shape. **23.** At
224 West Church is a fine Italianate house built in the mid-1800s by
W.H.H. Johnson. It has a small porticoed entrance, hooded windows, and an enclosed bracketed porch that matches the cornice.
24. Farther east between Second and First Streets on the south side is
127 Church, an Italianate house built in 1865 by A.C. Gray. This
clapboard house has a long veranda, east bay windows, bracketed
roof line, and fancy window treatment. **25.** The Queen Anne house at
113 Church was built by Fred Colony in the 1880s. It has a steep hip
roof decorated by iron cresting, as are its east bay and porches. Of
note is the variety of window styles, including a semicircular attic and
two Gothic windows. **26.** Across the street at 102 Church is the 1850s
Congregational church, which was remodeled in the 1880s in the
Picturesque style by adding Gothic windows and a decorative brick
frieze. **27.** On the south side of Church at First Street is the 1903
Romanesque Revival-style brick First Baptist Church. Its three-story
balconied tower protrudes from the building, and its round-arched
windows have distinctive leaded-glass panels. **28.** In the middle of the
next block between First and Madison Streets at 23 Church is the 1854
Free Will Baptist Church, the oldest remaining church in town. It was

originally built in the Greek Revival style, and the corner tower was added around the turn of the century. **29.** On the west side of South Madison is the cream brick Queen Anne City Hall. Built in 1892, it has a four-story tower. **30.** On the same side of the street is the 1867 high-Victorian Gothic Methodist-Episcopal Church. The ornate towers were built at different times. **31.** From this vantage point on the south side of Main look across at the Union Bank and Trust Company. The second-story facade is ornamented by original sheet-metal bay windows, pediments, and cornices displaying the names and dates of the buildings. All of these are original. **32.** Cross Main and look at the south side of the street. Part of the West Main block burned in the 1897 fire. A limestone fire wall stopped the fire. Turrets, parapets, friezes, and metal bay windows decorate the second floors of many of these buildings. **33.** Look at East Main Street's south side. There are a number of interesting second-story facades. The Eager Block, 5–9 East Main, was built in 1900. The architect was William Meggott. The structure at 11 East Main was built by Byron Campbell in 1877. The Central Building, 101 East Main, was constructed in the 1880s. Its frieze and brick arches are of some interest. **34.** The Second Empire house next door, designed by architect B.S. Hoxie of Cooksville, was built in 1874 for E.W. Beebe. **35.** The early Italianate brick house at 42 Montgomery Court has a bracketed cornice and two wings, one of which is older than the main two-story section. A small columned entrance porch and eyebrow windows are features of the older wing. **36.** A block north, on Garfield, is St. Paul's Catholic Church, built in 1906. This white Rhineland Romanesque structure has narrow, pointed windows and a block tower. **37.** Across the street at 51 First, is the Queen Anne Dixon house, built in 1902. Its architect was a local builder, William Meggott, who built numerous commercial structures but only two houses in Evansville, where he worked from 1867 to 1912. This three-story house has an intersecting gable roof, a three-window bay in its upper gable, and a garlanded Adamesque porch. **38.** A little farther south on First Street is another late Queen Anne, built between 1885 and 1900. It is notable for its Eastlake porch, a form of ornamentation named for British designer Charles Locke Eastlake that features fancy porches and balconies with ornaments produced on power-driven lathes. **39.** At the northeast corner of First and Main Streets is 44 West Main, a late Queen Anne house with a prominent three-story tower and rounded front bay windows on both stories. **40.** Across the street at 39 West Main is the Prairie-style Eager Free Public Library. The library is on the National Register of Historic Places. **41.** On the north side of Main, 32 is the Neoclassical Spencer building dating from 1907. **42.** On the south side of Main is the Neoclassical Grange store, built in 1904. It is cream brick with Ionic columns. The building supervisor was once again William Meggott.

Festivals, Tours, and Other Places of Interest

A public house tour is held in September in even-numbered years. If you would like a tour at some other time, contact the Historic Preservation Commission at City Hall, 31 South Madison Street, Evansville, WI 53536, 608–882–4424.

Historical Information

The Historic Preservation Commission, City Hall, 31 South Madison Street, Evansville, WI 53536, 608–882–4424. The Eager Free Public Library, 39 West Main Street, Evansville, WI 53536. Evansville Chamber of Commerce, P.O. Box 11, Evansville, WI 53536, 608–882–5860. The Historical Society publishes a *Historical and Architectural Walking Tour of Evansville's Historic District*, 104 West Main, Evansville, WI 53536.

Restaurants

Plescia's Coachhouse, 155 East Main Street, 608–882–4300, handicapped accessible.

Cooksville

ROCK COUNTY
Wisconsin

J OHN and Daniel Cook founded the village that bears their name in 1842. New England influence shaped the town's land pattern, which includes a town common. Today the town bears a startling resemblance to its appearance one hundred years ago.

Directions

On a day or weekend trip to south-central Wisconsin you should consider a stop in Cooksville. Evansville is close by, so you can visit both in a day. From Evansville follow U.S. 14 north to State Route 59, then turn east to Cooksville. The road becomes Rock Street, the main east-west thoroughfare.

ARCHITECTURAL TOUR

Unlike most of the historic districts in this book Cooksville is not an incorporated village or a town but a hamlet. At its largest it harbored 175 people; it now has about 85. A walk around the public square and down Main Street would be a nice half-hour stroll. Be sure to look carefully at the more than a dozen Greek and Gothic Revival houses, dating from 1846 to 1856, many of which are very well preserved. 1. The large open space on Rock and Webster Streets is the public square, or common, which in the original plat was designated as a public space belonging to the town's residents. 2. The Lovejoy-Duncan house across Webster was built in 1848–49. It is a simple brick Greek Revival structure. 3. Known as the Backenstoe-Howard house, the Gothic Revival double home next door was built in two sections. The earlier is the one-story wing, built in 1848. The one-and-one-half-story addition was built in 1865. 4. Next door is another brick Gothic Revival cottage, built in 1852 by local carpenter and architect Benjamin S. Hoxie. A frame wing with mansard roof on the rear was added in 1873, as was a bay window later. 5. The Cure-Van Vleck house, just north on the southwest corner of Dane and Webster, was built in 1852. It is a one-and-one-half-story frame Greek Revival

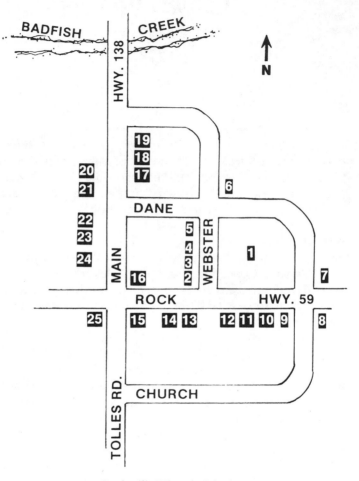

Cooksville Historic District

structure. **6.** The Isaac Porter house was probably built by John Chambers, who was a partner in Daniel Lovejoy's construction firm (see 2). A small two-story Gothic cottage which stands next door was probably built around 1856. **7.** At the northeast corner of Rock and Dane Streets, facing the public square, is a vernacular frame schoolhouse built in 1886. **8.** Across Rock Street on the southeast corner is the frame Greek Revival Thomas Morgan house, built in 1848–50. **9.** Across the street on the southwest corner is the one-and-one-half-story brick Greek Revival Frank Seaver house, built around 1850. An enclosed front porch, added in the 1940s, obscures the original lines. **10.** West on Rock Street is an 1849 frame Greek Revival house. **11.** The house to the west was probably built by John W. Fisher, who also built the house next door (10). The brick Gothic Revival cottage dates from around 1854. In the 1970s it was enlarged, but the original design is not injured. The original carpenter's lace, sometimes called decorated bargeboard, ornaments the porch and gable. **12.** The Blackman-Woodbury Gothic frame house to the west was built in 1853. Late Picturesque additions were made in 1893 and 1897. **13.** The Greek Revival Parker-Newell house next door was built around 1848. Over time the frame was covered with stucco, and a compatible addition was built to the rear. **14.** The Gunn-Breckenridge house next door is a collection of additions to a small 1852 gabled oak house which was moved to this site in 1924. **15.** The last house on this block is the 1848 Greek Revival Van Buren house. It was probably built by carpenter-builder John W. Fisher. **16.** The Greek Revival house across Rock on Main was probably built around 1852 by John W. Fisher. Wings on either side and a front porch were added in the early twentieth century. **17.** In the next block north is the Lovejoy-Chambers house, built sometime between 1851 and 1854. Unfortunately, this Greek Revival house has been altered. **18.** Next door is a Greek Revival brick house built by John Collins around 1856. A new Doric porch was added about twenty years ago, as was the disappointing carport. **19.** Next door is a two-story vernacular frame house with Late Picturesque porch, probably built in the early 1850s by Lovejoy and Chambers. Brown shingles now cover its original siding. **20.** On the other side of Main Street is the Betsy Curtiss house, built around 1845. This Greek Revival house has been adversely changed by aluminum siding and a picture window. **21.** The Cooksville general store was originally built around 1847 and remodeled in 1864 and 1890. The original builder was either Charles Smith or John W. Fisher. It is one of the few general stores remaining in the county and is remarkable for maintaining its turn-of-the-century facade. **22.** The one-and-one-half-story frame saltbox Smith-Galt house is next to the blacksmith shop to the south of the general store. Its builder, again, was either Charles Smith or John W. Fisher. Its exterior has not been altered with the exception of an architecturally consistent two-car-garage addition on the rear. 23. Next door is the house of the town's founder, John Cook, built about 1842. It is a one-and-one-half-story vernacular cottage with a one-story wing to the north. 24. On the south side of the Cook house on Main Street is the 1885 William Porter farmhouse. The house's facade has been clad in aluminum siding and its style changed with the addition of a Victorian porch. 25. On the southwest corner of Main and Rock Streets is the 1879 Cooksville Congregational Church, designed and built by Benjamin S. Hoxie. A combination of Italianate and Gothic Revival styles, it is now painted in its original nineteenth-century colors, tan with brown trim. The facade, including the spires and belfry, has been restored and a new bell installed. You are now one block west of the public square where you started the tour.

Historical Information

Larry Reed, Cooksville historian, 608–262–4741. Stephen Ehle, R.R. 1, Evansville, WI 53536, 608–873–7600. Richard P. Hartung, author of *Cooksville: A Guide*, Rock County Historical Society, 10 South High Street, P.O. Box 896, Janesville, WI 53547, 608–756–4509.

II:1

Sycamore

DE KALB COUNTY
Illinois

S YCAMORE glows with self-confidence. Its residents still reflect on the struggles of the past from which their town emerged triumphant. Carlos Lattin arrived in 1835 as the first settler, and the small settlement began to grow around his log cabin. Just to the west, Rufus Colton settled and named his fledgling hamlet Coltonville. Soon political intrigue arose when Colton, clerk of the board of commissioners, began lobbying for his town as county seat. This struggle between Coltonville and Sycamore went on for years, but in 1856 the Illinois General Assembly selected Sycamore as county seat and a courthouse was built.

The next struggle involved the Northwestern Railroad which bypassed Sycamore. The merchants knew that this meant death to Sycamore. They raised the princely sum of seventy-five thousand dollars for their Sycamore, Cortland, and Chicago Railroad to connect with the Northwestern. Today the fine Greek Revival limestone station they built still stands.

Directions

A day trip to this unspoiled town west of Chicago is most pleasant. It can be combined with a visit to Woodstock. To reach Sycamore from Chicago, you can take the East-West Tollway west to De Kalb, where you should change to State Route 23 north to Sycamore. Another way is to take Interstate 90 west to Carpentersville, turn south on State Route 47 to State Route 64, and follow it west into Sycamore.

ARCHITECTURAL TOUR

Sycamore has a fine collection of mid- and late-nineteenth century homes, principally along Somonauk, with some on North and South Main. The wide tree-lined streets with their well-spaced houses give an air of grace and gentility. Parking is not usually a problem. It is available in front of the courthouse and on the residential streets. It

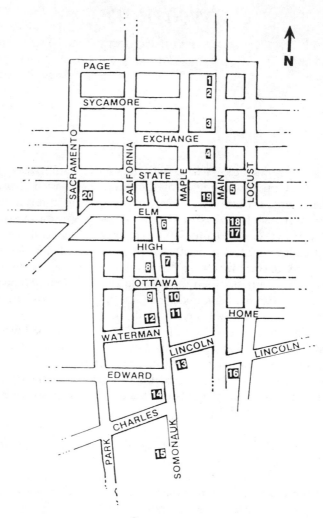

Sycamore

will take about an hour to walk the district. **1.** At 331 North Main Street is an elaborate Queen Anne house, designed and built in 1892 by George O. Garnsey for Frederick B. Townsend. It is remarkable for the variety of materials used in the facade, the Palladian windows in the third story, and the gables and tower. **2.** The Boyton house next door at 307 North Main Street was designed in 1886–87 by the same architect, George O. Garnsey. It is less elaborate but does have some of the earmarks of a Queen Anne house, with tower and turret, bay windows, and porte-cochere. **3.** The cheerful yellow Greek Revival house at 107 West Exchange was built around 1862 by Daniel B. James. It has "Jerkin Head" gables on the front and west sides of the house and a porch, which is a later but compatible addition. **4.** The grandiose De Kalb County courthouse, which dominates the square, was built in 1903 by architects Watson and Hazelton of Chicago. The courthouse square was laid out in the late 1840s. The building is a Neoclassical and Baroque structure of Indiana limestone whose imposing columned facade has not been altered. **5.** East of the courthouse, across State Street at its intersection with Main Street, is the imposing, heavy brown limestone Carnegie Library. Built in 1903, it boasts an imposing Classical-columned portico entrance and a distinctive rotunda with beehive roof. Walk west a block and a half to Somonauk. Notice the streetscape on Main: the two- and sometimes three-story commercial buildings preserve the turn-of-the-century flavor, particularly in the upper-story facades. Some show signs of Classical Revival and others of Italianate design. Turn south on Somonauk. **6.** The oldest church in De Kalb County is St. Peter's Episcopal Church at 206, a block and a half south and a half-block west. Its interior and exterior are exactly as designed by architect George O. Garnsey in 1877. It is Gothic Revival in style, featuring a bell tower with steeple and a large, round stained-glass window, both facing the street. **7.** On the southeast corner of Somonauk and High Streets is the old Congregational church, now the Sycamore Baptist Church. Designed by George O. Garnsey in the mid-1880s, it is also a limestone Gothic Revival structure, but it has two towers, one taller than the other, and two fine stained-glass windows, a round one and a huge arched one facing Somonauk. **8.** At 319 Somonauk is a fine Italianate house built before the Civil War by O.M. Bryan. Although some features have been removed, it still retains the fine Classical portico, heavy bracketed roof, and tall narrow front windows on both the first and the second story. **9.** Abram Ellwood built the Gothic cottage at 421 Somonauk about 1877. **10.** Another splendid Queen Anne house is 420 Somonauk, built for David Syme and designed by George O. Garnsey. In some ways it resembles both the Townsend and Boyton houses (1 and 2), products of the same architect, but it is smaller and has a less spacious setting. It has both a tower and a second-story bay in the form of a turret. The front porch has carpenter's lacework, and a second-story balcony protrudes above the porch's roof. Of particular note are the fountain and benches on the front walk, which give a Victorian look to the entrance walk even though they are more recent additions. 11. The elaborate Italianate house at 450 Somonauk was built for George P. Wild and designed by Chicago architect Ackermann. Its plans were studied by architects and builders for years as an example of a fine Italianate style. Notice the elaborate window treatment, the heavily bracketed cornice, and the wraparound porch which, although not original, complements the house. 12. Across the street at 453 Somonauk is the Willard house of similar style, built in 1871. 13. An identical twin to the Wild house was built at 804 Somonauk in 1875 for Joseph B. Stephens. 14. Another house in the same style was built for Ohlin H. Smith at 813 Somonauk. 15. The simple Italianate house at 821 Somonauk was built sometime before 1871 for Chauncey Ellwood. At the rear of the house there is a pond that mirrors a flower garden. 16. The house at 612 Main is the oldest house still standing in Sycamore. It was built in 1847 by Ellzy Young. Basically a Federalist structure, it has been embellished by a Classical portico and a horizontal beaded cornice. 17. On the northeast corner of Main and High is 232 South Main, a low, rambling cottage currently painted blue with white trim. It has an abundance of carpenter's lacework decorating its roof line, gables, and entries. 18. The old Universalist church at 212 South Main is of Italianate design, obscured by the addition of a front porch. 19. The Colonial brick house at 127 South Main was built around 1862. 20. At the intersection of Elm and Sacramento on the northeast corner is the Chicago and Northwestern Railroad's abandoned depot. Completed in 1880, the station's good Italianate facade remains unchanged.

Festivals, Tours, and Other Places of Interest

The Ellwood House Association of De Kalb holds a tour of De Kalb and Sycamore houses the first weekend in October. The houses vary each year. Information on the tour can be obtained from the museum. The museum itself can be toured Tuesday–Sunday, 1:00 P.M.–3:30 P.M., and is located in the Ellwood mansion, 815–756–4609. The Illinois Railway Museum at Union, located east of Marengo on Union Road south of State Route 176 (north of U.S. 20) makes a good addition to a trip to Sycamore or Woodstock. A steam train operates only on Saturday, Sunday, and certain holidays, from the beginning of May to the end of September; electric cars operate on Sundays from mid-April to the end of October, Saturdays, from the beginning of May to the end of September, and on Memorial and

Labor Days. There are also special events on holiday weekends. To fully appreciate this unique outdoor repository of railroadiana requires considerable walking, but casual visitors can savor the view from the train rides. For further information call 815–923–2488, 312–262–2266, or the business office, 815–923–4391.

Historical Information

The Greater Sycamore Chamber of Commerce, 206 West State Street, Sycamore, IL 60178, 815–895–3456. Carnegie Public Library, State and Main, Sycamore, IL 60178. Stephen J. Bigolin and Nancy Beasley's fifty-six-page booklet, *Sycamore's Architecture: A Walk Through History*, can be purchased for $5.00 plus $1.00 postage from the Chamber of Commerce. The National Bank and Trust Company offers a map of the historic district, with narrative on the back, also available from the Chamber of Commerce.

Lodging

Stratford Inn, 355 West State Street, 815–895–6789.

Restaurants

Carl's Coach Room, at the Stratford Inn, 815–895–6789, handicapped accessible.

El Matador, 1001 State Street, 815–895–9520.

II:2

Woodstock

THE early history of the county changed when Lake County split from McHenry County and a new county seat for McHenry, Centerville, was established in 1844. The next year the name of the county seat was changed to Wood-stock, honoring the Vermont town from which some of the early settlers came.

Woodstock Square is ringed with signs and buildings of the past, some presenting new and different uses. Over it all presides the Opera House. This important churchlike structure is back in business presenting plays, operettas, and dance companies, as well as hosting community meetings.

Actor Orson Welles, a native of Woodstock not given to excess verbiage, made this observation about his birthplace: "Like a wax flower tree under a bell glass in the paisley and gingham county of McHenry is Woodstock, grand capital of Mid-Victorianism in the Midwest."

Directions

A tour of Woodstock is a leisurely day's trip from Chicago. Combine it with a visit to Sycamore, if you'd like. From Chicago take the Illinois Tollway, Interstate 90, to just south of Huntley; then take State Route 47 north to Woodstock.

ARCHITECTURAL TOUR

The first part of the tour basically comprises the area around the public square. This area appears to be dated from around the turn of the century. A careful inspection tour will take about an hour. 1. The Woodstock square was platted in 1844 by Alvin Judd. In 1858–59 it was graded and landscaped. A Civil War monument and a replica of the 1873 spring house are on the square. 2. The Phoenix block, 103–13 Van Buren, was constructed in 1852. The fourth floor was removed in the 1930s and the facade altered. 3. The Oddfellows lodge was erected in 1907 at the southwest corner of Jackson and Jefferson. The cornerstone of the original building remains. **4.** The Murphy block and the Richmond hotel were built at 100 Benton in 1873 by John Murphy. This three-story brick Italianate building has been restored. The rounded sash windows on the second and third floors and the frieze decorating the cornice add a distinctive touch to the facade. **5.** At 110–14 Benton is a two-story Italianate building erected in 1873. Its neighbor at 118–24 Benton was erected in 1872. **6.** The Hoy block, at the northwest corner of Cass and Benton, was built about 1855. In the 1880s the building was raised four feet during street grading, and the cornice and windows were altered. **7.** The J.C. Miller theater was erected at 211 Main in 1927. **8.** The A.J. Zoia block at 138 Cass was built in 1905. **9.** Next door, the Elks post on the northeast corner of Throp and Cass was erected in 1923. **10.** The former McHenry County sheriff's residence was built at the southwest corner of Johnson and Cass in 1887. Notice the dark cornice and portico, the limestone arches decorating the windows, and the limestone quoins accenting the building's corners. **11.** The former McHenry County courthouse and jail were built on the northwest corner of Jackson and Johnson. The facade is original. **12.** A little south at 124 Johnson is the U.S. Post Office, designed by James Whetmore and built in 1931. **13.** City Hall, across Calhoun, is a Classical Revival building, erected in 1906. **14.** The Opera House, one block north and west on Van Buren, designed by Smith Hoag and built in 1889, has been completely restored. The bell tower is a fanciful addition. Arched window treatments, especially on the square side, are a touch of Richardsonian Romanesque Revival. **15.** The northwest corner of Jefferson and Calhoun is the site of St. John's Evangelical Lutheran Church, designed by F. Alschlager and erected in 1898. A tour of the residential area is also worthwhile. Although maintenance has not been perfect, most of the houses retain their nineteenth-century charm. You can drive to South Dean and South Tryon (16–22), then to West Jackson (23–34) to complete the remainder of the tour. Allow a minimum of an hour. **16.** At 410 South Dean is the Queen Anne Silas Olmsted house, built in 1892. In 1985 it was painted a mustard color. Its fish-scale gables are dark brown, and the window frames are highlighted in white paint. **17.** Another house in the same style is 324 South Dean, the Anderson house, painted tan with windows outlined in dark brown. It has a porch that wraps around the north and east sides of the house as well as a turret and a modified bay window on the second floor. **18.** The Elijah Burbank house, 522 South Dean, is a Federal-style brick house painted gray with windows outlined in white. It was built in 1855. The one-story addition to the southwest is newer. **19.** At 517 South Dean is a brick two-story Greek Revival

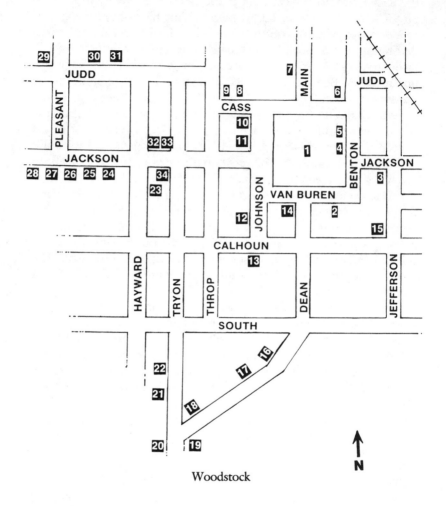

Woodstock

house with an interesting pediment and windows outlined in white. The one-story addition to the north is newer. Note the variety of brick in the latter's facade. **20.** The Homer Abbott house, 382–84 South Tryon, was built in 1884. It is Italianate-style, painted blue with white trim. The porch is decorated with elaborate carpenter's lacework. Two bay windows on the south side are also distinctive. **21.** The Frank Buell house, 336 Tryon, is a large Queen Anne three-story house with an ample porch across the front and a variety of window styles. It was built in 1905. **22.** At 344 Tryon is a modified cottage with an inset second-story balcony, unusual for Woodstock. **23.** Drive to the West Jackson area. At 123 Hayward is a small red-painted Greek Revival cottage, built in 1852. **24.** At 421 West Jackson is a Queen Anne house built in 1894. It is painted tan with its elaborate window treatment highlighted by white paint. It also sports a three-story tower with windows on three sides. **25.** A little farther west at 457 West Jackson is the Josiah Hyde house, built in 1895. It is a Queen Anne house with a small porch decorated with carpenter's lace in spindle form. **26.** Next door at 463 West Jackson is the A.J. Murphy house, built in 1903. The facade has been altered and not for the better. **27.** At 481 West Jackson, the Lorenzo Parson house is a simple white clapboard Greek Revival structure representative of the early houses. **28.** The David Robinson house at 535 West Jackson was built in 1858. It is a white clapboard Greek Revival house. Its original entrance door is complete with transom and side lights. **29.** On the northwest corner of Judd and Pleasant is the Freemont Hoy house, built in 1900. This combination Greek Revival and Italianate house is painted dark gray with windows and quoins outlined in white. The west wing has been altered on the first floor to enlarge a window. It has an attractive bay window on the east side. **30.** At 488 West Judd is the W.H. Stewart house, a brown shingle house with a balcony on the second story and a wraparound porch extending from the east around the south side of the house. **31.** The Edward Thompson house at 452 West Judd is a Queen Anne house with a curved porch across the front and side. **32.** On the northeast corner of Jackson and Hayward at 326 Jackson is a green Italianate house built in 1875. **33.** Farther east at 310 Jackson is an 1895 Steamboat Gothic house with tower and curving front porch. **34.** On the southwest corner of Jackson and Tryon at 301 Jackson is a fine deep gray Italianate house, built in 1862 and newly restored.

Festivals, Tours, and Other Places of Interest

See the description of the Illinois Railway Museum in the previous section, "Sycamore."

Historical Information
  Woodstock City Hall, 121 Calhoun Street, P.O. Box 190, Woodstock, IL 60098, 815–338–4300. Woodstock Public Library, 414 Judd Street, Woodstock, IL 60098, 815–338–0542. A good guide to Woodstock's residential buildings can be found in Ira J. Bach's *A Guide to Chicago's Historic Suburbs*, Swallow Press, Ohio University Press, Athens, Ohio, 1981.

III : I
Kankakee

KANKAKEE COUNTY
Illinois

ANKAKEE is one of those rare settlements that were first occupied by the white man and then by the Indians. Cavalier de la Salle, with his faithful scribe, Father Hennepin, came here in 1680. About a hundred years later a treaty between the United States and the Potawatomi tribe prohibited settlement by whites, and it was not until the Treaty of Tippecanoe in 1832 that white settlement began again. Indians and white men lived amicably in this rich bottom land, sharing the game and combining their two cultures.

Kankakee grew and prospered as a river port, rail center, and county seat. In 1904, businessman and civic leader Emory Cobb owned most of the land now known as the Riverview Historic District. Here entrepreneurs and professionals built a variety of houses reflecting their prosperity, the most notable of which are the two designed by Frank Lloyd Wright for Warren Hickox and his sister Anna Bradley. A chance to see these examples of the Prairie school is well worth a visit to this district.

Directions

Kankakee is about a two-hour drive from Chicago, a nice day's outing. Take Interstate 57 south from Chicago and leave the highway at the Court Street exit. Go west, turn left on Indiana Avenue, and proceed five blocks south to River Street. Turn left, or east, one block to Harrison and turn right.

ARCHITECTURAL TOUR

The Riverview Historic District was home to Kankakee's most prominent citizens at the turn of the century. The earliest houses were Queen Anne, but there are also Colonial and Tudor Revival, a few Mission, and a number of Prairie-style dwellings, including two outstanding Frank Lloyd Wright houses. 1. The house at 668 South Harrison is half of the original 1875 Clarke house, which stood a

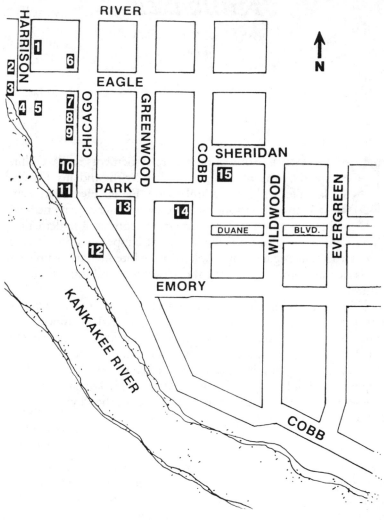

Riverview Historic District,
Kankakee

block north. In 1919 it was moved and divided. The house next door at 646–50 South Harrison is the other half. The first-floor facade dates from the division. **2.** The small white clapboard Queen Anne house at 667 South Harrison was built in 1920 by Louis E. Beckman. It has a high front gable, tower, and front porch with Ionic columns. **3.** The first of the Frank Lloyd Wright houses is 687 South Harrison, built in 1900 for Warren R. Hickox. This is the smaller of the two, but it has the characteristic stucco and horizontal wood trim and the leaded-glass windows. **4.** The much larger Bradley house, to which fate has not always been kind, remains a Prairie school jewel with its characteristic wide overhang, horizontal banding, and window treatment. **5.** Across the street is 762 South Harrison, built for Haswell C. Clarke before the turn of the century. In 1919 it was remodeled into a simple Queen Anne shingled house. **6.** Go east on Eagle one block to Chicago Avenue. On the northwest corner is the Queen Anne Magruder-DeSelm house at 691 South Chicago Avenue. This striking house has gables with lunette or eyebrow windows, two full-length bays, and a corner tower, as well as a large front porch with turreted roof. **7.** On the southwest corner at 711 South Chicago is a brick-and-shingle house built by W.K. Woodruff in 1896. All the rooms have rounded corners. **8.** John Buffum built the Colonial Revival house at 761 South Chicago Avenue in 1899. Its wide porch has Ionic columns, and the entrance is decorated by side lights and a fan-shaped transom. **9.** Frank Turk built the Prairie-style house at 783 South Chicago Avenue in 1902–04. The original front porch was removed in the 1950s; the side screened porch is an addition. **10.** William Hunter built the Queen Anne house at 825 South Chicago Avenue. The house has a massive cross-gabled roof, a two-story tower, and a wide wrap-around front porch. **11.** The Joseph Rondy house at 855 South Chicago Avenue has a low-pitched gabled roof and a wide front porch. This Craftsman-style house was built in the 1920s. **12.** Charles Cobb built the English cottage one block south on Chicago Avenue in 1911. The vine-covered house has a steeply pitched shake-shingle roof, two front gables, and a recessed doorway. **13.** The Spanish-style house at the southwest corner of Park and Greenwood was built in 1935 for Paul LeCour. Designed by the Chicago architectural firm of Carlson and Connley, its most interesting features are the pineapple finial capping the curved parapet and the red tiled roof. **14.** Go east one block to the southwest corner of Cobb Boulevard and Park Place, where you will see a Queen Anne clapboard house at 917 Cobb. This fancy representation of the style has dormers with Palladian windows, two-story bays, and a curved porch with Corinthian columns. Winfield S. Campbell built the house in 1898. **15.** Turn north on Cobb Boulevard to number 812, the Louis Suprenant, Sr., house, built between 1885 and 1895. This clapboard Queen Anne house has a wraparound porch, an attic gable with lunette window, and stained-glass windows in the first-floor bay.

Historical Information

Kankakee County Historical Society museum is open 10:00 A.M.–3:00 P.M. weekdays and 1:00 P.M.–4:00 P.M. weekends, Eighth Avenue and Water Street, Kankakee, IL 60901, 815–932–5279.

Lodging

Days Inn, 1975 East Court, 815–939–7171.
Fairview Motel, State Route 49 and Interstate 57, 815–933–7708.
Kankakee Hotel, 225 Merchant, 815–933–4411.
Winfield Inn, Bradley, IL 60915, 815–939–3501.
Scottish Inn, State Route 45 south, 815–939–4551.

Restaurants

Bennett-Curtis House, Grant Park, 815–465–6025.
Homestead Restaurant, 1230 South East Avenue, 815–933–6214.
Winfield Inn, State Route 50 north, Bradley, exit 315 off Interstate 57, 815–939–3501.
Leo's on the River, 650 West Station Steet, 815–937–4772.
Little Corporal, Kennedy Drive and Brookmont Boulevard, 815–932–6795.
Redwood Inn, Route 52 at I–57, 815–939–9446.

III:2
Lockport

WILL COUNTY
Illinois

THOSE who paddle on the existing twenty-seven miles of the old Illinois-Michigan canal often are not aware that the water beneath them is directly responsible for the rise of the mighty metropolis, Chicago. Those who bike or hike along Lockport's towpath are stepping in the tracks of the mules and horses that towed the bateaus barges en route to and from the Illinois River. The tourist with a sense of history might ponder on this link between the Atlantic Ocean and the Gulf of Mexico which opened up the Midwest to the world.

The Indians left no imprint on Lockport, though the Potawatomi used and controlled the river before the white man. The earliest settlers did leave their mark. The first hamlet, called Yankee Settlement, started in the 1830s, and the tiny town began to take on a New England look with a town square and Greek Revival–style limestone houses and churches. In the latter part of the nineteenth century, as the use of the canal declined, the town suffered. In the twentieth century it has shifted its economic base away from the canal, preserving many canal era structures. It is the best preserved canal town in the nation.

Directions

A trip to the canal town of Lockport can be a day's outing; it is also possible to include Princeton if you do not linger. If you want to take a weekend, you can add Peoria. Take Interstate 55 south to the Bolingbrook exit for State Routes 7 and 53. Go south through Romeoville and follow State Route 7 to State Street. Turn south and go one block to Eighth. Although Lockport is not congested, the flavor of the town is more easily savored if you explore the commercial center from Seventh to Eleventh on foot. It takes less than an hour.

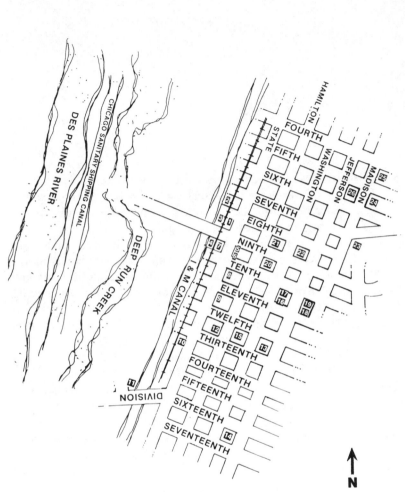

Lockport

ARCHITECTURAL TOUR

The distinctive attraction is the remains of the nineteenth-century Illinois-Michigan Canal, only a short block west of State Street. The National Register historic district stretches from the west side of the old canal east to the public square on Washington Street and from Seventh Street on the north to Eleventh Street on the south. The suggested tour includes areas outside the offically designated district, for there are a number of architecturally significant buildings on adjacent streets. If you drive to the outlying area, the entire tour takes a bit more than an hour. 1. The Illinois-Michigan Canal headquarters, 803 South State Street, was built in two sections. The northern one-story wing was the original Greek Revival clapboard building erected in 1837 while the canal was being built. The Queen Anne addition to the south was built in 1876. The building is oriented both to the canal on the west and to State Street on the east. Currently the Will County Historical Society operates it as a museum. 2. The Gaylord-Martin- Hyland building at the north end of the public landing between the railroad tracks and the old canal was the first canal warehouse, built in 1838, just two years after the town was founded. The western wing was added in the 1860s. The eastern three-story section is Italianate in style. The complex has been restored to its 1870s appearance. 3. The public landing was planned as an open space in the 1837 plat. The Will County Historical Society has established a pioneer village with buildings collected from around the county. 4. On the south side of Ninth Street is the large limestone Norton grain warehouse and shipping center, built about 1848. The eastern section was constructed in 1855. 5. State Street was a section of Archer Road, which connected Lockport with Chicago in the early nineteenth century. When the town was platted, it was designated as the widest street of the town. Today it is the commercial center, along with East Ninth Street. The east side of State Street between Ninth and Tenth Streets burned in 1895, destroying all but the building at the northeast corner of Tenth. The block was rebuilt within a few months. The first floors have been altered, but look at the upper stories to see the styles popular in the mid-1890s. Most of the buildings are two stories and have elaborate cornices. One has twin bay windows. 6. Miller hardware, on Tenth Street, is a limestone Greek Revival building, the only one on the block to survive the 1895 fire. 7. On the west side of State Street is 903 South State, built in 1876.It is a brick building with an elaborate Italianate cast-iron front, pop-ular in that period. Side walls and the rear were constructed of brick. 8. The limestone Norton Opera House at the southeast corner of State and Tenth, a multipurpose building, was probably of Greek Revival style originally. The third floor was added, and the original cornice replaced with the present brown one. **9.** On the southeast corner of Eleventh and State stands the Adelman building. The southern section was constructed in 1891; three years later the northern corner portion was added. The storefront is the original cast iron, as is the elaborately painted second-story turret on the corner. **10.** At State and Thirteenth Streets is the Chicago, Alton, and St. Louis Railroad depot, constructed in 1862. It is a limestone Italianate building with prominent brackets supporting the roof. **11.** North of Division is all that remains of the 1845 Lock Number One, the first lock built on the canal. The limestone walls were built of local stone. **12.** The limestone Greek Revival house at 1225 South Hamilton was built in the 1860s by John Heck. Lockport is noted for its limestone Greek Revival homes. This style, a simplified symmetrical box ending in a pediment at the roof line, was extremely popular in the Midwest. The wooden Greek Revival houses are distinguished by column-supported entrances and fanlights. The examples in Lockport run the gamut from the very plain to the more elaborate, which are not quite so fancy as the later Italianate. **13.** On the northwest corner of Thirteenth and Jefferson is a wooden Greek Revival house. The northern half is two-story and the southern one-story. It is painted bright red with window trim strikingly outlined in white. It is unusual not only for its color but also because it is a good example of the Greek Revival style in wood. **14.** Not in the historic district but worth a visit is the Catholic South Lockport Cemetery between Sixteenth and Seventeenth and Washington and Jefferson Streets. **15.** At the southeast corner of Twelfth and Hamilton is the Romanesque St. Dennis Roman Catholic Church, built in 1877. It was designed by Chicago architects Egan and Hill. The clock in the tower was moved here after the 1895 fire; the tower was extended to accommodate it. Despite the loss of the top of the tower in a 1965 tornado, the remainder is a landmark that can be seen for miles. **16.** At 326 East Eleventh Street is St. John's Episcopal Church, a limestone building constructed in the English Gothic Revival style. It was built in 1873 and designed by architect P.N. Hartwell. It is considered one of the Midwest's finest examples of this architectural style. **17.** At the southeast corner of Tenth and Washington is the original 1855 Methodist church, built of limestone in the Greek Revival style. It was designed by Julius Scheibe. The original tower has been removed. **18.** A block east and south at 1020 South Jefferson is a frame house built in 1848 in the Greek Revival style. Its balloon construction was a new technique that used lightweight wooden framing such as posts, joists, beams, and girders joined by nails. The siding is new. **19.** The Meyer house at 1006 South Jefferson is an Italianate-style building. It is made of limestone and was built in the 1850s. **20.** At Ninth and Washington is the former Congregational church, built of limestone in 1839. It is now restored to its 1880 appearance. **21.** In the middle of the village square is the Romanesque 1896 Old Central Grade School. It is a massive limestone building with large windows and a heavy entrance portico. **22.** A block east at 819 South Jefferson is a clapboard Italianate villa with an open cupola and ornate window trim. It is a good example of a style popular in the 1860s and 1870s. **23.** The limestone Greek Revival house at 535 East Seventh Street was erected in 1840 for Robert Milne. The first floor has three six-over-six windows, while the second-floor windows are about half that size. **24.** The Lockport City Cemetery is a collection of nineteenth-century monuments, including Gothic, Romanesque, early Georgian, and Egyptian Revival. **25.** North one block at 410 South Madison is the limestone stucco Arnold house, built in the 1850s. **26.** St. Joseph's Church at Jefferson and Fifth is a simple limestone structure erected in 1874. The large freestanding cross in front of the church is unique. **27.** Three blocks west and two blocks south at 128 East Seventh is the Italianate O'Connell house. The decorations, particularly the heavy cornice brackets and the intricate ironwork outlining the porch roofs, are of particular interest.

Festivals, Tours, and Other Places of Interest

Old Canal Days is held the third weekend in June. For more information call 815–838–4744. Not to be missed is the Rialto Square Theatre at 102 North Chicago Street in neighboring Joliet, built by the Rubens brothers in 1926. In 1981 it was completely restored. Tours are available, and box-office hours are Monday–Friday, 10:00 A.M.–5:00 P.M., and Saturday, 10:00 A.M.–2:00 P.M., 815–726–6600 or 312–242–7171.

Historical Information

Illinois-Michigan Canal Museum and Will County Historical Society, open daily 1:00 P.M.–4:30 P.M., 803 South State Street, Lockport, IL 60441, 815–838–5080. Isle a la Cache Museum, Romeo Road (135th Street), just east of State Route 53 in Romeoville, IL 60441, 815–886–1467. Lockport Chamber of Commerce, 906 South State Street, Lockport, IL 60441, 815–838–3357. Lockport Old Canal Days Committee, 222 East Ninth, Lockport, IL 60441, 815–838–4744. John Lamb, Professor of History, Lewis University, Route 53, Romeoville, IL 60441, 815–838–0500. Illinois State Museum, Lockport Gallery, 200 West Eighth Street, third floor, 815–838–8400.

Lodging

Holiday Inn, 411 South Larkin and Interstate 80, Joliet, IL 60436, 815–729–2000.

Howard Johnson Motor Lodge, U.S. 52 and Interstate 55, Lockport, IL 60441, 815–725–0111.

Manor Motel, Interstate 55 and Route 6, Joliet, IL 60436, 815–467–5385.

Quality Inn, U.S. 52 and Interstate 55, Joliet, IL 60435, 815–725–2180.

Regal 8 Inn, 2219 ½ West Jefferson Street, Joliet, IL 60435, 815–744–1220.

Restaurants

Cafe Eclair, 117 East Ninth Street, 815–838–0044, handicapped accessible.

George's Restaurant, 990 North State, 815–838–7225, handicapped accessible.

Inglenook, Burdy North, 815–838–4181.

Johnny's Greek Restaurant, 1030 East Ninth, 815–838–2445, handicapped accessible.

Kualla Mexican Restaurant, 1026 South State Street, 815–834–1158, handicapped accessible.

Pagoda House Restaurant, 952 East Ninth Street, 815–838–5123, handicapped accessible.

Hotel President Dining Room, 933 South State, 815–838–1881.

Public Landing Restaurant, 200 West Eighth Street, 815–838–6500.

Tall Grass, 1006 South State Street, 815–838–5566, handicapped accessible.

III:3

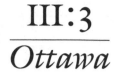

Ottawa

LA SALLE COUNTY
Illinois

JUST west of Ottawa stands Starved Rock where the last of the Illini Indians starved to death in the mid-eighteenth century rather than surrender to their enemies, the Potawatomi and their allies. Today you can climb the Rock or picnic in its shadow and imagine the Indians at war and the French trading post, long since gone.

The town of Ottawa was platted in 1831 as Carbonia; a year later it became the La Salle County seat. Settlers during the mid-1850s included English, Scottish, German, and Dutch people. Due to its silica deposits and central location along the Illinois Waterway, it remains prosperous today.

The first of the Lincoln-Douglas debates was held here. A marker in Washington Park commemorates the event. Some of the audience sat on the Reddick mansion's front steps while William Reddick, a loyal Democrat, sat with Stephen A. Douglas on the platform. Undoubtedly present for the confrontation were three of Lincoln's friends: Judge T. Lyle Dickey, a political opponent; his son-in-law W.H. Lawrence, a political supporter; and John Hossack, another supporter, whose houses you can see today.

Directions

In the fall or spring you could visit Ottawa on a day's outing. If you wanted to spend a long day, you could combine Lockport and Ottawa. From Chicago take Interstate 55 southwest to Interstate 80 west and exit on State Route 23 south into Ottawa. It will lead you right to Washington Park, where our tour starts. If you combine Ottawa with a stop at Lockport, you might consider taking U.S. 6, which parallels the old Illinois-Michigan Canal, now a historic industrial corridor. It also intersects State Route 23, which will lead you to Washington Park.

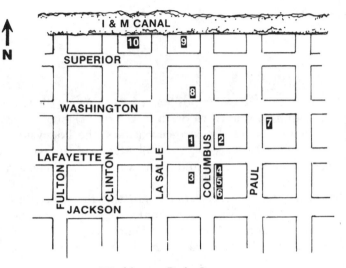

Washington Park, Ottawa

ARCHITECTURAL TOURS
WASHINGTON PARK TOUR

This three-by-four-block area is compact enough to walk around. Although the town was first laid out along the river banks, this area has been the center since the mid-nineteenth century. 1. The mansion on the northwest corner of Columbus and Lafayette was built by William Reddick in 1856. This ornate Italianate red brick and limestone mansion is one of the grandest ever built in central Illinois. Among its novelties were an elaborate bell system, an intercom, running water, gas lighting, and exceptionally fine plaster ceilings. The architects were William B. Olmsted and Peter Nicholson. 2. Across Columbus on the northeast corner is the imposing Greek Revival Illinois Appellate Court building, erected in 1856–60 with wings added in 1877. A grand staircase leads to a column-supported portico topped by a decorative pediment. 3. Washington Park was a gift of the Illinois-Michigan Canal Commission in 1831. Besides a monument to the first Lincoln-Douglas debate, the park includes a marble column dedicated to the town's Civil War casualties, cannon from the Civil War and World Wars I and II, a veterans' war memorial, and another to Boy Scout founder W.D. Boyce. 4. On the east side of Columbus is the limestone English Gothic Christ Episcopal Church, built in 1870–72. The church has a commanding side tower with spire and inside a handsome altar and impressive stained-glass windows. 5. Just a short distance south you will find the Masonic Temple. 6. A bit south and on the same side of the street is the First Congregational Church, erected in 1870. The Gothic Revival church has one prominent and one smaller tower and opalescent-glass windows. 7. One block east and one block north on the east side of Paul Street is Marquette High School. This Eclectic-Roman Revival building with central tower topped by a cross was opened in 1900. 8. Walk west on Washington, and between Columbus and La Salle on the north side of the street you will see St. Columba Catholic Church, begun in 1877 and finished in 1884. This limestone Gothic Revival church has a large corner tower with spire. 9. A block north at Columbus and Canal is 1217 Columbus, the original Illinois-Michigan Canal tollhouse. This small one-room structure has been covered by new siding. 10. Once the Illinois-Michigan Canal was here. Imagine a sixty-foot waterway connecting the Great Lakes with the Mississippi River via the Illinois River. You might well take a detour of several blocks to the east to the point on Michigan Street where it meets the Fox River. Here you can see the Fox River Aqueduct, which carried the Illinois-Michigan Canal over the river.

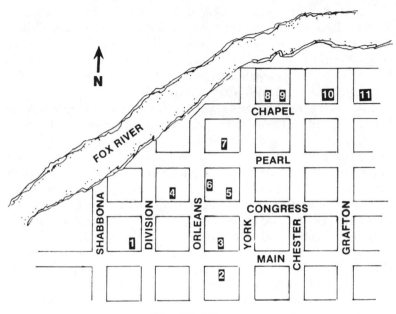

East Side, Ottawa

EAST SIDE TOUR

Drive south on La Salle Street to Madison, where you go east to view the La Salle County courthouse, built in 1881–84. This combination Renaissance-Romanesque Revival structure has prominent limestone piers, a heavily bracketed roof line, and an imposing three-arched entrance portico. Return to La Salle and go south to Main, where you turn left, or east, across the Fox River. Here you will find a five-by-four-block residential area bounded on two sides by the Fox River. 1. On an elevated lot at the northwest corner of East Main and Division is the Vincent J. Duncan house. This simplified late Queen Anne house has a prominent wraparound front porch, two-story bay, shingled second story, and gables with Palladian windows. 2. At 527 East Main is the J.O. Harris vernacular house. Its long first-floor windows indicate its age. The house was originally clapboard but has been covered with brick. 3. The vernacular Queen Anne house at 630 East Main Street was built by H.W. Johnson. This clapboard house has limestone foundations, a Classical front porch with Doric columns, and a pediment entrance. A square third-floor tower is its other prominent feature. 4. The clapboard house at 406 Congress Street was built in 1862 by John J. Nattinger. Its six-over-six windows and fanlighted entrance look original, but the siding appears new. 5. The handsome Italianate-Georgian Jeremiah Strawn house at 532 Congress was built in 1841. Not only does the house have distinctive lintels and sills and a bracketed gable roof, but it also has a Classical bracketed small entrance porch. 6. The E.Y. Griggs house is at 704 Orleans. This 1870 Italianate red brick house has a prominent circular entrance portico topped by a fancy ironwork balustrade. Arched windows, including one in the heavily bracketed roof line, are an elegant detail. 7. At 622 Pearl, Washington Bushnell built a French Renaissance-style brick house. A square three-story tower, rounded windows, and a small portico entrance are distinguishing features. The third-floor dormer was added later. 8. The Thorsen-Fleury house at 602 Chapel is an American Southern Colonial structure started in 1854 and completed in 1857. 9. The large Italianate house at 640 Chapel was built in 1864 by John Manley and called "Bellrose." It has a bracketed frieze punctuated with eyebrow windows, and small dormers protrude from the roof, giving light to the third-floor ballroom. The porte-cochere and the enclosing of the half front porch are obviously additions. 10. The Walter D. Strawn house at 702 Chapel was built in 1892. The large clapboard house has a three-story tower and gables as well as a wide columned wraparound front porch. 11. At 804 Chapel is the Hollister-Glover house, named "Montezuma." The house has Roman windows, an Italianate bracketed roof, and a small columned portico protecting the entrance. Return to Main Street and take

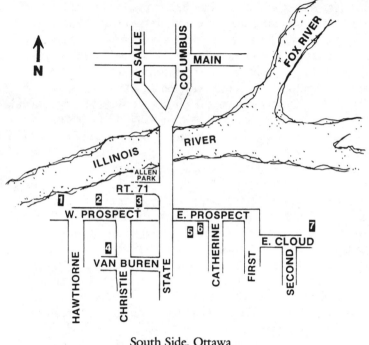

South Side, Ottawa

it west to La Salle Street. There turn south, or left, and cross the Illinois River to Van Buren Street.

SOUTH SIDE TOUR

The south bank of the Illinois River where it joins the Fox was the scene of early settlement. The original plat covered the area from the river to Van Buren Street. Houses along Prospect Street include some from the early settlement and others from the end of the nineteenth century. You can park and walk along Prospect to view the seven houses. Be sure to pause in Allen Park and take in the view of the city from the river's south bank. 1. The Eclectic Victorian house at 222 West Prospect was built in the 1890s by J.E. Porter. The three-story house has a central gabled section and two wings. The entrance is protected by a small portico. 2. In 1854–55 John Hossack built the Southern Colonial house at 210 West Prospect. Its distinguishing feature is the wide two-story porch stretching across the front. 3. The rambling three-story Queen Anne clapboard Pope house at 116 West Prospect sports a wide front porch, bays, dormers, and gables. 4. The Gothic Revival one-and-one-half-story cottage at 229 Christie Street dates from the early 1840s. The front section dates from 1887, hence the protruding bay window. 5. The Queen Anne house at 121 East Prospect was built in 1890 by Lester Strawn. One of its innovations is the second-story enclosed sleeping porch. A small Palladian window decorates its central gable, and a three-story tower with conical roof anchors its eastern end. 6. On the south side in front of 127 East Prospect is the site of Fort Johnson. 7. In 1837 Joseph Cloud built the house at 400 East Prospect. Basically Federalist in design, it is a forerunner of fancier styles in its bracketed eaves. The side- and fan-lighted entrance are particularly fine. The entrance portico is probably an addition.

NORTH BLUFF

Take State Street north over the bridge, where it becomes Columbus Street. Follow Columbus Street north to Norris Drive. Go west, or left, on Norris Drive one block to LaSalle Street. Turn north, or right, on LaSalle Street and go to the top of the hill. Now you are in the North Bluff district. Only two of the mid-nineteeth-century houses remain. 1. Erected in 1842, the T. Lyle Dickey house is at 2011 Caton Road. This rambling vernacular house may well be the result of numerous additions. It has both an east and a west wing and a center section. 2. The Gothic Revival stone house at 2101 Lincoln was built in 1858 for W.H.L. Wallace.

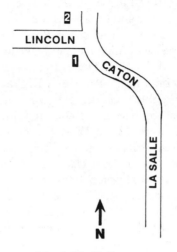

North Bluff, Otawa

Festivals, Tours, and Other Places of Interest

The Reddick Mansion Association offers tours and can be contacted at P.O. Box 563, Ottawa, IL 61350. The Chamber of Commerce provides a map for a self-guided tour, Reddick Mansion, 100 West Lafayette, P.O. Box 888, Ottawa, IL 61350, 815–433–0084.

Historical Information

Old Illinois Houses (1948) by John Drury. The official commemorative book *Ottawa Sesquicentennial*, available from the Chamber of Commerce, is a valuable source of information about the town's history, its historic buildings, and its business and social institutions, and it can be obtained by contacting 100 West Lafayette, P.O. Box 888, Ottawa, IL 61350, 815–433–0084.

Lodging

Ottawa Inn-Starved Rock, Interstate 80 at State Route 23, 815–434–3400.

Sands Motel, 1215 La Salle Street, 815–434–6440.

Starved Rock Lodge, ten miles west of Ottawa on State Route 71, also has twelve cabins, P.O. Box 471, Utica, IL 61373, 815–667–4211.

Surrey Motel, State Route 23 at Interstate 80, North Ottawa, 815–433–1263.

Restaurants

Casa Mia Restaurant and Lounge, 219 Eighteenth Street, Ottawa (Naplate), 815–434–0758.

Crowley's Steak House, 1321 La Salle Street, 815–433–2400.

Graffiti Ristorante, 1409 LaSalle Street, 815–433–9066.

Green Mill Restaurant, 100 West Madison Street, 815–434–6626.

Hank's, Highway 71 and Interstate 80, 815–433–2540.

Kickapoo Klub, Starved Rock Marina, Dee Bennett Road, 815–433–0275.

Monte's Riverside Inn, Routes 6 and 71 at the Fox River Bridge, 815–434–5000.

New Chiam Restaurant, junction of State Route 71 and Interstate 80, 815–433–3240.

Row House Cafe, 726 Columbus Street, 815–433–2233.

Tequila Eddy's, 209 Twentieth Avenue, Naplate, 815–433–4177.

III:4
Princeton

BUREAU COUNTY
Illinois

THE town of Princeton dates from the early 1830s when a group of settlers from Northampton, Massachusetts, arrived. It was incorporated as a town in 1837, and it is the Bureau County seat. It has maintained a gracious nineteenth-century atmosphere.

Slavery was an important issue here in Princeton. People were not united and the debate was fierce, but never fatal as in some Illinois towns. Early settlers John Howard Bryant, brother of poet William Cullen Bryant, and Congregationalist minister Owen Lovejoy were vocal abolitionists who practiced their beliefs by providing stations in their own homes on the underground railroad for escaping slaves. Bryant hosted Abraham Lincoln at a political rally on July 4, 1856. When war broke out in 1861, Bryant and others went to a great effort to raise and equip troops for the Union.

Directions

Princeton is a leisurely one-day trip from Chicago, or it can be combined with Lockport for a busy day. You might also consider a weekend trip, which could also include Ottawa and Peoria. From Chicago take Interstate 80 to the Princeton exit. You will be on State Route 26 going south, which becomes Main Street and leads you right to the courthouse. There you will find parking.

ARCHITECTURAL TOUR

We recommend that you walk around the area of Park Avenue East and West and the other streets near the courthouse and drive to the outlying areas, stops 15–27. 1. East of the courthouse between Church and Field Streets on the north side of Park Avenue East at 101 is the McConihe house. This brick Greek Revival structure was built in 1847. 2. At 125 Park Avenue East is the large brick Italianate Stevens house, built in 1854. 3. Known as "Keepsake Cottage," the vernacular Greek Revival house at 517 South Church Street was built about

70

1850. The porch is obviously a later addition. **4.** The Greek Revival one-and-one-half-story clapboard house at 112 East Peru was built before 1856. The porch may be more recent since it has fancy columns, and the two-story rear section is probably an addition. **5.** Walk south on Main or Pleasant two blocks to the courthouse. At the northwest corner of Pleasant and Park Avenue West, across from the courthouse, you will find 109, the Clark-Norris house, now the Bureau County Historical Society Museum. This Prairie Square house was built in 1900 and has third-story dormers, two of which sport balconies; a second-story sun porch and balustraded balcony; and a first-floor wraparound porch. **6.** At 303 Park Avenue West is the John H. Delano house. This nineteenth-century Gothic Revival house has bullseye windows in the gables, a protruding bay in both the first and second stories, and a wide-columned porch across the front. **7.** The Italianate Shepard house at 323 Park Avenue West was built in 1862. The columns supporting the porch are more recent, as is the rear addition. **8.** At 432 Park Avenue West is the Italianate Ferris house. This beautifully preserved house has bracketed eaves and a wide front porch. **9.** The large red brick Italianate house at 414 Park Avenue West was built in 1863. Known as the Kendall residence, it has bracketed eaves, a small classical entrance porch, a first-floor corner porch, and a bay window. **10.** The Windsor house at 128 Park Avenue West at South First is a Prairie-style building reminiscent of the Oak Park and Chicago houses designed by Frank Lloyd Wright. **11.** Turn south on First Street. At 904 is the Burr house, built in 1892. This Queen Anne house has an Eastlake front porch and double-front third-floor gables, one with a bullseye window and the other with a large half-circle window. Both gables have fish-scale shingles. **12.** At the corner turn east onto Boyd to 212. Built in the 1880s, it is a fine Second Empire three-story house with bays on the first two floors and a wide front porch with a pediment entrance. It is called "Round Grove." **13.** Walk east to Main Street and turn right, or south. The Gothic Revival brick house at 1110 was built for Cyrus Bryant, brother of poet William Cullen Bryant, in 1844–45. It has a wide front porch and a third-story arched window in the gable. **14.** At 1120 South Main is the Cairo A. Trimble house. This late Victorian Eclectic house has gables, dormers, a crownlike decoration above its center second-story bay, and various window trims. The landscape was designed by a Richmond, Virginia, architect. **15.** The Gothic Revival red brick house at 1324 South Main was built in 1867. It has remarkable gingerbread trim. **16.** John Howard Bryant, another of the poet's brothers, built the fine Gothic Revival house at 1518 South Main in 1844. It is built of brick and has a wide front porch and an arched window in the front gable. **17.** Proceed two miles south on

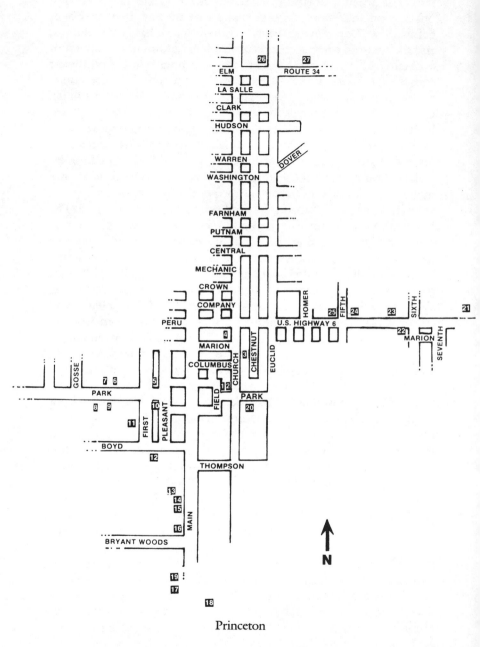

Princeton

Main Street, which is the Princeton-Tiskilwa road. There you will find the Arthur Bryant house, built in 1855. It is known as "Persimmon Grove" after the nursery which originally adjoined it. **18.** South and east of it is the home of another Bryant brother, Austin. Built in the mid-1800s, it is red brick. **19.** Returning to Princeton on Main Street, notice the large two-story Greek Revival red brick Clark house. Built in 1837, it has a two-story front porch. **20.** Continue into Princeton and turn east onto Thompson to Church Street. Take it north one block to Park Avenue East. Just one half block east on Park Avenue you will find 302 on the south side of the street. This red brick Greek Revival house was built in 1834 by William Carse. **21.** Proceed east on Park Avenue East to Fifth Street, then one block north to Peru Street, which is also U.S. 6. Turn right, or east, and proceed to the Owen Lovejoy home on the north side of the street. This rambling two-story vernacular house was built by Butler Denham before 1838. It is now a museum, renovated to appear as it was in the mid-1800s. It is open Saturday and Sunday from 1:00 P.M. to 4:00 P.M. from May to October. **22.** Go west on Peru. "Paddock Hall," a late Victorian house, is at 652. **23.** On the north side of Peru Street is the Second Empire three-story Skinner house at 627. It has a wide front porch and east bay window. **24.** At 609 East Peru is "Evergreen Lodge," built in 1860 by Martin Ballou. This Victorian house has an ornate columned front porch. **25.** The Gothic Revival cottage at 543 East Peru was built in 1852 by J.I. Taylor. It has a wide front porch decorated in carpenter's lace and topped by a balustrade. The second-story front dormer has a large Palladian window. This cottage still has the beautiful English garden that was created by the original owner. **26.** Proceed west two blocks to Euclid and turn right, or north, onto Elm Place. On the northwest corner of Elm and Euclid is 323 Elm Place, the Brown house, built in 1890. This fanciful Queen Anne house has a wraparound front porch with pediment entrance, all decorated in Stick style. Over the entrance on the second floor is an inset balcony showing a Near East influence. There are gables, bay windows, and stained-glass windows, as well as a balcony projecting from the third-story gable with Stick-style decoration. **27.** In the next block east is 425, the fine red brick Italianate Virden house, with bracketed eaves, bullseye windows in the gables, a wide wraparound front porch, and hooded windows.

Festivals, Tours, and Other Places of Interest

A self-guided tour map is available at the Chamber of Commerce, 435 South Main Street, Princeton, IL 61356, 815-875-2616, or from the

Bureau County Historical Society Museum, 109 Park Avenue West, Princeton, IL 61356. The Owen Lovejoy Museum (see 21).

Historical Information

Big Bureau and Bright Prairies by Doris P. Leonard. Bureau County Historical Society, has a museum and a library. Contact curator Mary W. Williams, Bureau County Historical Society, 109 Park Avenue West, Princeton, IL 61356, 815–875–2184. Matson Public Library, Princeton, IL 61356, 815–875–1331. Princeton Chamber of Commerce, 435 South Main Street, Princeton, IL 61356, 815–875–2616. Princeton City Hall, Princeton, IL 61356, 815–875–2631.

Lodging

Lincoln Inn, south of Interstate 80 on Route 26, also Main Street, 815–875–3371.

Princeton Motor Lodge, one block south of the Lincoln Inn, 815–875–1121.

Restaurants

Bonnelli's, 924 North Main, 815–875–6018, handicapped accessible.

Coffee Cup, Railroad Avenue, 815–875–8272.

Kristi-Jean's Tea Room, 1101 North Main, 815–872–0508.

Oriental Gardens, 428 South Main, 815–875–2560, handicapped accessible.

III:5
Peoria
PEORIA COUNTY
Illinois

ARLY settlement took place along the river front, but with
the development of industrial and transportation facilities,
businessmen began to build their houses along the river
bluffs above the smoke and the noise. Early development
was along Randolph, Moss, and High Streets, and many of these
early mansions remain today, reminiscent of an affluent time when
owners could afford to express their whims in many styles. Some of
these buildings were designed by such top architects as William Le
Baron Jenny, Daniel Burnham, Holabird and Root, and Frank Lloyd
Wright.

The city of Peoria, named after a local Indian tribe, dates from a
stop on Marquette and Joliet's famous 1630 exploration. The earliest
settlement was the French Fort Creve Coeur, built in 1680 on the east
side of the Illinois River. Fort St. Louis II, constructed near the
"narrows" between upper and lower Peoria Lakes, was established by
LaSalle and Tonti in 1691–92 and may well be the oldest continuous
settlement in Illinois. The French continued to live in the area until
1811. Americans arrived in 1819, and the town was incorporated in
1834.

Peoria seems to have the motto "Use what you can." It was built on
the ruins of Fort Clark in 1819, and has survived Prohibition and the
recent decline of the agricultural and heavy machinery industries.

Directions

One day would hardly do justice to this river town. It can be
combined with Lockport and Princeton for a weekend trip. From
Chicago take Interstate 80 west to the Hennepin exit, which is Interstate 180 south. Proceed south a few miles to State Route 29, which
follows the west bank of the Illinois River to Peoria.

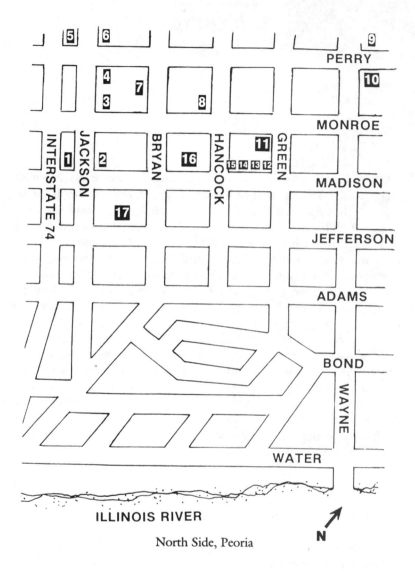

North Side, Peoria

ARCHITECTURAL TOURS

Peoria boasts two historic districts: the North Side and the West Bluff.

NORTH SIDE TOUR

The area east of I–74 called the North Side became a desirable residential area in the 1850s. Its growth was limited by the bluff, so by the end of the century it was completely settled. It remains today a neighborhood frozen in time. From the downtown area go northeast, crossing I–74 on NE Madison, and park. **1.** Between I–74 and Jackson at 321 Madison NE is the Cornerstone Building. This 1889 Richardsonian Romanesque church was designed by the architect W.W. Boyington, who built Chicago's famous water tower. It has an ornate limestone east facade and massive tower; the hardware is highly artistic. This building has recently been restored and is used as a catering hall. **2.** Across Jackson is the 1899 Notre Dame High School South at 401 Madison NE. Its architects, Reeves and Baillie, were the designers of City Hall. Sometimes described as Chateauesque or German Manor House style, it retains its original facade though the entrance doors have been modernized. Highly decorated dormers adorn its roof, and two large limestone statues seem to guard the entrance from their second-story perches. **3.** One block northeast at 401 Monroe Street NE is the Michael D. Spurck house. This Queen Anne house, now badly in need of repair, has a wraparound front porch, and smaller second- and third-story balconies rise from the porch pediment. A fish-scale tower adorns one corner, and a second-story bay window gives a fine view. **4.** At the southwest corner of Jackson and Perry is the Scottish Rite cathedral at 400 Perry NE. This brick Gothic Revival building has flying buttresses and an interior with heavy wood paneling in the Gothic style. The architect was Walter Jameson of the Peoria firm of Jameson and Harrison, which also designed the Shrine Mosque. **5.** Diagonally across the street at 331 Perry NE is the partially restored Wheeler-Woolmer house. Of a remarkably eclectic Victorian design, this 1877 house features Eastlake-style wood posts and Italianate-style windows, and a central tower rises above the roof line over an ornate Gothic-style gable. This house is indicative of the ostentatious lifestyle of the era. **6.** The Gertrude Oakford house at 403 Perry NE was built in 1899. The brick facade is constructed so that it appears to be a solid color. There is a porch across the front, which carries out the Georgian Revival style. Other styles are represented: the bracketed roof line is reminiscent of the Italianate; and the columned bay window, flanked by two round side lights, is a Queen Anne touch. **7.** A block southeast on Bryan at 601–7 are the Sandmeyer Flats. The style is Queen Anne with corner towers and twin gables. **8.** Go southeast to Monroe, where at 521 you will find the Christian Assembly Church. It was built as a Jewish temple in 1898. This Norman Gothic building has two crenelated Norman towers, sandstone buttresses, and stained-glass windows. **9.** At 803 Perry NE is the Ira D. Buck house, built in 1899. This Queen Anne house has a wide front porch; second-story bay; and two third-story dormers, one with a fancy gable and the other an oyster shell. **10.** Across the street at 802 is the Flavell Shurtleff house, another more elaborate Queen Anne structure. It has a remarkable third-floor fish-scale gable, which includes a recessed pillared porch with heavy bracketed overhang. A three-story tower with decorative window treatment dominates the southwest corner. A wide porch covers half the front. **11.** The only remaining farmhouse in the district is at 517 Green Street. This plain clapboard house has no ornamentation. **12.** Go southeast on Green Street to Madison, where you will find St. Mary's Cathedral, built in 1885–89. This Neo-Gothic church has fine twin spires and heavily paneled front doors; buttresses and stained-glass windows were added in 1935. **13.** Next door is the Diocesan chancery. This ornate limestone Italianate building has prominent quoins, decorative window hoods, third-floor dormers, and a recessed portico entrance flanked by polished marble columns. The most prominent feature is the curving French Renaissance stairway climbing from the street, where a columned portico rises to become the stairway's top railing. **14.** Farther southwest on the same side of Madison is 605 Madison NE, built in 1879 by Herbert F. Day. Little remains of this Italianate building's elaborate facade except the original first-floor front bay and the portico entrance. **15.** Next door at 603 Madison NE is the Phillip Zell house. Most of the ornamentation has been removed from this 1866 Italianate house and it has been covered with asbestos shingles, but the fanlight in the front gable and the columned front porch remain. **16.** One block southwest at 511 Madison NE is the house built by Valentine Jobst in 1902. It is a transitional house with some elements of Queen Anne, such as an implied tower on the southeast corner and a decorated pediment on the front porch, but in general it is a simplified facade. **17.** At 403 Jefferson NE is a much earlier house built in 1840 by Jacob Gale. Rumored to be the oldest house in the North Side area, this simple Federalist house has a Greek Revival entrance porch, which was added later. Plans are under way for restoration of this significant old home. Just around the corner on Jackson Street you again find the Cornerstone Building where your tour began.

WEST BLUFF TOUR

Coming into Peoria along State Route 29, which becomes U.S. 24, exit at Main Street to reach the Bluff historic district. Proceed west to North Street; take it north a short block to Randolph. High Street intersects Main from the south. You can tour the Randolph/Roanoake area by foot and then drive to High Street to walk that area. The suggested tour is of part of the area known as the West Bluff, which was settled after 1850. It was a fashionable residential area until the suburban migration of the 1950s. 1. The Paff residence at 209 Randolph NE was built in the mid-1880s. This Second Empire-style house has a turn-of-the-century porch, but its mansard roof is original. 2. Across the street at 234 Randolph NE is an Eastlake-style house built in 1887 by Walter Reyburn. This style is an offshoot of the Queen Anne. It features elaborate woodwork such as the latticed porch. This house has a second-story balcony, a third-story tower, and an elaborate gable. 3. The Ballance house, built in the mid-1880s at 240 Randolph NE, was in the Eastlake style. The second-story retains traces of this style, but the remodeled porch is Classical. 4. The house at 245 Randolph NE retains its Eastlake character especially in the front door and window trim. 5. At 255 Randolph NE is one of those wonderfully fanciful Queen Anne houses that combine almost every element found in the style. It was built in 1888 for John C. Wynd. The house has a wide front porch, a fish-scale second-story facade with protruding square bay over the front entrance, and a rounded bay on the south corner. The third floor has a gable with balcony and numerous other gables. Its chimneys are tall and decorated. 6. Proceed along Randolph to 256, a fine Queen Anne house designed by Warren H. Milner. The first-floor facade is brick and stone, rising to fish-scale on the upper floors. It has gables, bay windows, and stained-glass windows as well as a wraparound first-floor porch. 7. Across the street the house at 259 Randolph was built in 1890 by George P. Sandmeyer. This Queen Anne house has a wide variety of facade materials: brick, stone, wood, pressed metal, ornamental glass, and iron grille railings. The first floor has a wraparound porch and bay windows. The second has bay windows and, between them, a small balcony. The third has a large fish-scale gable and tower, behind which rises a tall chimney. 8. At 262 Randolph NE is an early twentieth-century Tudor house. 9. The house at 266 Randolph NE was built by architect W.H. Reeves. It contains elements of both Prairie School and Gothic Revival. 10. On the southeast corner of Randolph and Columbia Terrace at 270 Randolph NE is the 1910 California Bungalow built by J. Frank Ziegler. The facade is unchanged except for the green tile roof. Wide cement and stone steps

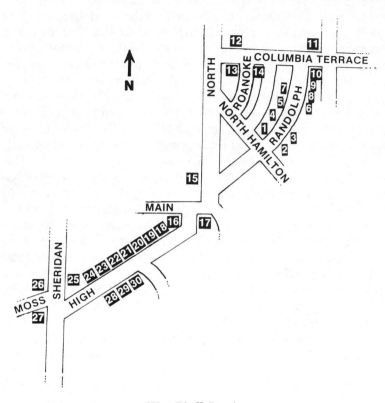

West Bluff, Peoria

capped by round urns rise to the wide entrance porch. A wide second-floor dormer and a high stone chimney are prominent features of the front facade. **11.** Across Columbia Terrace is 201, a simple Georgian Revival brick house built by Mrs. D.H. Proctor. It has three third-floor dormers, symmetrical windows, and a simple columned front portico balanced by a large second-floor window. **12.** At 305 West Columbia Terrace is an Eastlake house built in 1914. It has fine carpenter's lace trim, including an ornamental front porch. **13.** Across the street, 111 Roanoake NE is a Richardsonian Romanesque residence built by Sara A. Holman. This heavily rusticated green stone structure has a tower, gables, a green tile roof, and many beveled glass windows. Instead of a front porch it has a wide entrance terrace. The whole effect is rather fortresslike. **14.** Built about 1903, 112 Roanoake NE is a Tudor Revival house. **15.** The south end of North Street was developed in the 1870s. The house at 1101 is a fine brick Italianate with distinctive front bay window topped by grillework, as is the columned porch roof. The facade remains intact. **16.** On the southwest corner of Main and High is the former Methodist church. The original church was dedicated in 1869 and replaced in 1900 by the present Gothic structure, which is topped by a pressed-metal tower painted to resemble stone, a common practice. **17.** Opposite the church on the southeast corner of Main and High, the elaborate house at 1125 Main Street was built in 1882 for Edward Easton. The mansard roof with hooded windows marks it as Second Empire. Its bay windows, towers, grillework, friezes, and porches give it some Queen Anne elements. Drive to Giant Oak Park and park across from 423 High Street. Begin your walking tour on the north side of the street. **18.** The Queen Anne-style house at 429 West High was built in 1874 by John H. Francis. Its most prominent feature is a third-story belvedere, or open cupola, with an onion dome. A wraparound front porch with entrance pediment, bay windows, and many gables enrich the facade. **19.** The Clarke house at 437 West High Street was built in 1877 in the Italianate style. In 1901 it was remodeled in the Classical style with a porch, bay windows, and a new entrance; only the roof brackets remain to attest to its original appearance. **20.** J.M. Quinn's house at 443 West High is an even fancier Queen Anne than its neighbor (18), built four years earlier. Not only does it have a third-story tower; it also has a recessed balcony in its broad front gable. The original facade has been retained. **21.** The house at 509 West High was designed by architects Reeves and Baillie in 1906. Its elaborate Georgian Revival facade remains intact. **22.** Erastus D. Hardin built 511 West High in 1859. The original design was Second Empire, with the characteristic mansard roof with protruding dormers and square tower. In 1904 it was remodeled and the ornate portico, porte-cochere, and new third-floor windows were added. 23. Benjamin Langford Bourland built the house at 519 West High around 1850. This Gothic Revival cottage had a front-porch addition, but otherwise the facade is original. The symmetry is not characteristic of this style. 24. The Tudor Revival house at 611 West High was built in 1909 by E. Bethard. 25. The stable and carriage house at 816 Sheridan are all that remain of the imposing establishment of Joseph Benedict Greenhut. The Queen Anne stable and carriage house have numerous gables, a variety of window styles, and two prominent cast horse heads on the south and west walls. 26. William Bush constructed the house at 703 Moss Street in the 1860s. It is a brick Italianate house with white trim and a heavily bracketed roof. 27. The Leisey house across the street at 708 Moss was built in 1909. It is a Tudor Revival with an unusual red tile roof. Now return to the south side of High Street. 28. John H. Francis built the house at 600 West High in 1888. The first floor is heavily rusticated stone; the second shingles; and the roof, from which many dormers protrude, including one with a recessed balcony, is slate. The facade is further enlivened by bay windows, stained-glass panels, and wood and terracotta friezes. The exterior is original. 29. At 518 West High is a house built by Richard W. Kempshall in 1894. This Flemish Renaissance house has a full columned front porch with stamped-metal pediment, stepped gables, and third-floor balcony. 30. The Asahel Hale house at 510 West High is Queen Anne with a little bit of everything on its facade. The first floor is shaded by a wide front porch complete with elaborate pediment. Jutting out of the second story is a small balcony, a bay window, and a tower terminating in the third-floor steeple. Numerous dormers of different sizes and shapes dot the roof. You are now a half block from your car parked here at Giant Oak Park.

OTHER HOUSES OF NOTE

Our Bluff tour stopped at 700 Moss; however, a number of houses five to eleven blocks west on Moss have considerable architectural and historical merit. A few are described below.

The Tobias S. Bradley house at 802 West Moss was built in 1843. Lydia Moss Bradley, founder of Bradley University, lived here until her death. The facade of this home has been greatly changed since that time.

At 1212 West Moss is a house built in 1868 by Moses Pettengill. This Second Empire house has an Italianate bracketed cornice and hooded second-story windows. The porch with pressed-metal pediment was added later.

The Murray Baker house at 1222 West Moss is Georgian Revival in style. The brick house has a small columned portico, and three dormers jut from its roof.

The Little house at 1505 Moss Avenue was designed by Frank Lloyd Wright in 1903. The ground-level main entrance is outlined in stained glass with the pattern repeated in the door. Stained-glass panels light the living room, and vaulted ceiling windows are used in the dining room. The house is unchanged except for the porch enclosure and another bedroom.

At 1802 West Moss is the Benjamin Parker house. This white clapboard Greek Revival house has two front porches flanking a gabled center section.

Northeast of downtown Peoria on the east bluff section at 942 Glen Oak NE is the John C. Flanagan house, built about 1837. The symmetrical, simple style is Colonial, but it has the limestone lintels of the Greek Revival and the bracketed eaves of the Italianate. It originally faced the river, but in 1852 the house's entrance was changed to the street side and ornamental ironwork was added to the facade. It is now the headquarters of the Historical Society.

Festivals, Tours, and Other Places of Interest

The Peoria Historical Society holds an annual candlelight and poinsettia party the last weekend in November and the first weekend in December. The event may include visits to the Glen Oak Conservatory at 2218 North Prospect Road and the Pettengill-Morron house. Hours are Friday and Saturday 7:00 P.M.–9:00 P.M. and Sunday 2:00 P.M.–4:30 P.M. For further information contact the society, 942 Glen Oak NE, Peoria, IL 61603, 309–674–1921. The Peoria Historical Society conducts bus tours of historic places. Information about these narrated half- or full-day tours can be obtained from the Society, 942 Glen Oak NE, Peoria, IL 61603, 309–674–1921. The 1837 Flanagan house, headquarters for the Peoria Historical Society, is open for tours by appointment at 942 Glen Oak NE, Peoria, IL 61603, 309–674–1921. The Pettengill-Morron house at 1212 West Moss, Peoria, IL 61603 is open April–October on Sundays 2:00 P.M.–4:30 P.M. The Museum of Central Illinois Agriculture features a turn-of-the-century farmhouse, barn, and general store and is located at the Exposition Gardens, Northmore Road and Imperial Avenue, Peoria, IL 61603, 309–691–6332.

Historical Information

Cullom-Davis Library at Bradley University, Peoria, IL 61603, 309–677–2822. American Institute of Architects: contact Leslie Kenyon, Kenyon and Associates, for *Architectural/Historical Surveys*

(1976), 735 North Knoxville, Peoria, IL 61602, 309–674–7121. The Central Illinois Landmarks Foundation, P.O. Box 495, Peoria, IL 61651.

Lodging
Continental Regency, 500 Hamilton Boulevard, 309–674–2500.
Jumer's Castle Lodge, 117 North Western Avenue, 309–673–8040.
Hotel Pere Marquette, Main and Madison, 309–637–6500.

Restaurants
Ciota's Deli, Madison between Fulton and Main, 309–674–9000.
River Station, 212 Constitution Avenue, 309–676–7100, handicapped accessible.
Somerville's Restaurant, 456 Fulton Street, 309–676–6600.
Sully's Irish Pub, Adams between Liberty and Main, 309–674–0238.

IV:1

South Bend

ST. JOSEPH COUNTY
Indiana

THE first European settler in the South Bend area was a fur trader named Pierre Navarre, who arrived some time prior to 1820. With water power at their feet and boundless timber at their backs, the earliest white inhabitants turned to farming. By 1831 the town was platted and chosen as the county seat. Father Edward Sorin founded Notre Dame University in 1842.

James Oliver of South Bend took his place in agricultural history when he invented a chilling process which prevented the build-up of soil on the plow face, a major breakthrough in taming the prairie. His fellow townsmen, the Studebaker brothers, first produced spring wagons and later automobiles. In the second half of the nineteenth century, South Bend was a manufacturing center dominated by the Studebaker and Oliver companies. These two tycoons and many others built castlelike houses, turreted and bristling with bay windows, jutting roof lines, and an air of permanent superiority. They are still there. Since the end of World War II, the industrial base of the inner city has declined—but not the historic preservation movement.

Directions

If you are traveling through northern Indiana you might well stop and see South Bend, Elkhart, and Goshen. You have a choice of routes from Chicago. Take Interstate 94 to U.S. 20 into South Bend or leave U.S. 20 and take the Indiana Toll Road, Interstates 90 and 80, and exit at 77. Go south to the city's center and turn right, or west, on Washington Street to 620 West Washington. If you opted for U.S. 20, turn right on Main Street and go south to Washington and then right, or west, to 620 West Washington.

ARCHITECTURAL TOURS

The Washington Street area was favored by businessmen and professionals early in the history of South Bend for its proximity to the city center. Along Washington Street from the old courthouse west to the

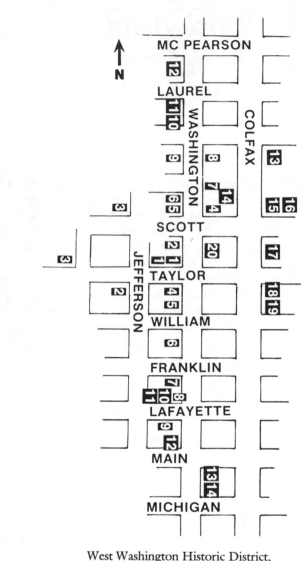

West Washington Historic District,
South Bend

1000 block you can see a parade of mid- and late-nineteenth-century buildings that attest to the city's prosperity. We have divided the district into manageable segments. Walking time is an hour or less for each.

WEST TOUR

1. Perhaps the grandest house ever built in Indiana is the Clement Studebaker house at 620 West Washington. Designed by architect Henry Ives Cobb and built between 1886 and 1888, this Richardsonian Romanesque Revival castle has forty rooms, twenty fireplaces, towers, porches, and a grand entrance. **2.** In 1880 Lewis Pagin built the modest house at 630 West Washington; it was purchased in 1886 by James Oliver. He had it enlarged and remodeled into a striking Queen Anne structure with corner tower, Eastlake porch, and two-story bay. **3.** Turn left, or south, on Scott Street to 329, St. Hedwig's, the first Polish Catholic church in South Bend. This Romanesque Revival church, built in 1881, has a prominent bell tower rising from the basilica's front. **4.** Returning to West Washington, you will see 715. Designed for Kersey DeRhodes by Frank Lloyd Wright, the Prairie-style house was built in 1907. **5.** Across the street you will see the oldest extant house in the city at 720. This two-story brick Federal house was erected in 1850 for Joseph Bartlett. Designed by Jonathan Webb, the house has a simple classical entrance portico, topped by a balustrade. **6.** At 730 West Washington is an elaborate Stick-style house built in 1884 for Edmund Maegher. The porch and the second-story bay are worth examining. **7.** In sharp contrast is 739 West Washington, the Renaissance Revival-style house designed by Freyermuth and Maurer for John Gergacz in 1923. This brick house also sports a recessed second-story balcony and a tile roof. **8.** In 1890 the Romanesque Revival stone house at 801 West Washington was built for William Kizer. This substantial residence has two round towers, a colossal chimney, and a porte-cochere. **9.** Across the street, at 808 West Washington, is an even grander Queen Anne– Romanesque Revival house. Designed by the New York architect Charles Alonzo Rich for Joseph Oliver, this fieldstone house has a round tower, tile roof, stone porches, and a heavy arched entrance. Of particular interest is the stone wall on the corner. **10.** Another Queen Anne house with Stick-style decorations, at 916 West Washington, was built in 1880, for Isabelle Case. The square entrance tower, the elaborate two-story bay, and the second-story window hoods are prominent features. **11.** At 920 West Washington is the Bowman residence, built in 1902. This three-story late Queen Anne has a wide front porch and three gables in the third story. Of considerable interest is the original wrought-iron fence. **12.** At 1016 West Washington is another two-story Prairie-style house, built in 1907 for Frederick O'Brien. **13.** Go north one block to Colfax Avenue. There at 833 you will see a Swiss-chalet-type house built in 1910 for Francis Keefer. Besides its wide gable and third-floor balcony, it has a heavily decorated porch. **14.** A second Greek Revival house dating from the 1850s is at 724 West Colfax Avenue. It was moved to this location in 1900. The facade sports a front gable and entrance with side lights and transom. **15.** Take a short detour on North Scott Street to 223, a Prairie-style house designed in 1913 for Murrough O'Brien by the local architectural firm of Austin and Shambleau. The facade is decorated with different materials—board and batten, clapboard siding, and stucco—with a projecting front porch. **16.** At 227 North Scott Street is the Italianate Jacob Freyermuth house, built in 1865 and moved to this location in 1889. Two sides are protected by a wide columned porch, and the bracketed eaves are original. **17.** The local architectural firm of Austin and Shambleau designed the Renaissance Revival house at 615 West Colfax Avenue for Ferdinand Raff in 1910. Its brick facade is decorated with rafters and a broad porch with brick columns. **18.** At 511 West Colfax Avenue is the Queen Anne Joseph Birdsell house, designed by local architects Parker and Austin in 1898. This brick house has stone porches and chimneys and stucco and timber gables. **19.** In her eightieth year, 1913, Mary Louise Hine had architect Ernest Young design the two Tudor Revival houses at 521 and 527 West Colfax Avenue. **20.** Return to West Washington and see 627, the Italianate Julia Hine house built in 1863. The Neo-Jacobean front is an addition. You are now back where you started.

EAST TOUR

This area includes not only residences but also churches and commercial and public buildings. **1.** Turn right, or south, to 131 Taylor Street, the Charles A. Carlisle 1894 Shingle-style house. This large house is mainly Shingle with stone porch and chimneys and a Palladian window in the front gable. **2.** The Italianate house at 210 South Taylor was built in 1882 for J.A. McGill. Its windows are hooded and its cornice decorated. The addition of an office at the front is unfortunate. **3.** At 305 South Taylor St. Patrick's Church, modeled after Chartres Cathedral, has two bell towers of different heights, a large rose window, and a statue in its center gable. It was built in 1886. **4.** Return to 508 West Washington, the only Second Empire house left in the city. Built in 1872 for Albert Cushing, this brick house has a bracketed cornice and twin arched windows. **5.** At 502 West Washington is the Colonial Revival manse for the First Presbyterian Church built in 1907. A denticulated frieze and pediment, dormers, and front porch with Ionic columns decorate its facade. **6.** The large

Classical Revival house at 420 West Washington was built in 1893 for Samuel Good. In 1982 it was moved from 518 North Lafayette when threatened by demolition. 7. The 1895 George Morey house at 322 West Washington is a Queen Anne with elaborate front porch, second-story balcony, massive chimney, corner tower, and stained-glass bay window. 8. The former First Presbyterian Church at 101 South Lafayette, designed in 1888 by J.P. Bailey, is the only Richardsonian Romanesque church in the city. It has a massive corner entrance tower with arched entries. 9. The Greek Revival Second St. Joseph's County courthouse at 112 South Lafayette was designed by John Mills Van Osdel in 1855. This handsome building with its two-story portico and imposing clock tower was moved to this location in 1896. Since 1906 it has been the headquarters of the Northern Indiana Historical Society. 10. The building at 115 South Lafayette is the oldest office building in the city's center. Designed by George Selby in 1901, it has an interior courtyard, a device used in turn-of-the-century office buildings to provide added light and air. The facade with its Chicago-type windows is original. 11. The Gothic Revival St. James Cathedral, located at 117 North Lafayette and built in 1894, has a rose window and four Tiffany windows. 12. At 105 South Main Street is the third St. Joseph County courthouse, built in 1897. The Beaux Arts building shows the influence of Chicago's 1893 Columbian Exposition on the architectural scene. The architectural firm of Shepley, Rutan, and Coolidge designed the building. 13. The JMS building at 108 North Main was designed in 1910 by Solon S. Beman, the architect for Pullman, Illinois. The three-part composition of this eight-story building is designed to resemble a classical column. Such a decorative note was common in early skyscrapers. 14. The small Neoclassical commercial building at 111 West Washington Street was designed by the architectural firm of Virthum and Burns in 1924.

CHAPIN PARK

Take Lafayette Street north to the 300 block of West Navarre. This is a residential area settled toward the end of the nineteenth and the beginning of the twentieth century. Styles vary from Greek Revival to Prairie and from large to modest size. Although there are interesting houses scattered throughout the area, this small area off Park Avenue on Navarre and LaMonte Terrace is representative. Even the streets have their original brick paving. 1. En route to the Chapin Park district on Lafayette Street detour at the 400 block to 405 North Main, the First Church of Christ, Scientist. This elegant building, designed by Leon Stanhope in 1916, has a Greek-temple facade and a Roman dome. 2. At 304 West Navarre, the Tudor Revival house was designed in 1906 for William Miller by the firm of Austin and

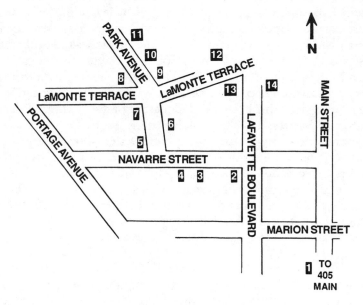

Chapin Park, South Bend

Shambleau. This stucco house has decorative half-timbering. **3.** A Queen Anne house at 328 West Navarre was built for Ricketson Burroughs. The gable decorations and the spindle porch are good examples of late-Victorian handiwork. **4.** The Eva Stover house at 330 West Navarre was built in 1894. This is a Stick-style house with a clapboard facade divided by six-inch bands and a forty-five-degree bay window. **5.** The beautifully preserved Gothic Revival-style house at 601 Park Avenue was built in 1856 by Horatio Chapin. His three-story house was copied from Andrew Jackson Downing's influential pattern book, *The Architecture of Country Houses*. A delicately decorated front porch is topped by a three-story gable with ornate bargeboard trimming. **6.** Across the street at 610 is the Queen Anne Campbell residence, built in 1904. The facade is painted in its original colors. Multicolored houses were popular with late Victorians. **7.** Walter Schneider, a prominent local architect, designed the George Ware house at 623 Park Avenue in 1900. This Classical Revival house has bracketed eaves, a classical porch with Tuscan columns, and a gabled entrance. **8.** A variation on the fanciful Queen Anne is the 1900 Richard Lyon Eclectic house at 405 LaMonte Terrace. It has a Bungalow roof sloping down to the front porch which is upheld by Tuscan columns. **9.** The Anderson Italian villa house at 710 Park Avenue, built in 1875, has a three-story tower with mansard roof, bracketed cornice, and wide front porch, added when the house was moved to its present location in 1901. **10.** The Stick-style house at 720 Park Avenue was built in 1878 by James DuShane. The house's most distinguishing feature is the delicate two-story front porch. **11.** The F. Lewis Stedman house at 730 Park Avenue, designed by architect Ernest Young, was built in 1911. The Northern Indiana Society of Architects gave the architect a design award for this Colonial Revival clapboard house with gambrel roof and pediment entrance supported by Doric columns. **12.** One of the early Prairie-style houses in this district was designed for Andrew Anderson by Ernest Young and George Selby in 1907, at 321 LaMonte Terrace. This duplex was built for rental purposes. **13.** Across the street is another Prairie-style house at 308 LaMonte, designed by the architectural firm of Austin and Shambleau for George Zinky. **14.** Turn south, or right, on Lafayette Boulevard to 708, a Prairie-style house designed by architect Ernest Young for Alexis Coquillard in 1916.

Festivals, Tours, and Other Places of Interest

For information about self-guided tours, write the Convention and Tourism Division of the Chamber of Commerce of South Bend and Mishawaka, P.O. Box 1677, South Bend, IN 46634, 219–234–0079. Southold Restorations, Inc., Leslie Choitz, director,

502 West Washington, South Bend, IN 46601, 219–234–3441. The Studebaker National Museum, open Tuesday–Saturday, 10:00 A.M.– 4:30 P.M., and Sunday 1:00 P.M.–4:00 P.M., Century Center, 120 South St. Joseph's Street, South Bend, IN 46634, 219–284–9714. The Old Courthouse Museum, otherwise known as the Northern Indiana Historical Society Museum, open Tuesday–Friday, 9:00 A.M.–5:00 P.M., Sunday 1:00 P.M.–4:00 P.M., 112 South Lafayette Street, South Bend, IN 46601, 219–284–9664. Amish Acres, southeast of South Bend at 1600 West Market in Nappanee, IN, open May–October, daily 10:00 A.M.–8:00 P.M. and Sunday 10:00 A.M.–6:00 P.M.; in November and April it is open weekends 11:00 A.M.–4:00 P.M., closed from December through March; from South Bend take U.S. 31 south to U.S. 6, then go east about 24 miles to Amish Acres, 219–773–4811.

Historical Information

South Bend-Mishawaka Chamber of Commerce, 230 Jefferson Boulevard, South Bend, IN 46601, 219–234–0051. Historic Landmarks Foundation of Indiana, 903 Jefferson Boulevard, South Bend, IN 46625, 219–232–4534. Historic Preservation Commission of South Bend and St. Joseph County, Lynette Jentoft Nilsen, director, Room 1123, County City Building, South Bend, IN 46601, 219–284–9798. Northern Indiana Historical Society, Kathy Mullins, director, 112 South Lafayette, South Bend, IN 46601, 219–284–9664. Southold Restorations, Inc., Leslie Choitz, director, 502 West Washington, South Bend, IN 46601, 219–234–3441.

Lodging

Downtown Holiday Inn, 213 West Washington Street, 219–232–3941.

Marriott Hotel, 123 North St. Joseph, 219–234–2000.

Restaurants

Barb's Restaurant, 214 West Jefferson Boulevard, 219–233–0892.

Captain Alexander's Wharf, 320 East Colfax, 219–234–4477.

Cornucopia Restaurant, 303 South Michigan Street, 219–288–1911.

Ice House Restaurant, 100 Center Complex, 700 Lincolnway West, Mishawaka, 219–259–9520.

Loft Restaurant, 112 West Colfax, 219–233–8711.

Senor Kelly's, 119 North Michigan, 219–234–5389.

Tippecanoe Place, 620 West Washington, 219–234–9077.

IV:2
Elkhart

ELKHART COUNTY
Indiana

THE beginning of the town of Elkhart coincided with the Removal Act of 1830, which moved the Indians who were living here to Kansas and allowed Crawford, Noffsinger, and Rush to move in as the first permanent settlers, cautious men as pioneers go, but still adventurous enough to find and take prime farming land with good water transportation. They were soon followed by Havilah Beardsley, the developer who purchased the site of Elkhart from Pierre Moran in 1832 and platted the town. Beardsley soon had mills, dockage, and a dam built. Elkhart became a busy river town, and Beardsley operated a ferry on the St. Joe River.

Unlike some of the towns featured in this book, modern Elkhart hums with activity. The old restored portions of the town are incorporated in the new.

Directions

On a trip to Goshen, or a weekend spent in north-central Indiana visiting South Bend and Mishawaka, you might wander through Elkhart. From Chicago take Interstate 80 and 90 east to exit 92, then drive south. In Elkhart you will be on Cassopolis Street. At Beardsley Avenue turn right, or west, and you will be in the Beardsley Avenue Historic District. To reach downtown and the other historic districts, turn south, or left, at Main and cross the St. Joe River. If you are coming from South Bend-Mishawaka, take Interstate 80 and 90 east and proceed as above or opt for U.S. 33 east. You will enter Elkhart on Franklin Street. At Main Street you will find parking. Or, you may turn left and take Main Street across the river to Beardsley Avenue and its historic district.

ARCHITECTURAL TOURS

Although there are several pleasant residential enclaves, we shall describe the Downtown-Fourth Street district, the Beardsley Avenue district, and the Jackson Boulevard-St. Joseph historic district.

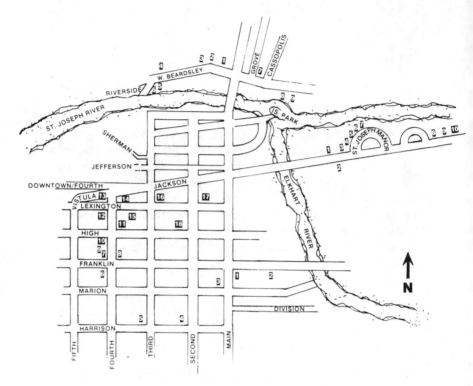

Beardsley Avenue Historic District,
Elkhart

BEARDSLEY AVENUE HISTORIC DISTRICT
The area directly north of downtown on the north bank of the St. Joe River was a favorite residential area for early settlers. The earliest house dates from the late 1840s. The range of architecture runs from the early Italianate to the turn-of-the-century Prairie style. You will get a better view of the houses if you turn west at Main and Beardsley and park. Four houses on Beardsley and two on Riverside Drive all have fine views of the St. Joe River. 1. The earliest house, at 102 West Beardsley, built in 1848 for Havilah Beardsley, is a simple Italianate house with bracketed eaves and a wide front porch. 2. At 114 West Beardsley is a Colonial Revival-style house, built in 1912. 3. The Prairie-style house at 120 West Beardsley was designed by a follower of Chicago architect Frank Lloyd Wright. It stresses the horizontal lines and overhanging roof. 4. Another popular turn-of-the-century style was the Classic Revival. The 1892 house at 130 West Beardsley is an example of this. 5. Near the intersection of West Beardsley and Riverside Drive is number 760 Riverside. The architect, E. Hill Turnock, was in the Chicago School tradition when he built this handsome Prairie-style house in 1910 for George E. Harter. 6. Another Prairie-style house, built in 1915, is nearby. 7. Cross Main and go east to Grove Street. A little farther east is 302 East Beardsley, known as "Ruthmere," built in 1908 by Albert Beardsley. This elaborate Italian villa was designed by E. Hill Turnock, who was the architect for some of the other Prairie-style houses. This elaborate house is now a museum maintained by two foundations. 8. Just east of Cassopolis Street on the south side of Beardsley is a Shingle-style house built in the 1890s. 9. Near the above is the earliest Prairie-style house in the city, built in 1905. If you drive east to Pulaski Park, you may leave your car and walk over the Miles Centennial footbridge to Island Park. The park is open from dawn to 11:00 P.M.

JACKSON BOULEVARD-
ST. JOSEPH HISTORIC DISTRICT
East of downtown is the area along East Jackson Boulevard, which became a residential area in the 1920s. 1. The George Boreman house at 1126 East Jackson is a Prairie-style building dating from 1905. 2. On the south side of East Jackson at 1501, versatile architect E. Hill Turnock designed a Prairie-style house for B. C. Godfrey in 1927. 3. At 1600 East Jackson is a Modernist house built about 1925. 4. Follow St. Joseph Manor, which makes a half-circle detour from and back to Jackson Boulevard. In the house at 6, architect E. Hill Turnock combines the Prairie and Neoclassical styles. It was built in 1925. 5. An entirely different style is the Spanish Revival house at 7 St. Joseph Manor. It was built in 1925 for William R. Trocken-

broder. **6.** Next door is still another Prairie-style house, built in 1910 for Gus Bisher. **7.** At 9 St. Joseph Manor is an imposing Neoclassical house designed for W. H. Foster by architect E. Hill Turnock. It has a handsome two-story semicircular entrance pediment supported by substantial columns. **8.** Another example of E. Hill Turnock's work is the 1920 Bungalow at 1906 East Jackson Boulevard. **9.** Another example of Turnock's Bungalow is the Charles Colbert house at 2002 East Jackson Boulevard, designed in 1926. **10.** Architect Turnock's versatility is again revealed in the Prairie–Georgian Revival Hossick house, built in 1920 at 2324 East Jackson.

DOWNTOWN AND THE
FOURTH STREET HISTORIC DISTRICT

This area contains residential buildings erected between 1870 and 1917 as well as commercial structures. Parking is available on South Main between West Franklin and West High. The area is roughly five-by-five blocks from South Lexington on the north to South Harrison on the south and from West Fifth to Main on the east. **1.** The Elco theater, 410 South Main, is housed in a monumental Classical Revival building erected in 1924. **2.** The Franklin station at 131 East Franklin Street was built in 1895 as a combined city hall, fire station, and police station. **3.** The Midwest Museum of American Art at 429 South Main Street is located in the 1922 St. Joseph Valley Bank building. **4.** At the northwest corner of West Second and South Harrison is the Knickerbocker house, built in 1916. **5.** A block west between South Third and South Fourth Streets on West Harrison is the Central Memorial Square. **6.** Walk two blocks north on South Fourth to the southwest corner of West Franklin and South Fourth, where you will find the imposing Italianate Franklin Miles home, built in 1885. In 1902 it was remodeled to fit the then popular Colonial Revival style. **7.** Across the street is a Second Empire house built in 1875. **8.** One block east at 328 West Franklin is another style, Dutch Colonial, popular at the turn of the century. **9.** Return to South Fourth Street and walk north to 309, a Carpenter-Builder house erected in 1875. **10.** On the southwest corner of South Fourth and West High is 403 High, the stately Italianate A.R. Beardsley house, erected in 1870. It has a wide front porch, arched windows, and heavily bracketed eaves. **11.** On the northeast corner is the well-preserved Broderick house, built in 1874. **12.** A block north at 401 West Lexington is a good example of the Queen Anne style, built in 1890. **13.** A bit north on Vistula Street is a Prairie-style house, designed by architect Turnock for Fred Gampher in 1917. **14.** In the next block east at 330 West Lexington is the colossal Romanesque Revival Samuel Strong school, built in 1892. **15.** On the south side of West Lexington at 317 is a good example of Neo-

Jacobean, built in 1910. This is essentially a much embellished late Italianate. **16.** At the northeast corner of West Lexington and South Third Streets is St. John's Evangelist Episcopal Church. This imposing Gothic structure was built in 1895. **17.** Walk east toward Main and you will see the former YMCA at 120 West Lexington. This Eclectic structure has a handsome arched first-floor entrance, matching windows, and a heavily bracketed roof line. **18.** On the northwest corner of South Second and West High is the new city hall, a sharp contrast to its Franklin Street predecessor (2). You are now a block from your parking place.

Festivals, Tours, and Other Places of Interest

Midwest Museum of Art, open Tuesday–Saturday, 11:00 A.M.–5:00 P.M., Saturday and Sunday, 1:00 P.M.–4:00 P.M., 429 South Main Street, Elkhart, IN 46515, 219–293–6660. Ruthmere Museum, tours Tuesday–Friday, 11:00 A.M., 1:00 P.M., and 3:00 P.M., 302 East Beardsley, Elkhart, IN 46515, 219–264–0330.

Historical Information

Elkhart Historic and Preservation Commission, City Hall, Second and High Streets, Elkhart, IN 46515, 219–294–5471. Greater Elkhart Chamber of Commerce, P.O. Box 428, 514 South Main Street, Elkhart, IN 46515, 219–293–1531. Elkhart County Historical Society, P.O. Box 434, Bristol, IN 46507, 219–848–4322.

Lodging

Days Inn, 2820 Cassopolis, 219–262–3541.
Holiday Inn, 2725 Cassopolis Street, 219–264–7502.
Midway Motor Lodge, 300 South Main Street, 219–295–0280.
Ramada Inn, 3011 Belvedere Road, 219–262–1581, handicapped accessible.

Restaurants

Casey's Restaurant, 411 South Main Street, 219–293–4232.
Gropp's of Elkhart, 573 East Jackson Boulevard, 219–293–0648.
Patriot House, 231 South Main Street, 219–293–9151.

IV:3
Goshen

ELKHART COUNTY
Indiana

GOSHEN, called Maple City for its quiet tree-lined streets and located about 15 miles south of Elkhart, is the county seat of Elkhart County. The Mennonite church is an important influence in Goshen. The church established Goshen College in 1894 as a four-year co-educational college, owned and supported by the church. Both the Mennonite archives and the church's research library are located on the campus.

Directions
In a day you could visit Elkhart and Goshen, or take a weekend and include South Bend. You reach Goshen from Chicago via Interstates 80 and 90 to the State Route 19 exit through Elkhart, where you take U.S. 33 to Goshen; or, go farther east on the Interstates to the State Route 15 exit, south through Bristol, to Goshen.

ARCHITECTURAL TOUR
The historic district covers the area from Pike on the north to Plymouth on the south and from the Pennsylvania Railroad tracks on the east to the canal on the west. It is an area too large to traverse by foot, and buildings of special merit are scattered on the periphery. Between the Pennsylvania Railroad tracks and the vestiges of the "hydraulic" canal lies a four-block-square area of interesting old houses. They range from Italianate to Queen Anne to Prairie School in style, from 1870 to 1910 in date. A drive or walk up Washington Street, crossing Main, Fifth, Sixth, and then south to Jefferson or Madison will provide the visitor with a delightful feeling for the early days of this town. **1.** Of particular note is the imposing red brick Italianate house built in 1875 by John H. Baker at the southwest corner of Fifth and Madison Streets. The house has a stately white portico, elaborate window decoration, and an ornate cornice. Its facade appears to be original except for the enclosed side porch and garage in the rear. **2.** Another architectural gem is the Stick-style house between Jeffer-

son and Madison on Fifth Street, built by J.A.S. Mitchell in 1870.
3. You can also view the Neoclassical Goshen Carnegie Library,
completed in 1901. It is on the southeast corner of Washington and
Fifth. 4. Not to be missed is the elegant Renaissance Revival Elkhart
County courthouse in the center square at Lincoln, Clinton, Main,
and Third, built in 1870 and remodeled in 1905. Its facade is of brick
and limestone, heavily decorated with columns and window hoods as
well as an entrance portico. A conical clock tower dominates the
square, which is well landscaped with bushes and trees and the Nep-
tune fountain.

Historical Information

Goshen Public Library, 601 South Fifth Street, Goshen, IN 46526,
219–533–9531. Goshen Historical Society, P.O. Box 701, Goshen, IN
46526. Elkhart County Historical Society, P.O. Box 434, Bristol, IN
46507, 219–848–4322.

Lodging

Best Western Inn, 900 Lincolnway East, 800–528–1234 or 219–533–
0408.

Goshen Motor Inn, U.S. 33 southeast of Goshen in Millersburg,
IN, 219–642–4388.

Holiday Inn, U.S.33, 219–533–9551.

Restaurants

Azar's Big Boy Family Restaurant, 1105 West Pike Street, 219–534–
1004.

Dandino's Restaurant and Lounge, 1407 Elkhart Road, 219–533–
9248.

Pagoda Inn, 2820 Elkhart Road, 219–533–2568.

Plain and Fancy Restaurant, 117 South Main, 219–533–4748.

Rustic Inn, U.S. 33, 219–533–4265.

Smalley's Old Mill Inn, State Route 15, 219–533–6503.

Super Steer Restaurant, U.S. 33, 219–534–2646.

Yoder's Restaurant, 103 North Fifth Street, 219–533–1339.

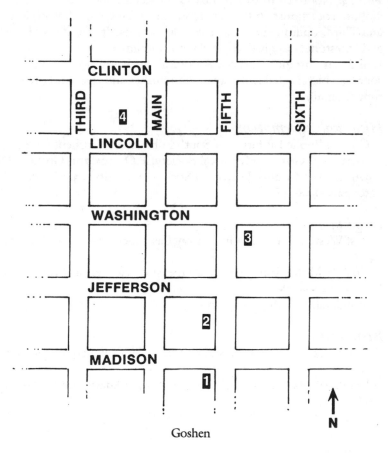

Goshen

N

PART TWO

Weekend Trips

V:I
Green Bay
BROWN COUNTY
Wisconsin

REEN Bay's recorded past extends back to the mid-1600s. The ubiquitous Father Nicolet passed through here, and in his wake came fur traders who bartered pelts with the Indians. In "La Baye," the French name for Green Bay, a fort was built in 1717, and after the 1750s the British influence in the form of the Hudson's Bay Company was very strong. John Jacob Astor and his American Fur Company became the principal and practically only trader here after 1824 when Congress ordained that only American citizens could deal in pelts and thus shut out foreign competition.

As the fur business diminished in the 1840s, lumber and shipbuilding expanded. The new fortunes of the Horners, Morgans, and Barkhausens began to grow, and the town became more sophisticated. It is now the proud home of the Green Bay Packers' football team, whose owners are area residents.

Today we can see the results of the lumber and shipbuilding barons' success in the well-preserved houses in the Astor district, in the restored and reproduced images of early life at Heritage Hill, and the charming downtown district with winding one-way streets lighted by Victorian gas lamps and filled with antique shops.

Directions
To do justice to this old trading post and river port, spend a weekend here and include a tour of De Pere and a ride on the river. Take Interstate 94 north to Milwaukee. There change to State Route 57, which takes you to Green Bay.

ARCHITECTURAL TOUR
The Astor Historical District stretches from East Mason Street on the north to Grignon on the south and from South Adams on the west to Webster on the east. The north-south streets are named for the U.S. presidents through Van Buren (leaving out the second Adams), and

Astor Historical District,
Green Bay

the east-west streets are named for early settlers. The tour has been planned so you can park at the first stop and walk; it will take about two hours on foot. If you wish to drive, examine the area south of Porlier and then drive to the 700 block of Jefferson or Madison and walk the remainder. There are many late Victorian buildings, and even a few in the twentieth-century Prairie style. The Astor neighborhood has always been a residential area. 1. The house at 1008 South Monroe, built by lawyer and legislator Morgan L. Martin in 1837–38, is known as "Hazelwood"; it is on the National Register. Here Martin and his co-workers drafted Wisconsin's first constitution. The house is a two-story Greek Revival building. Its fluted Doric columns supporting the porch give it a majestic air. It originally had two wings; the north wing was removed and the south made into a garage. The main section of the house has been restored. 2. Architect Thomas Stevens Van Alyea designed the house at 1101 South Monroe, built in 1928 for Cecil Baum. Van Alyea was a noted designer of Colonial, Georgian, and Tudor styles; this house is an example of the last. Surprisingly, the exterior is unchanged except for the conversion of the sunroom into a garage. 3. The large brick Georgian Colonial Revival building at 628 Emilie was built in 1919 by Edward A. Meyer. The landscaping adds to the gracious appearance of this house. 4. Walk east on Emilie to Van Buren. The house at 1120 South Van Buren, constructed in 1917 by Enos Colburn, is basically Georgian Revival with Prairie School touches such as leaded windows and plate-glass windows with muntins. The portico was added to protect it from winter weather. 5. At 1125 South Van Buren is a house built about 1916 by Charles M. Hasseler. It has the rare distinction of having retained its original exterior. In addition, it is the only house in the district of German Baroque style. 6. In 1905 Green Bay architect Henry A. Foeller built 918 Emilie as his own home. 7. The house at 1036 South Webster was also designed and constructed by the architect Henry A. Foeller as his second residence. It is Mediterranean style, modified for the harsh winters by adding a balcony over the front door. It has a red barrel-tile roof. 8. The Prairie-style house at 1040 South Van Buren was built by Agnes S. Jorgensen in 1921–22. 9. The Mediterranean-style house at 1045 South Jackson was built by Emile G. Nadeau in 1927. It has a centered entrance with balcony above; the semicircular arch is used throughout the facade. 10. The house at 1013 South Jackson was built in 1896 by Rowland T. Burdon. This Queen Anne house has a centered turret stretching from the first through the second story, false widow's walk, and second-story porch. In 1982 it was painted wedgwood blue with white trim. 11. Go west on Eliza Street to Madison and turn north. At 931 South Madison is a house built in 1923 by Warren C. Schillings. It was designed by architect Harry W. Carr. The style is English Tudor Revival. The first story is brick and the second stucco with stickwork. It has casement windows throughout. **12.** The Queen Anne-style house at 902 South Madison was designed by architect Henry A. Foeller and built about 1900 for Mitchell Joannes. It has elements of vernacular Romanesque Revival in its decorated facade, which gives it a fortresslike appearance. It also boasts a Tuscan porte-cochere, multistory bay windows, and semicircular portico. **13.** The house at 825 South Adams was probably built around 1900 on Doty Street; in 1956 it was moved to this location. The two-story Gothic frame cottage, with a pitched roof that sweeps down over the recessed front porch has a large centered dormer window above the porch. The house is built of hand-hewn timbers held together by square nails. **14.** The house at 402 Lawe between Madison and Jefferson was built in 1850–56 by Charles R. Tyler. Later, the Gothic Revival cottage was moved to the corner of Jefferson. It closely resembles the "Gothic Cottages" in Andrew Jackson Downing's 1850 design book, *The Architecture of Country Houses.* The original clapboard exterior has been covered with stucco, but the eaves are still decorated with carpenter's lacework. **15.** The building at 746 South Jefferson was built around 1859 by Guillaume Servotte for Timothy Otis Howe. Originally it was Greek Revival, and four Doric columns once supported the front porch. The porches have been removed and asbestos siding added. **16.** Proclaimed to be the finest house in the city, 736 South Madison was built for Patrick Martin in 1898–1900. The architect was probably the renowned Henry Foeller, and the contractor Joseph Servotte. The Martin house had such modern features as gas, electricity, and hot running water. The Queen Anne house has a wide variety of decoration, including a three-story turret, many types of siding, balconies, and a wraparound veranda (removed in 1925). **17.** The house at 701 South Adams was built in 1829, probably by Pierre Grignon; in 1834 it was forfeited to John Jacob Astor. This two-story, double-gable-roof house has gone through many alterations. The front porch has spindle columns and decorative trim as well as clapboard siding, none of which is probably original. **18.** The structure at 645 South Jefferson was probably built as a fur trading post before 1859. **19.** Go east on Cass to Monroe and then south. The house on the northwest corner, numbered either 702 South Monroe or 522 Cass, was built by Linus B. Sale in 1880. This fine Italianate house has wide projecting bracketed eaves and ballustraded balconies. The western addition dates from 1927. **20.** The Queen Anne-style house at 712 South Monroe was built for Frederick L.G. Straubel in 1898–99. The architect was the versatile Henry Foeller, and the builder the well-known William Servotte. The fanciful facade boasts dormers, bay windows, and a turret with an octagonal bell-cast roof. **21.** The two-story Queen Anne house at 500 Congress was built by Oscar Hathaway in 1895. The house is memorable because the facade has no right angles and is highly decorated with attic dormer windows, bay windows on both floors, a turret, and a variety of siding including clapboard and fish scale shingle. **22.** The house at 843 South Monroe is basically Federalist in style with Italianate features such as a bracketed roof. It was probably built in 1868 by Alma Earle. The east wing is the earlier and the west the later addition. **23.** The large house located at 904 South Monroe and built for Harry E. Eastman was originally Queen Anne with wraparound porch and porte-cochere. With some of the detail removed, it appears more Italianate. **24.** Arthur C. Neville built the large Queen Anne house at 905 South Monroe in 1890. **25.** At 945 South Monroe is the home built in 1905 by John F. Martin. The Dutch Colonial Revival structure has an open veranda and second-story porch, one of the few examples of this style in Green Bay. **26.** The Prairie-style house at 500 Eliza Street was built in 1910 by William Evans. This massive two-story stucco house has lost its original front porch.

Festivals, Tours, and Other Places of Interest

The Neville Public Museum, open 9:00 A.M.–5:00 P.M., Monday, Tuesday, Friday, and Saturday, 9:00 A.M.–9:00 P.M. on Wednesday and Thursday, and noon–5:00 P.M. on Sunday, 210 Museum Place, Green Bay, WI 54305, 414–436–3767. "Hazelwood," the home of Morgan L. Martin, open May–September, 10:00 A.M.–5:00 P.M. Tuesday–Saturday, 2:00 P.M.–5:00 P.M. on Sunday, October–March, 1:00 P.M.–5:00 P.M. Tuesday–Saturday, closed on Mondays and holidays, 1008 South Monroe, Green Bay, WI 54305, 414–436–3768. Rail America, the National Railroad Museum, open daily 9:00 A.M.–5:00 P.M., May 1–October 1, Shawano Avenue between Taylor Street and Military Avenue, 414–499–4281.

Historical Information

Brown County Library, current librarian, Mary Jane Herber, Local History Section, Pine Street, Green Bay, WI 54305, 414–497–6222. The authoritative source on the buildings and history of the Astor neighborhood is *The Astor Street District: Its History and Houses* by Sylvia Hall Holubetz and George Nau Burridge, available through interlibrary loan. Green Bay Area Visitors and Convention Bureau, P.O. Box 10596, Green Bay, WI 54307–0596, 414–494–9507.

Lodging

Coachlight Inn, 899 South Webster, 414–432–6391.
Downtowner, 321 South Washington Street, 414–437–8771.
Imperial 400 Motel, 119 North Monroe, 414–437–0525.

Restaurants

La Bonne Femme, 123 South Washington, 414–432–2897.
Paul's Carriage Inn, 119 North Adams, 414–437–2622.
Prime Steer Supper Club, 100 South Monroe, 414–432–8878.
Stein Lounge and Supper Club, 126 South Adams, 414–435–6071.
Town Room Supper Club, 347 South Washington, 414–437–5744.

V:2

De Pere

BROWN COUNTY
Wisconsin

I N 1836 De Pere was the first county seat of Brown County, the first county established by the first territorial government of Wisconsin. De Pere remained the county seat until 1854, at which time the county seat was moved to Green Bay. However, the charm of its vintage homes remains undimmed.

Directions

A weekend trip could include Green Bay and its neighbor De Pere, Wisconsin. From Chicago go north on Interstate 94 to Milwaukee. Take State Route 57 or Interstate 43 north to De Pere. From Green Bay, take State Route 57 south.

ARCHITECTURAL TOUR

The five blocks north of the business district along Broadway have traditionally been De Pere's finest residential area. Houses in this North Broadway Historic District span the years from 1836 to 1923; the styles range from Greek Revival to twentieth-century Bungalow, the sizes from small early nineteenth century to large turn-of-the-century Queen Anne. A leisurely tour will take about an hour. Parking is available adjacent to the museum described below. **1.** The Greek Revival one-story building known as "White Pillars," located at 403 North Broadway, was built in 1836. It was moved to its present site in 1867. In 1922 the fancy pediment and portico were added. It is the oldest extant building in De Pere and is now the home of the museum of the De Pere Historical Society. **2.** Across the street, the typical Wisconsin farmhouse at 400 North Broadway has a simple columned pediment protecting its entrance and two partial dormers in the second story. **3.** As you walk north, at 409 North Broadway you will find the second oldest building in De Pere, the William Elder Sharp house. This plain Greek Revival house was built in 1852. Somewhat altered after a 1915 fire, its facade is essentially original, including the leaf-pattern bargeboard gable trim. Although the entrance

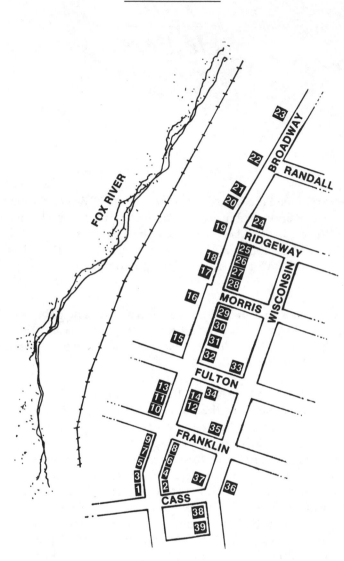

De Pere

pediment may be original, its pillars have been replaced. **4.** The small house at 432 North Broadway is a combination Gothic Revival cottage and vernacular Italianate. Its gables are Gothic and its bracketed roof line Italianate, reflecting the popularity of both styles in 1870. **5.** At 435 North Broadway is the old St. Anne's Episcopal Church, built in 1927. This Gothic Revival structure was altered in 1941 by the addition of the tower. **6.** Across the street at 434 North Broadway is a combination Queen Anne and Colonial Revival house. The attic dormers and the different siding on the first and second floors are elements of the former, the colonnaded front porch of the latter. **7.** On the other side of the street is 443 North Broadway, a vernacular Italianate with Gothic gable. This wood-frame building has small pediments over its entry doors; they are not original. **8.** At 448 North Broadway is the Merrill Greek Revival New England farmhouse, built in 1849 and moved to this site in 1947. It has a wide columned front porch and a period picket fence. **9.** The modified Bungalow at 449 North Broadway has Gothic touches in its gable, Queen Anne elements in its dormer and balcony, and reflects the Bungalow style in the sloping roof and front porch. **10.** The house at 503 North Broadway is transitional, retaining dormers and a two-story bay from an earlier Queen Anne style and adding a Colonial Revival columned wide front porch. **11.** Another example of the mixture of Colonial Revival and Queen Anne is at 515 North Broadway. The Queen Anne two-story bay and dormer remain, but the different facade materials have vanished. A Colonial Revival wide columned front porch has been added. It was built in 1886 by William E. Kellog. **12.** Across the street at 514 North Broadway is another more simple example of the same style, which was popular not only in De Pere but in many parts of the country. **13.** At 519 North Broadway, the Edward Lee house is a fine example of the Bungalow style which swept the country in the period just before and after World War I. Built in 1918, the house has the sloping roof, prominent dormer, and wide porch characteristic of this style. **14.** The small house at 524 North Broadway is thought to be what remains of an early De Pere church that was moved to this site. The entry enclosure, the front picture window, and the siding are obviously not original. **15.** At 621 North Broadway is a simple Queen Anne multi-family dwelling. It has a conical roof over one portion and a gable over the other. Its entrance porch is upheld by spindle pillars. **16.** The Stick-style house at 639 North Broadway was built in 1889 by Joseph C. Lawton. The south end of the house is a two-story tower, and the north a Gothic pavilion with attic. These are connected by a Second Empire section complete with mansard roof and dormer. The front entrance, which is in this section, is protected by a small open pedimented porch. The transoms over the outside doors and many of the windows provide added ventilation. **17.** The Greek Revival house at 707 North Broadway is one of the first of this style built in Wisconsin, erected in 1836 for Randall Wilcox. The two-story main house is flanked on the north and south by one-story-plus-attic wings. The small pedimented entance is original. **18.** Built in 1882 by E. E. Bolles, the massive Queen Anne house at 721 North Broadway has a remodeled veranda that has been widened and simplified, but it retains most of the embellishments of the style, including dormers, heavy chimneys, and a front bay. The designer was the locally distinguished architect William Waters of Oshkosh. **19.** In 1909 architect William de Geeche of Milwaukee designed 809 North Broadway for A. G. Wells. The three-story Eclectic–English Tudor manor is built of stone with timber and stucco trim. A large roof overhang shields the front entrance; a second-story balcony overhead, large stone chimneys, and a projecting front two-story bay enliven the facade. **20.** Next door at 813 North Broadway is the Queen Anne John P. Dousman home, built in the 1890s. Most of the first floor is shielded by porches. Clapboard, fish-scale, and sawtooth shingles cover the facade, which also includes a porte-cochere, a two-story bay, dormers, and both Palladian and beveled-glass windows. **21.** In 1895 John S. Gittens built this Queen Anne–Colonial Revival house at 823 North Broadway. A porch stretches across most of the front, as do dormers on the second floor. **22.** The Georgian Colonial Smith house at 903 North Broadway was built in 1922. It has a half-circle portico supported by columns and topped with a balustrade, forming a balcony in front of the large, arched second-story window. The semicircular brick driveway complements the house. In the rear is a terrace overlooking the Fox River. **23.** The large stone house at 935 North Broadway, known as "Crow's Nest," was built sometime between 1858 and the 1880s by Joseph Lawton. It was extensively remodeled after World War I and now bears almost no resemblance to the original. Originally the house faced the river, but later the entrance was moved to Broadway. A long rear veranda provides a splendid view of the river. The front porch has a porte-cochere and balustrade so that the second-story French windows have access to an open porch. First- and second-story balconies decorate the ends of the house. **24.** Now turn south on Broadway and proceed to the northeast corner of Ridgeway, where you will find a two-story Dutch Colonial Revival shingle house at 806 Broadway, built in 1905 by J.P. Lenfestey. It has a gambrel roof, a recessed entrance, a small bay, and an enclosed sun porch. Dormers protrude from the second floor, and three windows illuminate the third-floor gable. **25.** The simple Queen Anne house at 726 North Broadway was built in 1885. It has a wide front porch and a central tower which culminates in a pointed roof. It was remodeled into a two-family house in 1956, but the facade was not changed. **26.** Although built in 1930, the house at 720 North Broadway is a duplicate of an earlier house. This Colonial Revival house retains many exterior pieces from the earlier one. **27.** The house at 712 North Broadway was built by the Marcott family in 1912–14. It is in Bungalow style with a front dormer and a sloping roof that covers the front porch. A bay window protrudes from the first floor. **28.** The house at 704 North Broadway was erected in 1868. This Italianate structure appears unchanged except for the small front portico. **29.** The Italianate house at 640 North Broadway, built in 1884 by R. Jackson, has a wide front porch, big bay window, and widow's walk on the rooftop. **30.** The Jackson house at 632 North Broadway is another building that has been extensively remodeled since it was built in the 1880s as a Victorian mansion. All the fanciful Queen Anne decorations have been removed, and it is now a southern Colonial mansion, patterned after a Natchez, Mississippi, house. The two-story front porch is indeed grand. **31.** At 620 North Broadway is the Second Empire Wheeler house, dating from 1878. Its mansard roof envelops both the third-story tower and the second story. Hooded windows protrude from this roof. The front entrance is protected by a spindle corner porch. A similar smaller porch covers a rear entry. **32.** The Queen Anne-style house at 602 North Broadway was built in 1892 by J.S. Chase. A square tower, gables, and a wrap-around porch are its distinguishing features. **33.** Turn left, or east, at Fulton Street. The Italianate Rueben Field house was built in 1859 and moved to its present location at 410 Fulton in 1930. Its annexes have been removed, restoring it to its original condition. A wide columned porch stretches across the front, and eyebrow windows ventilate its second-story attic. **34.** The house at 417 Fulton was originally erected in 1875 for J.S. Chase. The Greek Revival house has a porch and second-story eyebrow windows across its front facade. **35.** At the northwest corner of Wisconsin and Franklin, 503 North Wisconsin is a Queen Anne Cape Cod house built in 1867. It has a wide front porch covering the first floor and three dormers protruding from the second story. On the south side is a tall bay window. **36.** On the other side of the street is 432 North Wisconsin, a Queen Anne house built in 1906 by Gustave Fleck. In keeping with the style, it has a number of imaginative elements, including a third-story gabled balcony, a two-story corner columned porch, a third-story dormer, and a two-story bay. **37.** The Gothic-style house with a Queen Anne square towers across the street at 425 North Wisconsin was built in 1881 by E.F. Parker. It has a simple front porch and bargeboard decorating the front gable. **38.** On the southwest corner of Wisconsin and Cass at 421 Cass is the F.E. White house. This Greek Revival house has a two-story front veranda topped by a pediment. This porch extends across the one-story west wing. **39.** The Jacob Falk house at 321 North Wisconsin is Queen Anne-style with conical tower, deep gables, wraparound front porch, and first-floor bay. Although there have been alterations, particularly to the porch, the original facade is essentially intact. You are now one block south and one block east of your starting point.

Festivals, Tours, and Other Places of Interest

Green Bay Area Visitors and Convention Bureau, P.O. Box 10596, Green Bay, WI 54307–0596, 414–494–9507. "White Pillars," the De Pere Historical Museum, open Wednesday–Sunday, 1:00 P.M.–5:00 P.M., 403 North Broadway, De Pere, WI 54115. The Oneida Nation Museum, corner of County Highways E and EE, open Monday–Saturday, 9:00 A.M.–5:00 P.M., April 1–November 30; Monday–Friday, 9:00 A.M.–5:00 P.M., December 1–March 31; take U.S. 41 south to County Highway EE and go west on EE to its intersection with Highway E.

Historical Information

De Pere Historic District on Parade. De Pere Historical Society Museum, 403 North Broadway, De Pere, WI 54115, 414–336–3877.

Lodging

Excel Inn, 2870 Ramada Way, 414–499–3599.
Howard Johnson's, U.S. 41 and Main Street, 414–336–0611.
Ramada West, 2750 Ramada Way, 414–499–0631.

Restaurants

Ivan's, 127 North Broadway, 414–337–0265.
Nicolet Restaurant, 313 Main, 414–336–8726.
Union Hotel, 200 North Broadway, 414–336–6131.
Ye Olde Charterhouse, 614 George, 414–336–7337.

V:3

Beaver Dam

DODGE COUNTY

Wisconsin

B EAVER Dam and Dodge County began to be settled in the
1830s, and the town was platted in 1846. Manufacturing
was the source of the town's income, and it remains so
today, with some twenty companies in business here. Reflecting the town's continuous prosperity are the fine late nineteenth-
century homes, the gingerbread spring house in Swan Park, and
co-educational Wayland Academy.

Directions

On the way to or from the Fox River cities, you could stop in
Beaver Dam. Another possibility is to combine your trip with a visit
to the Horicon Marsh, a resting place for thousands of migrating
Canada geese. From Chicago take Interstate 94 north around Milwaukee and west to Johnson Creek. Turn north onto State Route 26
to State Route 33, then west into Beaver Dam. You will be on east
Park Avenue. Drive to Spring Street, turn left, or south, and park at
the Williams Library, the site of the Dodge County Historical Society, from which you can walk the district.

ARCHITECTURAL TOURS

The neighborhood on Maple and Park between Lincoln and University was called Silk Stocking Hill because it was home to Beaver
Dam's most prominent and successful citizens. The walking tour will
take about an hour. 1. At 105 East Park Avenue, on the southeast corner of Park and Spring, is the Richardsonian Romanesque Williams
Free Library, now the headquarters of the Dodge County Historical
Society, built in 1891. The architect was W.A. Holbrook of the Milwaukee firm of E. Townsend Mix and Company. The massive sandstone building has a three-story corner tower with belfry, a recessed
arched entrance, another two-story corner tower culminating in a
pinnacle, and numerous large windows. The facade is unchanged,
and the fountain on the front lawn is also original. 2. Next door at 127

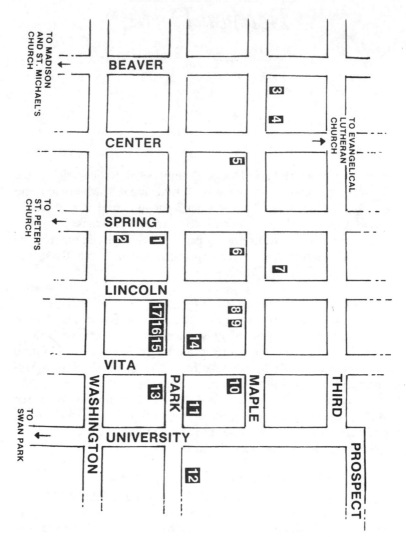

Beaver Dam

South Spring Street is the vernacular Chicago, Milwaukee, and St. Paul Railroad station, designed by prominent railroad-station architects Frost and Granger of Chicago. It was built of brick with two front gables outlined in plain white bargeboard, in 1900. It now houses the Beaver Dam Chamber of Commerce. The original hardwood floors, oak doors, and large fireplace are intact. 3. Walk west one block to Center Street and north to Maple Avenue. Turn left, or west, to 212 West Maple, the Bogart house, built in the 1860s or 1870s. This large vernacular Italianate house was a grand mansion with such innovations as running water, which was provided by large rooftop cisterns, and cesspools, the town's first example of interior plumbing. 4. Retrace your steps to 202 West Maple, the Eclectic Schemmel-Cullen house. This late-Victorian house's facade is dominated by a two-story bay, each floor boasting four windows. 5. The simple Gothic Revival church at 117 West Maple is St. Patrick's, built in 1907. 6. The house at 131 East Maple was built for Anna Shipman in the 1870s. This Greek Revival house has been somewhat altered, but you can see its handsome rounded windows and dentils outlining the cornice and front pediment. 7. St. Mark's Gothic Revival board-and-batten church at Lincoln and Maple is a good example of the church style publicized by American architect Richard Upjohn in his 1852 pattern book, *Rural Architecture.* 8. On another Maple and Lincoln corner is the former St. John's English Evangelical Lutheran Church. Devoid of its large corner belfry tower and stained-glass windows, it is still an interesting Romanesque building. 9. John T. Smith built the house at 229 East Maple in 1878. This restrained Second Empire house originally had a south wing, which has been detached and now stands as a separate house facing Vita Avenue. The house has a bracketed cornice, small entrance porch, and first-floor bay. 10. Turn right, or south, on Vita Avenue to 115, the Bonner-Vinz residence. This Queen Anne house has a generous wraparound front porch with pedimented entrance and two-story tower culminating in a bell-shaped roof. 11. Walk south one half block to Park Avenue and turn left, or east. A comfortable vernacular house at 330 East Park has a Gothic Revival front gable modestly decorated, a prominent front window, and a wraparound front porch. A quaint note is the fountain on the lawn in front of the big window. 12. Walk east on Park Avenue one block to Wayland Academy. The Greek Revival Wayland Hall was begun in 1855 but not completed until several years later. The handsome three-story building features an imposing portico upheld by Corinthian columns. Nearby Warren Cottage is a much remodeled Eclectic building. Lindsay Gymnasium was built in 1889 and has been remodeled, including a 1946 rear addition. Roundy Hall, a Georgian Revival building, was built in 1899. The other Classical Revival building is Linfield Hall, built in 1910. It, like Roundy Hall, reflects the American Renaissance movement initiated by the Chicago World's Fair of 1893. This imposing building has a center pediment and ornate hood over its entrance and columns rising from its second to its fourth floor. **13.** Walking west on Park Avenue, you will find 323, the Gothic Revival Carol Roedl house. Its sharp gables have Stick-style ornamentation. The front porch has column supports. **14.** On the northwest corner of Park and Vita is the Queen Anne George E. Swan house, built in 1898–99. This complicated, elegant house has a three-story corner tower with cone roof, a number of gables, a gabled porch entrance, and arched front and side porches. **15.** Across the street at 221 East Park Avenue is the very different Tudor Revival Edward Jacobs house, with a gabled front entrance and exterior boards suggesting, but not providing, support. This house was built in 1912. **16.** The 1866 Italianate S.P.K. Lewis house at 219 East Park Avenue is only slightly simplified from the original. The front entrance and the window above it on the second floor are devoid of their original decoration, but otherwise the facade is original. Of particular interest is the cupola. **17.** A bit west is 207 East Park Avenue, the Italianate Congdon-Canniff house. It has an unusual center front pediment with a bullseye window and a half-porch shielding its entrance.

SCATTERED SITES

Other noteworthy buildings are scattered throughout the town; it is best to drive to view them.

Swan City Park, at South and University, is remarkable for the spring house built by George E. Swan in 1880. Restored in 1985 to its original design, it is the only building of Dr. Swan's spa remaining. This elaborate Stick-style structure originally protected a spring.

One of the handsomest churches in Beaver Dam is St. Peter's, built in 1900. This Romanesque church at 503 South Spring Street was inspired by eleventh- and twelfth-century Italian churches. The facade is elegantly decorated and culminates in a high pinnacled tower with a clock in each of its four sides.

At 835 Madison Street is St. Michael's Church, built in 1904. Its front center tower has rose windows on all four sides as well as clocks.

At Mackie and North Center Street is the Gothic Revival First Evangelical Lutheran Church, built in 1893. It is dominated by a three-story pinnacled tower and simple front-corner buttresses.

Festivals, Tours, and Other Places of Interest

Ten miles east of Beaver Dam is the Horicon Marsh where migrating Canada geese rest from mid-March to mid-April and again from

September to November. The refuge can be approached from the town of Horicon on the south end or from Highway 49 and to County Route Z south 3.7 miles. Tours are available from Memorial Day to Labor Day and on weekends in September and October from Blue Heron Landing, Highway 33, Horicon, WI 53032. Dodge County Historical Society, open in the summer Tuesday, 10:00 A.M.– 1:00 P.M., Wednesday–Saturday, 2:00 P.M.–5:00 P.M., in the winter Tuesday, 11:00 A.M.–1:00 P.M., Wednesday–Saturday, 2:00 P.M.– 4:00 P.M., 105 East Park Avenue in the Williams Free Library, 414– 887–1266.

Historical Information

A Closer Look at Beaver Dam: Guide to Historic Architecture (1981) by Jean G. Messinger. Dodge County Historical Society, 105 East Park Avenue, Beaver Dam, WI 53916, 414–887–1266. Beaver Dam Chamber of Commerce, 127 South Spring Street, Beaver Dam, WI 53916, 414–887–8879.

Lodging

Grand View Motel, 1510 North Center Street, 414–885–9208.

Restaurants

City Lunch, 103 East Maple, 414–885–9451.

Cortina's Italian Cuisine, 110 South Center, 414–887–7782.

Los Gringos Mexican, 210 South Spring Street, 414–887–0800.

Sub Shop, 104 South Center, 414–887–3122.

Voelker's Steak House, 415 East South Street, 414–885–9924, handicapped accessible.

V:4
Appleton

ECORDED history in the Fox River valley began in the 1600s when the river served as a pathway from the Great Lakes to the Mississippi. In 1634 Father Jean Nicolet landed in the area after crossing Lake Michigan in the company of Indians. Nicolet thought he was headed for Cathay and clothed himself in suitable attire to meet the legendary Chinese. Instead he met the Winnebago Indians, laid claim to the area for the King of France, and established a flourishing fur trade.

At the north end of Lake Winnebago on the Fox River are three communities which have a particular flavor. Appleton, Neenah, and Menasha are all important paper producers and have been praised by national magazines as among the ten best places in the country to live and work. Appleton is also the home of Lawrence University, founded in 1847 as the second co-educational institution of higher learning in the country; the site of the nationally recognized Institute of Paper Chemistry; the birthplace of magician Harry Houdini; and was home to Edna Ferber when she wrote *Dawn O'Hara*.

Directions

A weekend spent in the Fox River area could include Appleton and Neenah. From Chicago take Interstate 94 north to Milwaukee, take bypass 894 north to U.S. 41, then north to Neenah, Menasha, and Appleton.

ARCHITECTURAL TOURS
COURTHOUSE HISTORIC DISTRICT

Proceed south to Prospect, then west one block to park. If you are coming into Appleton from U.S. 41, you might tour the Courthouse district first. Turn right, or south, onto Walnut and drive one block to park. You can make a leisurely tour of this district in about an hour.
1. Courthouse Square was built in 1851 for the village of Martin which later joined with other towns to form the village of Appleton.

The courthouse itself was erected in 1941. **2.** Across the street at 403 West Sixth is an Italianate double house with one section of two stories and another of two and one-half stories, built in 1878. **3.** The Schuetter-Baumruk house at 330 West Sixth is a Queen Anne-style building designed by architect C.A. Tenbusch in 1890. Its wealth of detail includes a wraparound corner porch, dormers, turret, and bay window. **4.** Turn north onto West Prospect to 312, the home of mural painter Francis Scott Bradford. **5.** The simple Queen Anne house at 300 West Prospect was built in 1869 for T.W. Brown. **6.** Turn south to 315 West Prospect, an elaborate Italianate house built by W.G. Whorton in 1870–76. The house has a three-story corner tower and fancy Eastlake front porch. **7.** The Italianate house at 325 West Prospect was built before 1873 for E. C. Goff. **8.** William Scheer, a church artist whose Stations of the Cross can be seen in St. Joseph's Church, built the Queen Anne house next door in 1901. It has third-floor dormers and a wide front porch. **9.** At 335 West Prospect is another large, ornate Queen Anne house, built in 1903. Its wide front porch has a pedimented middle entrance and a fancy third-floor dormer. **10.** Go west a block along Fifth Street to South Walnut. The large house at 601–3 was built in 1871 for Adam Mertes. Like others of the period, it has a wide front porch and third-story dormers. **11.** Across the street on the northwest corner is a large house built at the turn of the century by William Reilly. **12.** The Greek Revival Balliet house at 515 West Fifth, the oldest house in Appleton, was built in 1851 and moved to this location in 1934. **13.** Walk one half block west and one block south to Hearthstone. At the southeast corner of Prospect and Memorial Drive is an elaborate Queen Anne house built in 1881–82 by H.J. Rogers. The house has a wraparound front porch, numerous third-story gables, and two second-story balconies. **14.** Proceed north on South State Street to the twin houses at 414–16. They were built as one in the 1880s and divided in 1925. **15.** Half a block north are St. Mary's Catholic Church and its rectory at 522 West Seventh Street. The Queen Anne-style rectory was designed by Charles Hove. The small east wing and the front porch are later additions, but otherwise the facade is original. **16.** The elaborate Queen Anne house east and a bit north at 303 Walnut was built in the 1870s for James Lennon. **17.** Proceed a block north and then east to 415 West Eighth Street. This large Queen Anne house was built in 1895 for Peter Heid. It has a prominent third-story front gable and wraparound front porch. **18.** A block farther east is 340 West Eighth Street, a large house built for William Early in 1871. This two-story L-shaped house has a porch across half its front. **19.** Across the street at 327 West Eighth is a Queen Anne house built in 1874 by Joseph Rossmeissl. A prominent feature is the steep roof and third-story front gable. **20.** At the

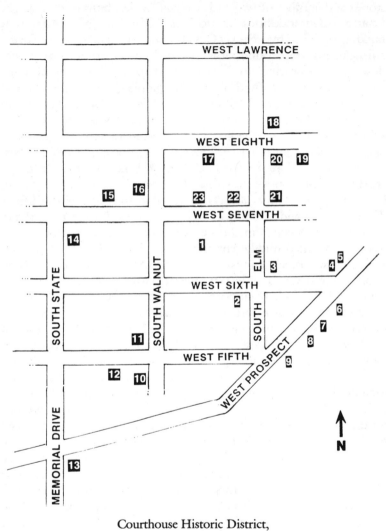

Courthouse Historic District,
Appleton

southeast corner of Eighth and Elm Streets is 302 South Elm, built in 1871. **21.** A block south at the northeast corner of West Seventh and South Elm is a rambling Eastlake–Italianate house built in the early 1880s for Julius Peerenboom. **22.** Turn west on Seventh Street to 402, a house built before 1872 for Gerhard Kamps. **23.** The larger house next door at 408 West Seventh was built in 1894 for J.H. Kamps. You are now a block and a half from where you parked.

CITY PARK HISTORIC DISTRICT
Take College or Lawrence Avenue east to Durkee Street. Proceed north to Washington Street. On the northwest corner is a parking facility. Allow about one hour for a leisurely walk through this district. **1.** The churchlike building at 320 North Durkee was built in 1883 as Temple Zion. Its rabbi was Houdini's father. **2.** Proceed north to the corner of North and Durkee; you will see the David Hammel Stick-style house at 417 North Durkee. This large house has a corner tower, massive central chimney, and ornamentation. **3.** Edna Ferber lived at 216 East North Street in 1909 while she wrote *Dawn O'Hara*. Like most of the houses in this area, it was built at the turn of the century. **4.** Go east to 413 North Drew Street, built in the 1880s for Leonard Bushey. **5.** At the corner of North Drew and East North is the Richardsonian Geenen house. This heavy stone house has a three-story bay ending in a third-story balcony, flanked by two dormers and a large first-floor veranda which is topped by a second-floor open porch. **6.** Next door at 418 East North Street is a much smaller house. **7.** Across Park Avenue on the northeast corner is 504 East North Street, built in 1899. It has a wide front porch and three second-story dormers. **8.** The twin houses at 510 and 516 East North were built about 1908 for Eva Hammel and Anna Kahn. **9.** The Tuttle house at 524 East North Street is built in a style called Eclectic Resurgence. Most prominent is its three-story crenelated turret tower. It also has a wide front porch and third-story dormers. **10.** The Queen Anne house at 414 North Union was built in 1890. It has steep gables and a wide front porch. **11.** The much smaller house at 602 East Eldorado was built in 1890 by Herman Heckert. **12.** Another Queen Anne house is located at the northeast corner of East Franklin and North Union at 304 North Union. **13.** A much larger Queen Anne house is found across Union Street on the southwest corner at 229 North Union. It was built for John Stevens in 1890. **14.** The elaborate house at 229 North Park was built in 1904 by George W. Jones. **15.** Across the street is another Queen Anne house, built for Charles Mory. **16.** The Eastlake house at 216 North Park was built in 1896 for P.M. Conkey. It has steep gables and a large wraparound porch. **17.** A block south and east is the Thomas Patten Stick-style house, built in

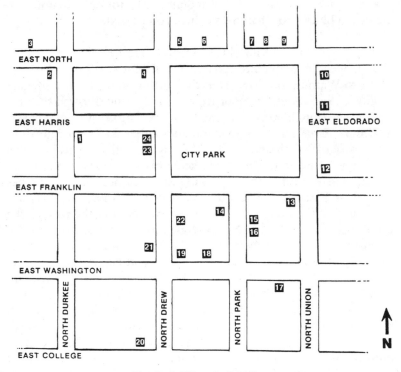

City Park Historic District,
Appleton

1890. It, too, has a wide front porch and very steep gables. **18.** Back on Washington Street at 410 is the home of William Montgomery, a friend of magician Harry Houdini. **19.** A bit west is 402 East Washington, a Picturesque-style house built in 1883. **20.** Walk south a block to the northwest corner of College and Drew Streets where you will find the Outagamie Museum, built in 1923. The building, designed by Milwaukee architect Cornelius Leenhouts, is in the eclectic Norman–English–medieval style. **21.** The fancy Queen Anne house at 211 North Drew was built by Fred Kutler in the 1860s. It has a wrap-around porch, decorated dormers, and bays. **22.** The simple two-story house at 224 North Drew Street was built around 1889 by Lorenzo S. Knox. The only apparent change is the sun porch to the south. **23.** The house at 315 North Drew was built for Allen E. Davis in the 1860s. **24.** Next door is 319 North Drew, the first home of Edna Ferber in 1897.

Festivals, Tours, and Other Places of Interest

Tours of the City Park and the Courthouse districts, including the interiors of a few houses, are occasionally held by the Outagamie County Historical Society office, 330 East College Avenue, Appleton, WI 54911, 414–733–8445. Outagamie County Historical Society Museum, 330 East College Avenue, Appleton, WI 54911, 414–733–8445. The Charles A. Grignon mansion, open Memorial Day–Labor Day, Tuesday–Sunday, 1:00 P.M.–5:00 P.M., Augustine Street, Kaukauna, WI 54130, 414–766–3122.

Historical Information

Outagamie County Historical Society, 330 East College Avenue, Appleton, WI 54911, 414–733–8445. City of Appleton, Department of Planning and Development, William A. Brehm, Jr., Director, 200 North Appleton Street, P.O. Box 1857, Appleton, WI 54913, 414–735–6460.

Lodging

Guest House Inn, 3730 West College Avenue, 414–731–9231.
Midway Motor Lodge, 3033 West College, 414–731–4141.
Paper Valley Hotel and Conference Center, 333 West College, 414–733–8000.
Roadstar Inn, 3623 West College, 414–731–5271.

Restaurants

Damorow's Restaurant, 1212 East College, 414–731–2951, handicapped accessible.

Dragon Gate Restaurant, 406 West College, 414–731–8088, handicapped accessible.

Good Company Restaurant, 110 North Richmond Street, 414–735–9500, handicapped accessible.

Karras' Restaurant, 207 North Appleton, 414–739–1122, handicapped accessible.

Koehnke's Lounge, 733 West College Avenue, 414–733–9917.

Peppermill Restaurant, 105 East College, 414–739–1233, handicapped accessible.

Pyszora's Coach Lamp Inn, 211 South Walnut, 414–733–9719, handicapped accessible.

Trim-B's Bar and Restaurant, 201 South Walnut, 414–734–9204.

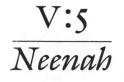

V:5
Neenah

WINNEBAGO COUNTY
Wisconsin

THE brightest star in the region known as the Fox River valley is Neenah. Not long after its founding in 1847, it was called the "paper city." The two Kimberly brothers came to this spot at the mouth of the Fox River to establish their paper business and to build houses side by side. The towering Bergstrom Paper Company smokestack anchors historic Wisconsin Avenue at one end, and at the other end are mansions of such dimensions that one wonders how a pre-Kleenex Kimberly Clark could have supported such elegance.

Directions

Appleton and Neenah are neighbors. You would have a rewarding weekend visiting them both. From Chicago take Interstate 94 north to Milwaukee and bypass 894 to U.S. 41 north to Neenah. Take the Winniconnie Avenue (State Route 114) exit and proceed east to Commercial Street. Turn left, or north, to the Wisconsin Avenue intersection. You are now in the center of the downtown historic district.

ARCHITECTURAL TOURS
WEST WISCONSIN AVENUE HISTORIC DISTRICT
The West Wisconsin street area became the commercial center of Neenah in the 1880s. Today, this section of West Wisconsin is a reflection of late nineteenth- and early twentieth-century architecture. We are calling attention to the important architectural buildings, but it is the entire streetscape that makes this district remarkable. You can cover the area at a leisurely pace in well under half an hour. Parking is available on both the northeast and northwest corners of Church Street and Doty Avenue, one block south of Wisconsin, and one block north of Wisconsin on the southeast corner of Church.
1. Regarded as the finest building on the street is the Winnebago Paper Company office at 225 West Wisconsin. This Romanesque

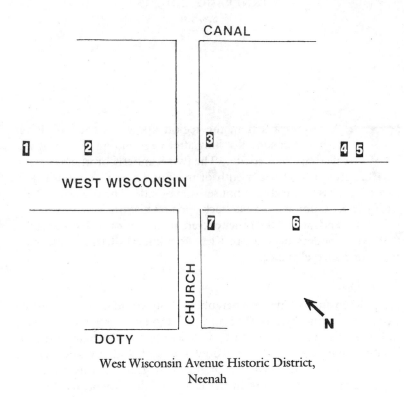

CANAL

1 2 3 4 5

WEST WISCONSIN

7 6

CHURCH

DOTY

N

West Wisconsin Avenue Historic District,
Neenah

commercial building has a decorated entrance on its southwest corner and a myriad of detail on its brick and limestone facade. The architect of this 1893 building was William Waters; his work can be seen in other Fox River cities. 2. A bit east is the Northwestern Distributing Company store at 205 West Wisconsin. This glass and stone building is the only example of Art Deco in Neenah. The first floor is black glass with decorative etching. The second story is stone with wrought-iron grilles beneath two of the three casement windows. Both the interior and the exterior are original. 3. On the northeast corner of Church and Wisconsin is the largest building in the area, 137–45. This commercial building is Queen Anne with Gothic touches, particularly the off-center tower. Although the first-floor storefronts have been altered, the second story and the attic are original. 4. Farther east is the Sherry-Tippens building at 111–15 West Wisconsin. This Victorian Gothic structure has been much altered at street level, but a look at the second story and roof line reveals a wealth of window and cornice detail. Its architect was Charles Hove, who worked here before moving to Appleton. 5. Next door is the National Manufacturers' Bank building. This limestone Neoclassical structure was erected in 1902 and is the only example of this style in Neenah. 6. Cross Wisconsin to 120, the Marketplace mini-mall's Sullivanesque building. Although the first floor has been altered, the second-floor facade with its large windows and terracotta panels is in the Louis Sullivan tradition. Oddly enough, this is the only Neenah commercial building reflecting the Chicago School of architecture. 7. At the southeast corner of Church and Wisconsin is the district's earliest extant block at 132–34. Built in 1858 by C.J. Wheeler and C.A. Leavens, this vernacular structure has its original central entry and cornice.

SCATTERED SITES

A variety of buildings including an opera house and the mansions of the four Kimberly Clark founders are scattered throughout the town. We suggest that you drive to view these important edifices. Depending on your speed, you can view these in an hour or so. 1. The oldest industrial building, dating from 1857, is the Bergstrom Brothers stove works at 636 Main Street. 2. At 336 Main Street is an octagonal house built in 1855 for Hiram Smith. Like others of its design, this house has a semicircular porch. 3. At 307 Tray Street is the Danish Lutheran Church parsonage, built in 1872. This vernacular brick house is the oldest church-related building in the city. 4. The Italianate Dewitt C. Van Ostrand house at 413 Church Street was built in the 1870s. 5. You are now in the West Wisconsin Avenue Historic District, discussed above. 6. The Prairie-style opera house, built in 1902 and designed by Chicago architect Sidney Lowell, was the first cultural edifice in

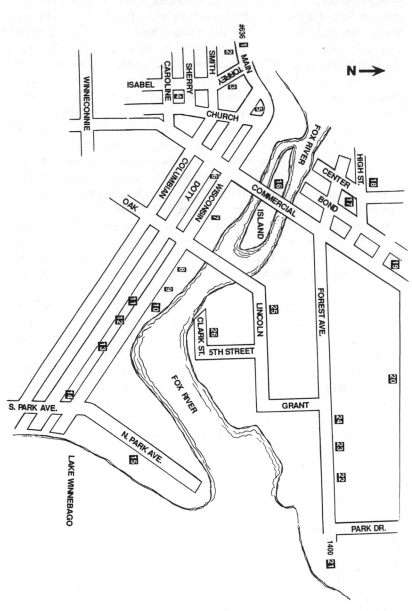

N →

#636

MAIN
TORREY
SMITH
SHERRY
CAROLINE
ISABEL
CHURCH
WINNECONNE
COLUMBIAN
DOTY
WISCONSIN
OAK
FOX RIVER
ISLAND
COMMERCIAL
CENTER
BOND
HIGH ST.
FOREST AVE.
LINCOLN
CLARK ST.
5TH STREET
GRANT
FOX RIVER
S. PARK AVE.
N. PARK AVE.
LAKE WINNEBAGO
PARK DR.
1400

Neenah

Neenah. **7.** The pavilion in Shattuck Park at 200 East Wisconsin is modeled after a Greek Revival market building. **8.** The Colonial Revival house at 402 East Wisconsin was built for Frank J. Sensenbrenner. **9.** The Greek Revival double house at 404–6 East Wisconsin was built in 1849 by John and Harvey Kimberly. **10.** John A. Kimberly, a founder of Kimberly Clark, built the imposing house at 410 East Wisconsin in 1874. **11.** The large Shingle-style house at 433 East Wisconsin was built in 1904 for Frank W. Hawks. It has an imposing entrance from which rises a second-floor bay and third-story dormer. **12.** The grandiose 1883 Queen Anne house at 537 East Wisconsin was built by Havilah Babcock, another founder of Kimberly Clark. It has a wide limestone terrace, Stick-style front porch, three-story tower ending in a pinnacle, and a porte-cochere. Some of the trim is Norman Revival. **13.** Another Kimberly Clark founder, Franklyn C. Shattuck, built the Georgian Revival house at 547 East Wisconsin. This large, imposing red brick house has a wide pillared front porch and third-story dormers. Its builder was the Milwaukee firm of Ferry and Clas. **14.** The Tudor-style house of John Nelson Bergstrom at 165 North Park Avenue was built in 1930. In 1958 this house became a museum. **15.** The Harrison Reed stone barn at 700 South Park Avenue was built by Neenah's founder in 1847. **16.** Drive west to Commercial Street and turn right, crossing the Fox River. The Reliance mill at 100 North Commercial Street, on an island in the Fox River, was built in 1868. **17.** Joseph Patzel's Italianate house at 238 Bond street was built in 1883. **18.** The Ernst Weickert Eclectic–Italianate house at 303 High Street was built in 1881. It has a broad wraparound front porch and decorated gables and window hoods. **19.** The Victorian Romanesque Chicago and Northwestern station at 500 North Commercial Street was built in 1892. **20.** The Queen Anne house at 417 Nicolet Boulevard was built for Louis Jourdain in 1888. The frame house has highly decorated Stick-style gables. **21.** The Ernst Mahler house at 1400 East Forest Avenue was designed by the Chicago firm of Childs and Smith and Milwaukee's A.C. Eschweiler. It is a Tudor Revival house, half stucco and half timber, built in 1921. **22.** The Alexander Syme house at 910 Forest Avenue was built in 1882. This Queen Anne house has a prominent three-story front bay culminating in a dormer, a three-story central square crenelated tower, a wide front porch, and a number of dormers. **23.** The Eclectic Charles R. Smith house at 824 East Forest Avenue was built in 1891. **24.** Henry Smith's Queen Anne-Shingle house is found at 706 East Forest Avenue. **25.** The James Doty double log cabin was moved to this location in Doty Park at Lincoln Street in 1926 and renovated in 1948 to its 1850s condition. **26.** At 515 Clark Street is the extravagant Mediterranean-style Frank Whiting boathouse, built in 1932.

Festivals, Tours, and Other Places of Interest

Doty Cabin, open mid-June–mid-August, Tuesday–Sunday, 1:00 P.M.–5:00 P.M., Doty Park and Lincoln Street, Neenah, WI 54956.

Historical Information

Fox Cities Chamber of Commerce and Industry, 330 North Commercial Street, Neenah, WI, 54956, 414–722–7758. Neenah Public Library, 240 East Wisconsin, Neenah, WI 54956, 414–729–4722.

Lodging

Valley Inn, 105 Walnut Street, 414–725–8441.

Restaurants

Caliban's, 134 West Wisconsin Avenue, 414–725–0573, handicapped accessible.

Hau's Restaurant, 111 West Wisconsin Avenue, 414–722–7998.

Marketplace Cafe, between Church and Commercial on Wisconsin Avenue, 414–725–2242, handicapped accessible.

Valley Inn, 105 Walnut Street, 414–725–8441, handicapped accessible.

VI:1

Bishop Hill

HENRY COUNTY
Illinois

THIS small town was founded in 1846 by Swedish dissidents at odds with both their church and their state. Their leader was Erik Jansson, who believed himself to be the second Christ, designated by the Lord to lead his people in both religious and material matters.

Under Jansson's leadership, the living arrangements as well as the work were communal in Bishop Hill. Adults were assigned rooms. The children ate in one dining room and the adults in another. The boys herded the cattle and lived in the boys' house above the shoemaker's shop. The girls milked the cows and made the butter and lived in the dairy building. Unlike some American utopian communities, the Janssonites did not try to eliminate the family, but the family did not work as a unit; members participated as individuals.

Although Erik Jansson was murdered in 1850 for trying to keep his niece from following her husband out of the community, the trustees kept the community together. They were most successful in promoting economic prosperity, but they could not completely fill the religious void left by Jansson's death.

A combination of the 1857 depression, the growing appetite of colony members for democracy, and the decline of religious fervor resulted in the decision on February 14, 1861, to divide the property. The dissolution of the commune brought about the decline of the village.

Due to the efforts of the Bishop Hill Heritage Association, private property owners, and the state's Division of Historic Sites, the village is being renovated and is on its way to being a center for nineteenth-century crafts.

Directions

You can combine Bishop Hill with a weekend trip to Galesburg. A day trip would be long, as Bishop Hill is about a four-hour drive from Chicago. From Interstate 80 west of Chicago exit at Geneseo on State

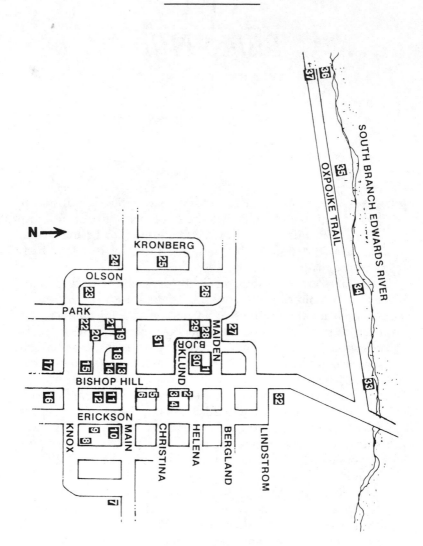

Bishop Hill

Route 82 and proceed south to County Route 233. Travel east approximately four miles, turning south at the Bishop Hill sign. This road will take you directly into the town.

ARCHITECTURAL TOUR

Most of the important buildings were constructed during the communal period or in the decade after it. The most striking difference between the two is the large number of single-family houses built in the latter. 1. Colony Church, on Maiden Lane, was built in 1848. It has been restored and is open to the public. 2. The dairy building, one block south on Bishop Hill Street, dates from 1855. It is a two-and-one-half-story brick structure. 3. The blacksmith's shop next door was built in 1857; it, too, is a two-and-one-half-story brick building. 4. The colony residence, just east toward Erickson Street, was built in 1848. First constructed as a timber-framed Shingle home, the addition was put on in the 1870s. 5. The carpentry and paint shop across Christine Street was constructed in 1852. This two-and-one-half-story brick building has the traditional high Swedish thresholds. 6. The 1854 steeple building, a three-story Greek Revival structure near Main Street, is the largest building in the village. 7. The Swedish Methodist Episcopal church three blocks east on Main, built in 1867, is the only surviving church in town. Its original structure is completely obscured by a later addition. 8. The 1867 Olof Pilstrand house one block south and one west on Knox Street has not been unduly changed by a one-story addition on two sides of the first floor. 9. The Erik Troil house north on Erickson also dates from 1867 and has been moved one block from its original site. A rear kitchen and front porch have been added. 10. The 1866 J.H. Westerberg house next door was originally I-shaped; a series of wings and gables have been added. 11. The 1868 boarding house one block west on Bishop Hill has a well-preserved exterior. 12. The 1867 Abraham Florine house next door is a cross-gabled residence, well preserved on both the inside and the outside. 13. The Greek Revival colony store and post office, across Bishop Hill, was built in 1854. 14. Neumann's tin shop next door dates from the 1870s. 15. The Peter Johnson house near Knox was built in 1867. It is a two-story frame gabled L-shaped building. 16. The Jacob Jacobson house on the other side of Bishop Hill, a Greek Revival T-shaped structure with a columned entrance portico and ornately bracketed cornice, was built in 1866. The only exterior change is the addition of a sleeping porch in 1916. 17. The Swan Swanson house across Bishop Hill Street, a slightly less elegant version of the Jacobson house, was built in 1862. 18. The administrative building on Main between Park and Bishop Hill dates from 1856. It is a three-story Greek Revival L-shaped building. 19. The apartment building next door was constructed in 1855. It is a mirror image of the Greek Revival administrative building. 20. The privy and wash house just south was built to serve the apartment building. It is preserved as the only remaining such structure in the village. 21. The Bjorklund Hotel, next door to the apartment building, was built in 1852. It originally looked much like the carpentry and paint shop (5). Between 1857 and 1861 it was remodeled with the addition of a third story and tower and a first-floor kitchen with rooms above, which made the building U-shaped. A barroom was added to the first floor and a hotelkeeper's apartment above it. It is open to the public. 22. The Olson barn just south was built in 1859–60. It was moved to the Bjorklund Hotel site in 1982. 23. The Krusbo building, across Park, is a one-and-one-half-story balloon-frame building. In 1975 it was moved to Bishop Hill. 24. The Colony School, one block north on the other side of Olson Street, was built in 1861. The bell tower and porch entrance were added to this Greek Revival building in the 1920s. 25. The hospital building across Main Street, dating from 1855, is a timber-framed Greek Revival two-and-one-half-story building. 26. The Erik Johnson residence at Olson and Kronberg Streets was originally a two-over-two-room timber-frame building. Around 1910 two wings were added. 27. The one-and-one-half-story brick meat-storage building, just east on Maiden Lane, was erected in 1851. The garage and porch were added in the 1950s. 28. The 1853 brewing cellar across Maiden Lane is all that remains of a bakery and brewery building. 29. Adjacent is the site of the "Big Brick," a dormitory built between 1849 and 1851. Unfortunately, it burned in 1928. 30. The 1847 boys' house across Bjorklund is a two-over-two-room balloon-frame dormitory. The west and south additions were built in 1922. 31. The bandstand just south is a 1976 reproduction of the 1860s original. 32. The Chaiser house, three blocks north on Bishop Hill, was built in 1866. 33. Continue up Bishop Hill to the Oxpojke Trail. Here you will find the site of the steam-powered second mill. 34. West is the site of the water-powered first mill. 35. Still farther west is the site of the tannery. 36. At the Weller Township Road is the site of the brick kiln. 37. Oxpojke, a trail along the Edwards River, connects the second mill site with the Red Oak Grove where some of the original colonists spent their first winter. Arrangements can be made by organized groups to walk the trail.

Historical Information

An authoritative book about the village, *Bishop Hill: A Utopia on the Prairie* by Olov Isaksson, 1969, LT Publishing House, Stockholm, Sweden, is available from the Bishop Hill Heritage Association, P.O. Box 1853, Bishop Hill, IL 61419, 309–927–3899.

Lodging

Country Hills, 309–932–2886.
Holden's, 309–927–9273.

Restaurants

All restaurants are handicapped accessible and are also closed during the winter.
Filling Station, 309–927–3355.
P.L. Johnson Dining Room, 309–927–3885 or 309–932–2623.
Red Oak, 309–927–3539 or 309–932–3115.
Valkommen Inn, 309–927–3531.

VI:2
Galesburg
KNOX COUNTY
Illinois

P LANS for the city of Galesburg came from the vision of
George Washington Gale, who led a colony of Congrega-
tionalists from upstate New York to 10,000 acres of land that
they had purchased to found a town and to establish a college
to train young men for the ministry and a female seminary to educate
their future wives. In 1837 Knox College received its charter. Knox
College's "great day," the Lincoln-Douglas debate held at the east
end of Old Main on October 7, 1858, is still held to be the most
spectacular event in the college and the town.

By the early twentieth century one third of the population was of
Swedish descent or birth. The most famous member of this popula-
tion was Carl Sandburg, midwestern poet, who was the son of a
Swedish-born railroad blacksmith.

Directions
A good weekend trip would encompass Galesburg and Bishop
Hill. The trip from Chicago is at least four hours each way. From
Chicago take Interstate 80 west to Interstate 74. Exit on Main Street,
the second Galesburg outlet; proceed west to Cherry; and turn left, or
south, onto Simmons, where there is parking.

ARCHITECTURAL TOURS
Architecturally and historically significant buildings are found in the
business district, south of Main between Chambers and Academy
Streets, and north of the Burlington Northern tracks, which includes
Knox College. North of the center of town and above North Street is
the fine residential area known as Society Hill, developed from about
1890 to 1905. Of special literary and sociological interest is the area
bounded on the north by South Street and east of the Burlington
Northern's tracks and yards, around Chambers and Third. Carl Sandburg was born in this working-class section. The downtown area is
best explored on foot. Many buildings are worth studying in this

138

fairly compact area. Allow about an hour for this trip. The other areas can easily be toured by car.

DOWNTOWN

1. Walk north on Broad Street to the public square, which is circular. The Central Congregational Church, located at the southwest corner, is a massive Richardsonian Romanesque edifice designed in 1897 by the Galesburg architectural firm of Gottschalk and Beadle. The building is rich in detail, including an impressive bell tower with wheel window and a handsome rose window over the triple-arched entrance. Now walk east around the square and along Main Street, noticing the scattering of nineteenth-century facades. The National Trust for Historic Preservation awarded Galesburg one of its original Main Street grants. 2. One block south and one and a half blocks east on East Simmons is the Romanesque Revival 1906 Central fire station. 3. The building at 147 Cherry was built in 1910 by J.F. Percy. 4. Adjacent on Cherry is the 1905 City Hall, designed by architect William Wolfe. This Neoclassical building's facade is original, including the restored central tower, complete with weathervane. 5. The First Baptist Church, at the corner of Prairie and Tompkins, was built in 1894. This massive Richardsonian Romanesque church, designed by Galesburg architect William Wolfe, has an unusual corner entrance. 6. Walk south on Prairie one block to South Street. On the northeast corner is Corpus Christi Roman Catholic Church. This 1885 Gothic Revival building has a landmark steeple. 7. A little farther south on Prairie is the 1874 Italianate Knox County Jail, designed by Peoria architect William Quayle. The building is embellished by limestone window hoods and quoins and, in the best Italianate style, has heavily bracketed eaves and a center pediment. 8. Occupying the west side of Cherry between South and Tompkins is the Knox County courthouse. This Romanesque Revival–Victorian Gothic structure was designed by Detroit architect Elijah E. Meyers, who also designed six state capitols and many courthouses. Its most prominent feature is the turreted clock tower. 9. Occupying the remainder of the block is Standish Park, dating from 1859. 10. In the next block across South Street is the Knox College Alumni Building, designed by courthouse architect Elijah E. Meyers. The impressive recessed arched entrance is topped by a pediment with a round window. 11. Directly across the college campus is Old Main, the original college building, dating from 1857. This Gothic Revival structure was designed by Peoria architect Charles Ulricson. Its entrance is flanked by twin towers and a fine arched belfry. 12. On the northeast corner of Broad and East Tompkins Streets you will find Whiting Hall, the Knox Female Seminary, built in 1857. The original Italianate middle

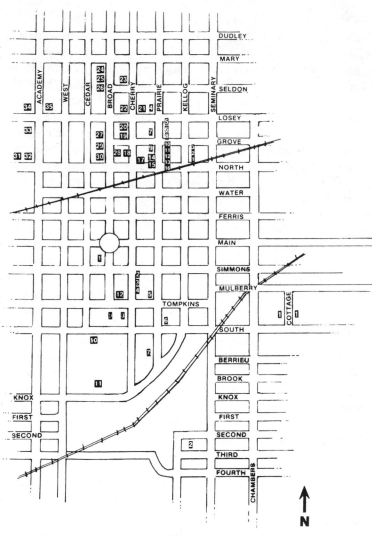

Galesburg

three sections were augmented by a compatible east wing in 1885 and a west one in 1892.

SOCIETY HILL

The area north of North Street adjacent to downtown, settled between 1890 and 1905, was home to Galesburg's most prominent residents. Many houses are prime examples of the late Victorian style known as Queen Anne, which allowed owner and architect freely to express their taste in towers, turrets, balconies, porches, and the newly developed porte-cochere, not to mention the facade combinations of stone, brick, and shingle. We suggest that you drive to the area, then park and walk on North Prairie. The trip should take about an hour. Leaving downtown, go north on Kellog to North Street. At the intersection you will enter Society Hill. 1. On the east side is 425 Kellog, an Italianate house built by James Short in 1868. 2. The Gothic cottage at 435 North Kellog was built in 1855 by Walter Patch. A wide veranda protects three sides of the house. It is resplendent with fine carpenter's lace trim, the result of the invention of the scroll saw. 3. At 483 North Kellog is an 1856 Federal-style house built by John C. Stewart. 4. Proceed one block north to Losey and a block east to North Prairie. On the northwest corner is 640 North Prairie. This Colonial Revival house was built in 1905 by Cyrus M. Avery. 5. Across Losey on the southeast corner is 591 North Prairie, a grand house built in 1891 by George Lawrence. This Queen Anne three-story monument has a Richardsonian Romanesque heavily arched entrance, a wide wraparound front porch, a two-story bay window, and partial porch and large gable with pediment jutting from the third story. Most houses of this style are made of a number of materials, but this is made of fine carved stone throughout with numerous decorative details including stained-glass windows. 6. On the east side of Prairie is the Queen Anne John C. Fahnestock house. Built in 1896, it is a simple structure with a three-story tower, two third-story gables, carved double-entrance doors, and a semicircular porch above the entry. 7. Another version of Queen Anne is the Clark E. Carr house at 560 North Prairie, built by Galesburg's first architect, William Wolfe. It has a myriad of details, such as bay windows, a stepped-pediment roof line, pressed-metal elements, varied window designs, and an ornate porch. 8. The Queen Anne house at 545 North Prairie, built in 1886 by John Hood, is another example of the style's variety. It has octagonal towers, round turrets, bay windows, and a dominant decorated third-story gable. 9. The Neoclassical W.S. Purington house, built at 464 North Prairie in 1876, features a columned porch across its front, a Palladian window above the porch, and two dormers protruding from the third floor. 10. The 1876 Second Empire house built by Mary Smith at 455 North Prairie is one of the few examples of this style still found in Galesburg. The porch replaces an earlier one and is more in keeping with the house's style. **11.** The house at 437 North Prairie was built by John Houston Finley in 1892. **12.** A stunning example of the Queen Anne style is found at 427 North Prairie in a small white house with a portico-porch entrance supported by Classical Corinthian columns, a many-windowed tower (now without its bulb dome top), a myriad of window types, and a fanciful second-story bay window. **13.** The shingled Queen Anne house at 343 North Prairie was built by Andrew Harrington in 1886. It boasts a porte-cochere, hipped roof, turreted side bay, first-floor bay window with balustrade, large semicircular window, and a prominent third-story gable. **14.** In 1876 this Federal-style house was built at 382 North Prairie by Robert Chappell. This is a rather late date for a Federal house, but by the 1870s there was considerable freedom of choice in architecture. **15.** On the west side of Prairie is 396 North Prairie, a Georgian house built in 1866. Its Classic proportions are highlighted by side windows flanking the entrance door. **16.** The Italianate house at 153 North Street was built in 1856 by Alfred Craig. **17.** Go west on North Street one block to Cherry Street. At 127 East North Street on the northeast corner of Cherry is the house built in 1840 by Galesburg's founder, George Washington Gale. Although much altered by subsequent owners, this clapboard house still retains some of its original Greek Revival detail. **18.** North on Cherry at 422 is a Prairie School residence, a significant departure from its nineteenth-century neighbors. Built in 1910, it has geometric-detailed leaded windows rather than Victorian stained glass, a roof with large projecting eaves, and a third-floor central gable reminiscent of the Queen Anne style. **19.** North on Cherry at the northwest corner with Grove Street is the 1910 Classical Revival O.N. Custer house. **20.** The Italianate house at 536–38 North Cherry was built in 1865 by A.J. Ostrander. It has the characteristic heavily bracketed eaves and long windows embellished by ornate hoods, but also a third-floor dormer. **21.** On the northeast corner of East Losey and North Cherry is a massive two-family house built in 1924. The most prominent feature of this Eclectic structure is its impressive tiled roof. **22.** On the northwest corner of North Cherry and East Losey is a Queen Anne house built in 1894. A three-story corner tower is topped by a pyramidal roof. Across the front is a wraparound Eastlake porch. **23.** One block north at 57 East Seldon is a house built by H.C. Gardner in 1914. It is in the Prairie style promoted by Chicago architect Frank Lloyd Wright and his followers. It stresses the horizontal rather than the vertical line and is characterized by a low sloping roof and wide overhanging eaves. **24.** The elaborate Queen Anne house at 774

North Broad Street, built in 1894, is an ingenious combination of fanciful details so dear to the hearts of Victorians. The third-floor gable is heavily decorated, and the offsetting second-floor gable has fancy shinglework. A prominent feature is the three-story tower with tent roof. The wide front porch has a pavilion at one end and a porte-cochere at the other. **25.** A little farther south at 756 North Broad is an even grander example of Queen Anne architecture. Not only does it have a tower and third-floor balcony but it also has an elaborate third-story gable complete with large columned balcony rising above a second-story bay window. The first floor shows the influence of Richardson in its arched stone entrance matched by the porte-cochere at the other end of the front porch. This magnificent house was designed about 1894 by N.K. Aldrich for George E. Luster. **26.** The Albert Felt brick-and-wood house at 738 North Broad Street was built in 1880. It has the prominent Gothic Revival gable and an extraordinary chimney. **27.** The Queen Anne John.W. Lescher house at 534 North Broad was built in 1895, based on a design shown at the Chicago World Columbian Exposition. It has a massive stone front porch with columned entrance, as well as third-floor gables and extraordinarily beautiful stained- and cut-glass windows. **28.** Another large Queen Anne house is at 441 North Broad Street, a bit south and on the other side of the street. It, too, has a wide columned front porch. A corner tower is decorated with a pressed-tin frieze. **29.** On the west side of Broad is a house built by Chauncey S. Colton in 1885. This substantial house has a wide front porch and prominent third-story gable. **30.** The Prairie-style apartment house called "Sanborn Terrace" was built at 316 North Broad Street in 1911. The horizontal lines are accented by the sloping roof with wide overhanging eaves and window groupings. Of some interest is its facade of Purington paving bricks. **31.** Go west on North two blocks. The William Bollenbach Queen Anne house at 337 West North Street was built in 1896. It has a steeply pitched roof accentuated by a front third-story dormer and a wide wraparound front porch. **32.** Next door at 319 West North Street is a Queen Anne house built in 1890 by D.W. Aldrich. The facade is resplendent with the steep decorated gables, cornice, bay windows, and tower so popular with late nineteenth-century builders. The porch, which stretches across the front, has a fine entrance portico. **33.** Around the corner at 444 North Academy Street is another house of the same style built in the same year by M.T. Perrin. **34.** Another Queen Anne house at 546 North Academy was also built in 1890, by George Prince. It, too, has a three-story tower, wide front porch, and conspicuous third-story gable. **35.** "Wedgwood House" at 537 North Academy was built around 1895 for Edward J. King. The house, built in the Cottage style popular on the East Coast and in western Chicago suburbs, was unique in that its second-story dormers and its octagonal tower were decorated with a blue and white Wedgwood design.

CARL SANDBURG BIRTHPLACE

No visit to Galesburg would be complete without a stop at Carl Sandburg's birthplace. Proceed south on Academy to Main. Turn left and proceed eight blocks to Chambers. Turn right onto Chambers and go south for three blocks. Turn left onto South Street and turn north onto Cottage. 1. On both sides of this short street are houses built by the railroad to house strikebreakers in the late nineteenth century. The street looks much as it did when originally built. The whole area from Mulberry to Fourth and east of the railroad tracks was settled by people who worked on the railroad. This nineteenth-century working-class area is generally untouched by the passage of time. Turn left onto Mulberry and go one block to Chambers. Turn left again and proceed to Third Street, where you turn right. 2. The small white three-room cottage at 331 East Third Street is the birthplace of poet Carl Sandburg. The state of Illinois now operates this cottage as a museum. It is open Tuesday–Saturday, 9:00 A.M.–noon and 1:00 P.M.–5:00 P.M.

KNOXVILLE

From Galesburg take either Interstate 74 southeast or U.S. 150, which becomes Main Street in Knoxville. Removal of the county seat to Galesburg in 1873 spelled the end of Knoxville's growth. Today, with a population of around 3,000, it is a rural residential town frozen in time.

In traveling around Knoxville, notice the original brick-paved streets, particularly Division and Market Streets south of Main, around the public square, and on Hebard north of Main. 1. On Main between Market and Timber you will find the 1840 courthouse. The handsome Greek Revival structure reflects the Jeffersonian ideal that the architectural style of the first democracy, the Greek city-states, was best fitted for the public buildings of the American Republic. Its Doric-column portico and pediment are as grand today as they were in 1836 when designed by architect John Mandeville. The second floor is now a museum. 2. The Hall of Records next door was built in 1845 in the Classical Revival style. It, too, has a portico and columned entrance. 3. On the northwest corner of the public square is the old Knox County Jail, built in 1842. This Federal-style building has its original facade except for the cornice, which was added later. 4. The John G. Sanburn log cabin, built in 1832, was the first commercial enterprise in the town. Discovered inside a larger building, it was

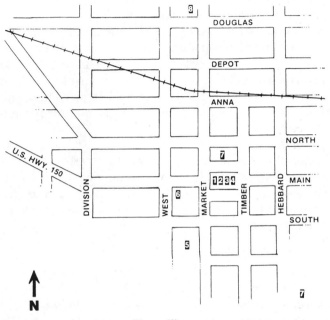

Knoxville

removed to the public square and restored to its original state.
5. Along Market Street there are a number of fine houses of different
architectural styles. 6. On Main Street west of the public square there
are a number of commercial architectural gems. A Federal-style commercial building which once housed Knox County's first newspaper
was built in 1849. The decorative second-floor window hoods, cornice, and frieze are later additions. 7. One block north of the public
square is a Federal-style brick house dating from the 1830s. The porch
and a rear addition are recent. 8. Continue north to Douglas Street
where you will find a chapel and attached cloister, all that remains of
St. Mary's Episcopal School for Girls, built in 1859. The design is
similar to eastern architect Richard Upjohn's small country churches
and also reminiscent of High Gothic architecture. The stained-glass
windows are fine examples of both European and American work of
the 1880s.

Festivals, Tours, and Other Places of Interest

The Galesburg Railroad Museum, South Seminary and Mulberry
Streets, 309–342–9400. Knox County Historical Sites Museum,
open Sunday afternoon, in the Old Courthouse in the public square,
Knoxville, IL 61448.

Historical Information

Remnants of the Nineteenth Century Landscape: Knox County, Illinois
(1979) by Richard C. Welge. Galesburg Historical Society, 325 North
Kellog Street, Galesburg, IL 61401. Galesburg Public Library, Galesburg, IL 61401, 309–343–6118. Knox College, Galesburg, IL 61401,
309–343–0112. Knox County Historical Sites, Old Courthouse, Public Square, Knoxville, IL 61448.

Lodging

Galesburg Inn, 5655 West Main Street, 309–343–3191 or
1–800–255–3050.

Grand Motel, 1777 Grand Avenue, Exit 48 west off I–74, east on
U.S. 150, 309–343–2812.

Holiday Inn of Galesburg, U.S. 150 at Henderson Street, 309–344–
1111.

Howard Johnson Motor Lodge, 29 Public Square, 309–343–9161
or 1–800–654–2000.

Jumer's Continental Inn, I–74 at East Main Street, 309–343–7151.

Regal Inn, 1487 North Henderson Street at U.S. 150, 309–344–
2401.

Starlite Motel, 1966 North Henderson Street at U.S. 34 and 150,
309–344–1515.

Restaurants

Cherry Street Brewing Company, 57 South Cherry Street, 309–342–4700.

Golden Corral Family Restaurant, 1707 North Henderson Street, 309–344–2029.

Jumping Bean, 41 South Seminary Street, 309–343–7074.

Landmark Cafe and Creperie, 62 South Seminary Street, 309–343–5376.

Little King, 250 East Main Street, 309–343–4101.

Packinghouse, 441 Mulberry Street, 309–342–6868, handicapped accessible.

Steak House, 951 North Henderson Street, 309–343–9994.

Swedough's, Fremont and Broad Streets, 309–342–7517.

VI:3

Jacksonville

MORGAN COUNTY
Illinois

JACKSONVILLE was laid out in 1825 and became the county seat. The old and the restored sections exude an air of settled prosperity. Many antique stores are clustered on a street which forms one side of the town square. Nearby is a truly imposing mansion, a combination of stone fort and porticoed confection, the Strawn Art Gallery. This is the center for historical tour information. Another building affectionately called "Old Beecher" was named for Edward Beecher, first president of Illinois College and brother of Harriet Beecher Stowe. Built in 1829, this was the first college structure in Illinois. Nearby MacMurray College, then called the Illinois Conference Female College, was founded in 1846.

Jacksonville is surprising in that it grew around these college institutions rather than around the mill and brewery as so many other towns did. Jacksonville can also take pride in its caring past. As early as 1849, it had state institutions for the handicapped and the deaf. A mental health facility and a school for the visually impaired were also built.

Many statesmen have come from Jacksonville. Stephen Douglas was Morgan County prosecuting attorney in 1835, and William Jennings Bryan, an Illinois College graduate, practiced law in Jacksonville from 1883 to 1887. Three Illinois governors have also come from Jacksonville: Joseph Duncan, whose house still stands in Duncan Park; Richard Yates, Senior; and Richard Yates, Junior.

Directions

A rewarding weekend trip would be to visit Jacksonville and Petersburg. From Chicago take Interstate 55 to Springfield. Then go west on U.S. 36 to U.S. 67 north to Jacksonville. If you are coming from Petersburg, take State Route 97 to State Route 123 to State Route 125 west to Virginia, where you turn south onto State Route 78 to Jacksonville.

ARCHITECTURAL TOUR

The district is mainly residential. Streets are tree-lined, houses set back on spacious lawns, particularly on College and State Streets. The area is much as it was at the turn of the century. A leisurely walk along State and College will take about an hour. You can park at Duncan Park. 1. The house at 4 Duncan Place, built by the sixth governor of Illinois, Joseph Duncan, stands facing the park. Much has been altered on this house, built in 1834, thus its interest is largely historical. 2. At 2 Duncan Place is the F.J. Waddell Prairie-style house designed by Chicago architects Spencer and Powers. Built in 1911, it is one of two Prairie-style houses in Jacksonville. 3. The Rowe house at 1152 West State, built in 1872 and remodeled in 1902, is one of the handsomest houses in the city. A two-story front bay, elaborate front entrance portico, and latticed porch decorate the facade of this renovated house. 4. The Italianate Cyrus Epler house at 1106 West State, built in 1871, has been compromised by a front addition. 5. At 1042 West State is an entirely different type of house, a Shingle-style Queen Anne with center three-story tower rising from a semicircular front porch. A porte-cochere is at one end of the porch and a matching porch extension at the other. It was built in 1888 by William Hook. 6. At 876 West State is an Italianate house built in 1857 by Augustus E. Ayers. One of its prominent features is the glass-enclosed cupola. 7. It is well worth the almost four-block detour to see the Morgan County courthouse at 300 West State. This Eclectic building with its Second Empire towers, Italianate brackets, and Romanesque Revival arches and windows was designed and built in 1868 by Chicago architect Gurdon Randall. One of three Second Empire courthouses in the state, this impressive granite structure is the grandest. 8. An early house is the Greek Revival example built in 1846 by John W. Lathrop at 817 West State. 9. The double Queen Anne house at 845 West State was built by the Thompson brothers. 10. At 907 West State is a Gothic Revival house built in 1851 by Newton Bateman. The facade was originally board and batten; the shingles were added later. Some of the original bargeboard still decorates the eaves. 11. The only Richardsonian Romanesque house in Jacksonville is at 1135 West State. 12. The main building of the Illinois School for the Deaf was erected in three stages beginning in 1843 and unified by the Colonial Revival facade addition in 1871. 13. The second Prairie-style house, at 1146 West College, was built for Walter Bellatti in 1915 and designed by the same architects, Spencer and Powers of Chicago. 14. Samuel Adams built the Greek Revival house at 1120 West College in 1840–45. 15. The house built in 1874 by William E. Capps at 908 West College is a good example of the Italianate style, which is a popular style in Jacksonville. 16. On

Jacksonville

the northeast corner of College and Kosciusko is the Congregational church built in 1860. This building is more ornate than earlier Congregational churches, for it has a massive corner tower, Romanesque windows, twin-entrance doors, and a large front window; its simple interior is a reminder of the church's New England origin. **17.** The Second Empire Strawn Art Gallery at 331 West College was built in 1880. A three-story pavilion with heavily hooded windows, a side two-story bay, and a porte-cochere is crowned with a bullseye window. **18.** At 871 West College is another Italianate house erected in the 1870s. It has a porticoed corner entrance, a side sitting porch, hooded windows, and bracketed eaves. **19.** The Italianate Henry B. McClure house at 919 West College, built in 1853, was originally Greek Revival. In the 1860s it was remodeled to the then fashionable Italianate, and in 1902 the front porch was added. **20.** One of the oldest frame houses in Jacksonville, dating from 1838, is at 1005 Grove Street. It was built for Bezaleel Gillett. Except for the demolition of the shed used to hide fugitive slaves on the underground railroad, the property is unchanged. **21.** At the southeast corner is 1061 Grove Street, a Greek Revival house built in 1854 by David A. Smith. This handsome house has a well-proportioned entrance portico. **22.** At the northeast corner of Park and Grove is 252 Park. The Gothic Revival house was built around 1852 by Julian Sturtevant. **23.** An unusual house is the octagonal structure built around 1858 at 222 Park. This handsome house has a cupola and a two-story wraparound porch. This is a distinctively American style, and this house is one of nine octagonal houses in Illinois. **24.** On the Illinois College campus is Sturtevant Hall, a Gothic Revival structure built in 1857. **25.** Federal-style Beecher Hall, erected in 1829 and restored in 1950, is the oldest college building in the state. **26.** Another architecturally important building on the college campus is Crampton Hall, an Italianate structure built in 1873. **27.** Philip Gillett built the Classical Revival house at 1235 West College in 1900. You are now one block south of Duncan Park, where you parked.

Festivals, Tours, and Other Places of Interest

The Yesterday's House Tour of a number of buildings in the historic district is sponsored by the Art Association and the Historic Preservation Commission in the first part of June. Write 331 West College, Jacksonville, IL 62650. Tours of the Governor Joseph Duncan home, 4 Duncan Place, are available by appointment with the local chapter of the D.A.R., Jacksonville, IL 62650.

Historical Information

The Legacy of Historic Jacksonville: Its Homes and Buildings (1986) by Jo Ann Beard is available from the City of Jacksonville Historic

Preservation Commission, Jeff Radcliffe, Chairman, Jacksonville, IL 62650, 217–243–3391. Strawn Art Gallery, Art Association, 331 West College, Jacksonville, IL 62650, 217–243–9390. Jacksonville Chamber of Commerce, 155 West Morton, Jacksonville, IL 62650, 217–245–2174. Helen Hackett, Historic Commission member, 217–243–2421.

Lodging
Blackhawk Motel, U.S. 36, 217–245–2187.
Holiday Inn, 1717 West Morton, 217–245–9571.
Motel Six, 1711 West Morton, 217–243–5322.
Star-lite Motel, 1910 West Morton, 217–245–7184.

Restaurants
Good Time Doc's, 222 South Main, 217–243–4521.
Hoosier Lounge, 304 South Main, 217–243–4811.
Jolly Tamale, 601 West Morton, 217–243–5333.
Leo's Pizza, 230 South Main, 217–243–3413.
Same Old Steak House, 837 West Morton, 217–245–2714.
Smith's Cafe, 408 West Morton, 217–245–6761.
Tops Big Boy, 1000 West Morton, 217–245–4185.

VI:4
Petersburg

As you drive to Petersburg on State Route 29, go left at the sign for Lake Petersburg. At the top of the bluff carved by the Sangamon River lies the Oakland Cemetery. The simple boulder marking the grave of Abraham Lincoln's love, Ann Rutledge, is backed by a touching poem composed by Edgar Lee Masters, who wrote for Ann in his *Spoon River Anthology*:

> Bloom forever, O Republic
> From the dust of my bosom

Other famous people of Petersburg are artist and muralist Edward L. Lanning; the intriguingly named Bowling Green who, along with his wife, nursed Lincoln back to health after the death of Ann Rutledge; and Major B. F. Stephenson, founder of the mutual aid society of the Grand Army of the Republic.

Petersburg was first surveyed in 1833, and then was surveyed again in 1836 by Abraham Lincoln, deputy surveyor of Sangamon County at that time. Numerous New Salem residents such as Mentor Graham, teacher of Abraham Lincoln, and Peter Lukins, cobbler and tavern keeper for whom the town was named, moved into Petersburg when New Salem was abandoned.

Directions

A leisurely weekend trip to the Spoon River country should include a stop at Jacksonville and Petersburg. From Chicago you can take Interstate 55 to Springfield and then go northwest on State Route 97 into Petersburg. If you wish to see more of the countryside, you can bypass Springfield by leaving Interstate 55 at Lincoln where you take State Route 10 west to State Route 29 south to State Route 123 west to State Route 97 into Petersburg.

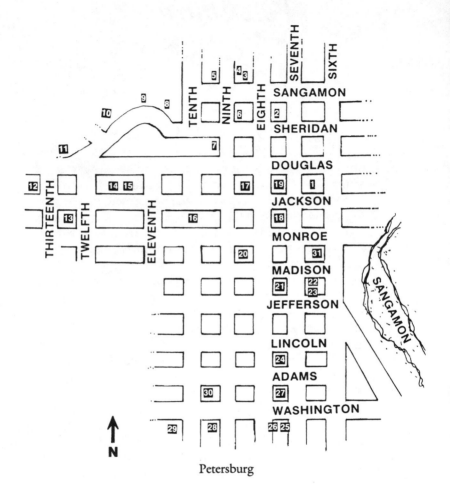

Petersburg

ARCHITECTURAL TOUR

1. Menard County courthouse, the second to occupy the site, is Romanesque in style and was built in 1897 of rose granite and red sandstone. It also has copper ornamentation and a dominating domed cupola. 2. At 121 West Sheridan is a handsome later Federal-style house, built in 1870. It displays Italianate eaves, balanced windows, and an original rusticated plaster finish on brick. 3. Built in 1839, 211 West Sangamon is the Samuel Hill house. The entrance has been moved from the east side of the second floor to the south side. It was originally a Greek Revival house, built in the southern style with a second-story entrance and exposed basement. 4. The unique many-gabled John Bennett house at 313 North Ninth is of early Victorian design, showing some Gothic detailing at the lintels over the windows. 5. On the corner opposite the Bennett house is the towering second house of Edward Laning, built in 1904 in the Queen Anne style. Its prominent feature is a three-story tower. 6. The Federal-style Bishop house at 217 West Sheridan was built between 1845 and 1849. 7. The Cumberland Presbyterian Church, originally built by the Disciples of Christ in 1876, is located at the southwest corner of Ninth and Sheridan and is of simplified Italianate style. It originally displayed a cupola tower. 8. The magnificent towered brick house across Sheridan where the road curves to form Snake Hollow Drive was built in 1875 by Edward Laning. It is a masterful Italianate with balconies, a tower, elaborate window treatment, and the original slate roof. 9. The house at 503 West Sheridan, which stands on top of a hill, was built during the Civil War by Dietrich Fischer, a noted Victorian contractor. It was originally intended to be a two-story house, but due to the wartime shortage of materials it was completed as a one-and-one-half-story house in the Greek Revival style with Italianate detailing. 10. On the next hilltop at 533 West Sheridan Road is the Harry Schirding house, built in 1910, which displays characteristics of the Prairie school style. 11. The large frame Queen Anne house at 605 West Sheridan Road was built by Andrew Jahl in 1910. 12. The Wesley Dowe house at 621 West Jackson on the corner of Thirteenth Street is an attractive late Federal-style home with Italianate touches and was built in 1888. 13. At Jackson and Twelfth is the Robert Frackelton house. It is a wood-framed Italianate house with bay windows on the first and second floors, ornamental iron trim on the porch roof, and a third-story cupola. 14. David Frackelton built the house at 527 West Jackson in 1868. This gracious Italianate brick mansion has elaborate carved stone lintels, a first-floor bay window, and an original columned porch. 15. The red brick Isaac White house at 521 West Jackson is Greek Revival and was built in 1860. 16. Where Tenth ends at Jackson is the Nathaniel Branson house. It is a white

clapboard Victorian Eastlake-style house with a prominent two-story square porch and an imposing tower complete with third-story balcony. **17.** At the northwest corner of Eighth and Jackson is the Edgar Lee Masters house, a simple Victorian era cottage. The house was moved here from its original location at 528 Monroe Street and has been renovated. **18.** The William White house, built in 1850, is located at 209 South Eighth Street. The house is Greek Revival with a small two-story porch on the front. **19.** On the northwest corner of Seventh and Jackson is the 1889 Frackelton Bank. It is of rusticated Romanesque style with a curved glass corner tower and now houses the headquarters of the Menard County Historical Society. **20.** The large red brick house at 319 South Ninth Street was built by Elijah Gault in 1865. It is an Italianate villa-style mansion. An original glass cupola has been removed, but the 1880s gazebo on the south lawn remains. **21.** The William Sullivan Conant house at 419 South Eighth Street was probably built in the 1850s. It is a red brick simple Federal-style house with a carpenter's lace front porch. **22.** The two-story gray brick house at 106 East Madison was built by Richard Bennett. This Federal-style house was erected in the early 1840s. The clapboard addition and the porch were built later. **23.** James D. Whitley built the home at 405 South Seventh Street in the late 1870s. The house is Italianate in design with more modern porches. **24.** The house at 112 East Lincoln was built by George Davidson in 1837. It is a one-story Greek Revival cottage reputed to be one of the oldest houses in the village. **25.** The J.M. Johnston house at 108 West Washington Street, built in 1886, is an interesting example of the Stick and Eastlake styles. **26.** The house at 120 West Washington is a red brick Italianate structure, probably built in 1861 by Boone Talbott. The porch is a modern addition. **27.** At 714 South Seventh Street is the Major Stephenson house, which was built in the 1870s for the widow of the founder of the Grand Army of the Republic. **28.** At 316 West Washington is the McNeely house, built in 1876. It is Italianate with a dominant three-story cupola, bay windows, and a fine bracketed cornice. **29.** At 404 West Washington is the Hobart Hamilton wood-framed Italianate house, built in the early 1870s. The house displays original heavily bracketed eaves, bay windows, a small entrance portico, and a columned side porch. **30.** The C.B. Laning house at 717 South Tenth Street was built in 1875. This large red brick Italianate house retains its original facade except for the addition of a solarium.

Festivals, Tours, and Other Places of Interest

There is a tour of historic houses on the second Sunday in June sponsored by the Petersburg Historic Preservation Association, P.O. Box 3, Petersburg, IL 62675, 217–632–2833. Two miles south of Petersburg on State Route 97 is Lincoln's New Salem Historic Site, an authentic reconstruction of the village as it was in 1831–37 when Lincoln lived there. For information contact Lincoln's New Salem Historic Site, R.R. 1, Petersburg, IL 62675, 217–632–7611.

Historical Information

Petersburg Historic Preservation Association, P.O. Box 3, Petersburg, IL 62675, 217–632–2833. The Chamber of Commerce, P.O. Box 452, Petersburg, IL 62675, 217–632–7363. Menard County Historical Society, 125 South Seventh Street, Petersburg, IL 62675. Petersburg Public Library, 220 South Sixth Street, Petersburg, IL 62675. *Some Interesting Menard County Homes* by Mathilda Johnson Plews is available on interlibrary loan in Illinois. Another source of historic preservation information is *Petersburg, Illinois, Sesquicentennial Historic Homes Guide* by Rodney B. Dimmick.

Lodging

McHenry's Country Motel, State Route 97 (one-half mile south of the entrance to the New Salem State Park), 217–632–7688.

Restaurants

Glena's Country Kitchen on the Square, 217–632–7544.

VII:1

Mineral Point

IOWA COUNTY
Wisconsin

I N the 1830s, Cornish lead miners tried to re-create in Mineral Point the whitewashed row cottages of their old home. Their mines were at the top of the ridge, their homes in the valley. The women would wave a cloth from their doorways to call the men home for dinner, hence the name Shake Rag Street for the principal historic street here. It includes the mining settlement called "Pendarvis," run by the State Historical Society of Wisconsin.

Two incidents in the 1840s made Mineral Point famous in the annals of crime. One was the November 1, 1842, hanging which was viewed by 5,000 people who sat on the hillside with picnic baskets. The prisoner rode to the scaffold upon his coffin, beating a tattoo with two empty beer bottles while the accompanying band played a funeral march. The other, although less spectacular, was an embarrassment to the town. Three burly prisoners on Jail Alley lifted their prison and crawled out from under it.

When ore deposits were exhausted in 1850, this mining town went into a long decline, which was reversed by its evolution into an artistic community in the 1970s.

Directions

Mineral Point is either a day trip or a weekend trip when combined with Galena and/or Mount Carroll, Illinois. If you have time for a long weekend, you could also include Dubuque, Iowa. From Chicago take Interstate 90 northwest to Monona, Wisconsin, where you will follow U.S. 18 and 151 west to Dodgeville. There, take U.S. 151 to Mineral Point. Total distance is 175 miles from Chicago. The historic district encompasses the entire town.

ARCHITECTURAL TOUR

In addition to the miners' log and limestone cottages, there are good examples of Federal, Italianate, and Victorian styles. Although the architecturally significant buildings are scattered around the town, you might park off Commerce Street between High and Fountain and walk around the town's business district. You can cover the remainder of the district by a combination of walking and driving. **1.** The Walker house at Water and Front Streets was built of limestone in three sections between 1857 and 1860. **2.** Pause and look across the valley opposite to the "point" where John Hood made his famous lead strike. **3.** The 1857 Mineral Point depot, the oldest in the state, is a two-story limestone structure with massive walls. **4.** At 20 Commerce Street is the Chesterfield Inn, dating from 1857. This two-story limestone building is a fine example of Cornish stonecutters' craftsmanship. **5.** Go north to Front Street and then left to State, where you will find the 1838 yellow frame Greek Revival Odd Fellows Hall and Museum. The facade is divided into three sections by Doric pilasters. **6.** Turn left on State Street and soon on your right you will see the Old Cemetery. **7.** On your left between Fifth and Sixth Streets you will see the tower of the crushing and flotation plant that extracted lead and zinc from local ore. **8.** Turn west on Sixth to Wisconsin and then right, or north, to Tower. On your left is the limestone Federal-style house built in 1853 by M.M. Cothren. **9.** Return to Wisconsin and turn left onto Front Street. The Flockhart Gothic Revival brick house is on your right facing Front Street. It has handsome arched windows, a bargeboard-trimmed front gable, and limestone corner quoins. **10.** Across the street is the brick Italianate William Lanyon house. Built in 1857, it is distinctive for its ornamental ironwork, particularly in the porch decoration. It has a prominent tower. You can either return to your parking place between Fountain and High and drive to a parking place off Chestnut between Jail Alley and Doty or proceed by foot to Jail Alley along Commerce Street. **11.** Jail Alley extends three blocks from Commerce Street on the east to Wisconsin on the west. The houses along the alley are made of brick, stone, and/or wood and have been well restored. The salmon-colored brick Federal-style house at 105 was built in 1847 by Parley Eaton. **12.** On High Street between Wisconsin and Iowa Streets is the Mineral Point Masonic Temple. This building is not the original but an 1897 replacement. **13.** A little west on the same side of the street is the 1852 Washburn and Woodman Bank building. Note the large metal dog atop the Wisconsin Power and Light Company, the symbol for the Gundry and Gray department store. **14.** On the north side of Fountain Street between Iowa and Center is the limestone Greek Revival Moses Strong house, built in 1867–68. **15.** Directly across the street is the James Brewer house, built in 1866. This clapboard Italianate structure has ornate eave brackets, large arched windows, a wide columned front porch, and a small Second Empire wing. **16.** One block west is the 1860 Gothic

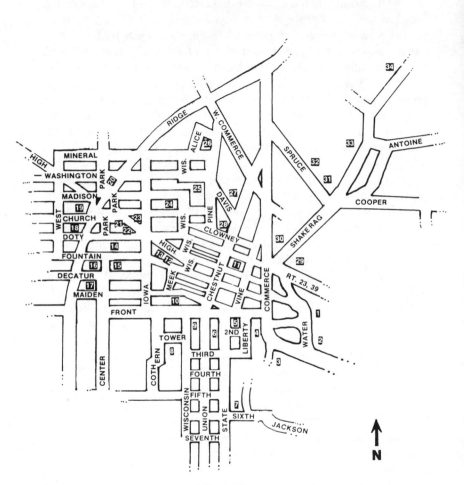

Mineral Point

Revival St. Paul's Church and beside it the 1842 limestone mission church that preceded it. Father Samuel Mazzuchelli probably designed this church. **17.** A block south on Maiden and Ridge is the clapboard Italianate house built by John Gray. Currently painted red with white trim, it has bracketed eaves, a wide columned front porch, and a first-floor bay window. **18.** Go north along Ridge; between Doty and Church is the 1906 William A. Jones house. This Georgian Revival house has a handsome handcarved Corinthian columned portico with balustrade, prominent third-story dormers, and limestone quoins. **19.** In the next block north on Ridge is the 1855 Henry Plowman house. This Federal-style limestone house originally had a front porch and a widow's walk. **20.** One block north is the three-story brick house built by Alexander Wilson in 1855. **21.** Where High and Church meet is the Thomas Priestly house. This 1850 Federal-style house is brick with limestone lintels. **22.** Farther east on High Street is the First Methodist Church. Completed in 1871, this fine English Gothic church with buttresses is constructed of local limestone. **23.** Across the street is the Trinity Episcopal Church and rectory. The Gothic Revival-style church was built in 1846. Next door is the rectory in the same style but it was built between 1860 and 1870. The eaves are decorated with carpenter's lace, or bargeboard, and the front entrance is protected by a porch. **24.** Go east a block to Wisconsin and then north to Madison to the Classical Revival Thomas Ansley house. **25.** The Mineral Point Historical Society is housed in the home built in 1867–68 by Joseph Gundry. This Italianate limestone mansion has arched windows and bracketed eaves with a bullseye window. Corinthian columns support the front porch, which also boasts a Classical pediment. **26.** Walk north two blocks on Pine to what was the home and studio of artists Max and Ava Fernekes. This Federal-style two-story limestone house was built in the 1830s. **27.** On Davis between Pine and Chestnut is the Greek Revival limestone Bracken house, reminiscent of other Mineral Point houses built in the 1840s. This style of limestone house was also popular in Lockport, Illinois, where there also was an abundance of limestone. **28.** Go south on Chestnut to Clowney and turn right to the limestone Henry Rodolf house. This Greek Revival house, built in 1840, has three dormers protruding from its second story, the middle of which is grandest. **29.** Go south on Chestnut to Doty and then left across Commerce to Shake Rag Street. If you want to park, there is a lot one block north on Cooper. On your left is a one-story limestone house built in the 1840s, now operated as a gift shop called the Welsh House. **30.** Shake Rag Alley is a collection of restored buildings with lovely gardens and has become the setting for artisans and craftworkers. Among the shops of interest are those of Bernard Klais, built in 1858, and Brown Ellery, built in the 1840s. The Coach House, across the Federal Spring from Brown Ellery's cabinet shop, was built between 1838 and 1842. Next you will see the Pendarvis complex on Spruce and Shake Rag Street, which is owned by the State Historical Society of Wisconsin. **31.** Across the street is the Merry Christmas mine, the last surviving mine shaft. **32.** On Spruce Street you will find Tamblyn's Row. Dating back to the early mining days, it includes a "kiddlywink," or pub. The two-story log section was built in 1841 and the two rock units in the 1840s. **33.** North on Shake Rag Street you will find Polperro, a three-story log and rock house; Pendarvis, a small one-story limestone cottage; and Trelawny, a two-story limestone house. Polperro was built in 1843 by George Kislingbury. The stone root cellar, attached to the second floor, was added later. Pendarvis and Trelwany are also nestled into the hillside and connected to Polperro by a garden. **34.** The Mineral Springs brewery was built in 1847. It originally had twin towers, but one was destroyed in 1878 by a tornado and never replaced.

Festivals, Tours, and Other Places of Interest

The Pendarvis Complex (Tamblyn's Row [32] and Polperro, Pendarvis, and Trelawany [33]) are open to the public, 9:00 A.M.–5:00 P.M., May 1–October 31. The cottages are furnished with period antiques and lead mining artifacts. For information contact Mark Knipping, Curator, Pendarvis, 114 Shake Rag Street, Mineral Point, WI 53565, 608–987–2122. Shake Rag Alley, an early settlement area (30), provides a guided or self-guided tour May–October, 10:00 A.M–5:00 P.M.; contact Marion Carey, Curator, Shake Rag Alley, 18 Shake Rag Street, Mineral Point, WI 53565, 608–987–2808. The Odd Fellows Hall (5) is open for guided tours daily June–September, 9:00 A.M.–5:00 P.M., and weekends in May and October, Mineral Point, WI 53565. Orchard Lawn, the Joseph Gundry House (25), now the museum of the Mineral Point Historical Society, is open for tours Memorial Day–September 30. Group tours can be arranged in May, September, and October; contact the Mineral Point Historical Society, P.O. Box 59, Mineral Point, WI 53565.

Historical Information

The Chamber of Commerce sells Frank Humberston, Jr., and Anne D. Jenkin's book *The Homes of Mineral Point*, Mineral Point, WI 53565, 608–987–3201. Mineral Point Historical Society, Orchard Lawn, the Joseph Gundry House Museum, P.O. Box 59, Mineral Point, WI 53565. Pendarvis, 114 Shake Rag Street, Mineral Point, WI 53565, 608–987–2122. The Mineral Point Room of the public library, which is in the basement of the Municipal Building on High

Street, has a comprehensive collection of material on the town and the state, open Saturday, 2:00 P.M.–5:00 P.M. and Thursday evenings by appointment, 608–987–2447. Water Tower Park Tourist Information Center, May 1–October 31, 9:00 A.M.–5:00 P.M., State Route 151, Mineral Point, WI 53565, 608–987–3201.

Lodging
Dairyland Motel, Ridge Street, State Route 151, 608–987–3141.
Duke Guest House, 618 Maiden Street, 608–987–2821.
Point Motel, Ridge Street, State Route 151, 608–987–3112.
Redwood Motel, Ridge Street, State Route 151 north, 608–987–2242.
Walker House (1), 1 Water Street, 608–987–2033.
Wilson House (20), 110 Dodge Street, near the Water Tower Park, 608–987–3600.

Restaurants
Donna's Pizzeria, Commerce between High and Jail Alley, 608–987–9932.
Mineral Point Mining Company, High near Vine.
Pillings Pub, High near Commerce, 608–987–3025.
Red Rooster, High near Chestnut, 608–987–3616.
Redwood, Ridge Street, State Route 151 north, 608–987–2242.
Royal Inn, Jail Alley at Vine, 608–987–2770.

VII:2
Mount Carroll

CARROLL COUNTY
Illinois

W ITH tree-lined brick and cobblestone streets and carefully preserved nineteenth-century houses, the quiet town of Mount Carroll emanates cheer. Its early existence centered around a flour mill, a dam, and Mount Carroll Seminary, later Shimer College. When the college closed in 1978, the Campbell Center was established in the handsome administration building with a grant of $100,000 from the Campbell family. Its mission is to preserve and disseminate knowledge of decorative arts and historic preservation.

Directions
A trip to Mount Carroll can be combined with one to Mineral Point or Galena for a pleasant weekend. Count on three to four hours to reach Mount Carroll from Chicago. The quickest route is via Interstate 90 to Rockford and then west on U.S. 20 to State Route 78 to Stockton. Turn south, and you will reach Mount Carroll, which is twenty miles away. State Route 78 brings you to Main and Market Streets and the Courthouse Square. A shorter but more time-consuming route is to leave U.S. 20 at Freeport and go south on State Route 26 to State Route 72 to Shannon and Lanark, then on State Route 64 to Mount Carroll. Turn right onto State Route 78 at the junction and continue on to the business district and Courthouse Square.

ARCHITECTURAL TOUR
You can park around the courthouse on three sides of the square. No parking is allowed on the east side, which is State Route 78, but off-street parking is available on the east side next to the drive-in bank area. We suggest that you park here and cover the blocks between Market and Center Streets on foot. Then drive south on Clay Street to Benton, park, and tour the rest of the historic district. The tour will take you between one and two hours. 1. The Hotel Glen View on

Market Street faces the courthouse. It was built in 1886 in vernacular Italianate style. Note the ornate cornice incorporating the date. 2. The War Monument and Annex commemorate the 1,284 Mount Carroll soldiers who died defending the Union. The famous sculptor Lorado Taft designed and sculpted the figure of the Union soldier that tops the shaft. 3. Adjacent to the monument is the courthouse. The section on the north was built in 1843, before the rest of the building. It is a simple brick Greek Revival structure with a limestone English basement. The second section to be built was the southern one, and the middle section is the most recent. 4. On Main and Market Streets you can see typical mid-nineteenth-century commercial buildings. On Main across from the courthouse is a stunning collection of cast-iron fronts. On the northwest corner of Main and Rapp is the early twentieth-century City Hall, which is distinguished by its corner bell tower. 5. On the opposite corner is the Classical Revival library, built in 1906. 6. At the end of the block at 202 North Main is a house built by S. J. Campbell, Sr. This red brick Italianate house has a white bracketed cornice with eyebrow windows and white hoods over the front windows and entrance doorway. 7. The house at 115 North Clay Street was built in 1867 by Robert Hawk. The two-story vernacular Italianate house has a southern bay window and half front porch. 8. At 105 North Clay is the Uriah Green house, built in 1873. Its former grandeur is revealed in its handsome enclosed cupola, bracketed cornice, and elaborate front porch. 9. Take Center Street west to Main. On the northeast corner is the Greek Revival community house, originally built as the English Evangelical Church in 1860. It has elongated windows on either side of the entrance and a fine fanlight in the gable. 10. On the other side of Main a half-block north is 108, a house built by John Christian in 1856. This brick Italianate house has been marred by its beige paint with white trim. It has a bracketed cornice, eyebrow windows, and an entrance pediment without the column supports. The numbering system changes when you move from the north to the south section of the town. The even numbers on the north are on the west side of the street and the odd on the east side; in the south it is the opposite. 11. The Hallett Federal-style house is at 209 South Main. This simple red brick building, built in 1856, has two large floor-to-ceiling windows on the first floor, an entrance with side lights, a fanlight, and a porch across the front, which may not be original. 12. In the next block south on the other side of the street at 306 South Main is the Nelson Rinedollar house. Built in 1877, it has Greek Revival lines and Italianate hooded windows and entrance. 13. Go east on Franklin to Clay Street; at 302 is the James O'Brien home, built in 1856. This red brick Greek Revival house has a columned portico shielding its front entrance which

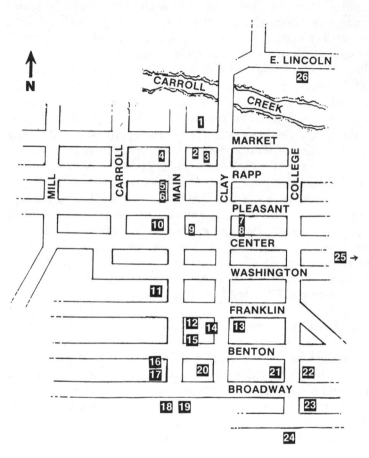

Mount Carroll

is topped by a second-story window **14.** John Lafferty built 311 South Clay Street in 1870. It is a Queen Anne-style house with a carriage house in the rear. **15.** Returning to South Main via Benton, you will find the 1860 Hiram Colehour house at 316. **16.** In the next block south on the west side is 401 South Main. The house was built in 1871 for Nathaniel H. Melendy. The brick Italianate house has a portico entrance and a porch across half the front with fancy ironwork trim on its roof line. The stucco is a recent addition. **17.** Farther south on the same block is 413 South Main, built in 1860 for John M. Stowell. **18.** Where Main terminates at Broadway, you will find the large S.J. Campbell II house at 111 West Broadway. Built in 1925, it is a Tudor-style house. **19.** A little east at 107 West Broadway is the Italianate house built in 1873 for Owen P. Miles. **20.** Across Broadway on the northwest corner where Clay Street ends is 415 South Clay, the James Shaw house. The Queen Anne house has a two-story tower with a conical roof. The architect was Joseph Lyman Silsbee, by whom Frank Lloyd Wright was at one time employed. **21.** At the end of the next block east at 210 East Broadway is the John B. Blake house. The excellent Italianate house, built in 1861, has a heavily bracketed cornice, a pillared porch across most of the front, and a bay window on the east. **22.** Across College Street is 304 East Broadway. This house was built for Jesse M. Shirk in 1867. **23.** Turn south and go a half block on College to 512. This Italianate house was built in 1856 for Philander Seymour. **24.** The administrative offices of the Campbell Center for Historic Preservation Studies occupy part of the Georgian Revival red brick building, formerly part of Shimer College. **25.** If time permits, you might go north to Washington Street, then west to 728. This well-preserved Italianate house was built in 1854 for a town founder, Nathaniel Halderman. The house has a large enclosed cupola, bracketed cornice, double-door front entrance, floor-to-ceiling first-floor windows, and wide front porch. **26.** Another building off the beaten path is the brick Caroline Mark home, built in 1906 at 222 East Lincoln.

Festivals, Tours, and Other Places of Interest

The Oakville Country School Museum complex consists of an 1888 one-room schoolhouse, two 1840 log cabins, an early granary, and a working blacksmith shop. It is owned and operated by the Carroll County Historical Society. Located four miles southeast of Mount Carroll on State Route 88, it is open to the public Sunday afternoons, 2:00 P.M.–4:00 P.M., June 1–Labor Day. The Campbell Center, founded in 1980 to provide educational programs in the fields of conservation and restoration of historic materials and places, is located in the former Shimer College. For more information contact the Campbell Center for Historic Preservation and Studies, P.O. Box 66, Mount Carroll, IL 61053, 815–244–1173.

Historical Information

Campbell Center for Historic Preservation and Studies, P.O. Box 66, Mount Carroll, IL 61053, 815–244–1173. Carroll County Historical Society, P.O. Box 65, Mount Carroll, IL 61053. Mount Carroll Chamber of Commerce, P.O.Box 94, Mount Carroll, IL 61053, 815–244–3111.

Lodging

Country Palmer House, RR 3, Box 254, Mount Carroll, IL 61053, 815–244–3111.

Mount Carroll Motel, one mile west of State Route 78 on State Route 64, 815–244–9581.

Quinn's Inn, 1 Quinn Place, Mount Carroll, IL 61053, 815–244–7666.

Restaurants

Barristers, 830 South Jackson Street, 815–244–2556, handicapped accessible.

Carroll Place, 110 West Market Street, 815–244–4023, handicapped accessible.

Cimino's, 119 West Market Street, 815–244–2401, handicapped accessible.

Courtyard Cafe, 312 North Main, 815–244–4255.

Myrna's Kitchen, 204 East Rapp Street, 815–244–2212, handicapped accessible.

Sievert's, 121 West Market Street, 815–244–7553, handicapped accessible.

VII:3
Galena

JO DAVIESS COUNTY
Illinois

INDIANS and French explorers were aware of the lead deposits in Galena, but it was not until the 1820s that mining and smelting began. The profitable lead business continued here until the deposits were depleted and the next strike, the California gold rush of 1848, drew the miners westward.

Galena was a most important source of military talent. Nine Union generals came from here, the most important of whom was Ulysses S. Grant, who later became the eighteenth president of the United States.

Historic preservation has done great things for Galena. Many grand and not so grand houses have been restored and the town abounds with antique stores and museums.

Directions

Galena either is a weekend trip by itself, or could be combined with a visit to Dubuque. It is about a three-hour trip from Chicago via Interstate 90 and U.S. 20 northwest.

ARCHITECTURAL TOURS

Galena has an excellent collection of public, commercial, and residential buildings dating from the days of its mid-nineteenth-century prosperity. They represent fine examples of Greek Revival, Italianate, Gothic, Second Empire, and Queen Anne styles from the 1820s to the 1890s. These buildings have recently been renovated and offer the visitor a glimpse of history in a town which is alive again. The center of the town on both sides of the river is the core of the historic preservation district. It is best to cover the downtown area on the west side of the river by foot. The outlying areas can easily be covered by car. There is public parking at the old train depot which is now the Tourist Information Center, across the river via the foot bridge, near downtown, and adjacent to the levee. We have broken the tour into three segments, each taking about an hour. First comes the northern

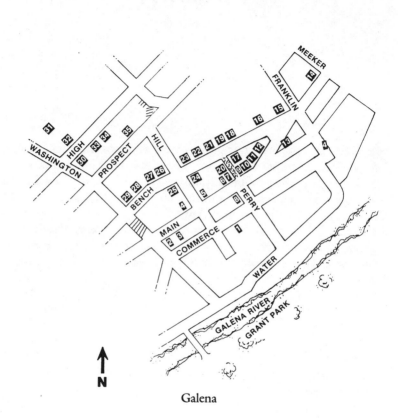

Galena

N

section of the business district, from Washington Street north. Next is the area south of Washington to U.S. 20. The third is the area east of the river, which is mainly residential.

NORTH TOUR

The tour north of Washington Street begins and ends at Market House Square, but you can join it at any point. **1.** Market house, built in 1845, was the central market for produce until 1910 and the seat of city government until 1938. This Greek Revival red brick building with white cupola and white clapboard wings has been restored to its original condition and now contains an exhibit of Illinois architecture. It is open to the public from 9:00 A.M to 5:00 P.M. **2.** Go south on Commerce Street to Washington and take a right onto Main Street. At this point you might stop and look at the streetscape both north and south on Main Street, for it has little changed since the nineteenth century. North on Main, the second building on your right is the Italianate Coatsworth-Barrows store, formerly the site of U.S. Grant's father's leather shop. **3.** On the same side of Main a little farther north is the Lucius S. Felt Greek Revival store, built in 1844. **4.** Across the street on the southwest corner of Hill and Main is the three-story red brick Greek Revival building erected in 1843 by Horatio Newhall. It sports eyebrow windows in the frieze. **5.** On the opposite corner is the Greek Revival store built in 1846 by Charles H. Hempstead. **6.** Continuing north on Main, on the west side of the street south of Perry is the first brick store built in Galena. This Federal-style structure was built by Reuben W. Brush in 1837. **7.** Next door on the site of the original stockade is the 1861 Italianate Richard Barrett store. **8.** Across Main on the southeast corner of Perry is the Burton Greek Revival stone warehouse, built about 1837. **9.** Cross Perry Street and notice the cobblestone paving. On the northwest corner is the Italianate store built in 1855 by Henry Clymo. **10.** Farther north on the same side of the street is another Italianate building, built by James A. Meusel in 1888. **11.** Next door is the Nicholas Dowling Greek Revival Sligo Iron store, built in 1849. **12.** The next house, set high above the street, is one of Galena's oldest buildings, the John Dowling home and trading post, built in 1828. This stone house shows the southern influence brought by the river trade in the two-story front porch. Now restored to its original state, it is open to the public. **13.** On the corner of Main and Diagonal Streets is the Flatiron Building, erected in the 1840s. Originally called the Tyler House, it was one of the largest hotels in the Midwest. **14.** Cross Franklin Street and walk one block north to the southwest corner of Meeker where you will find the Jo Daviess County courthouse, begun in 1839 and completed in 1844. When it was extended in

1900, the original Greek Revival facade was removed. It now has a Second Empire exterior. **15.** Retrace your steps across Franklin, and on the southwest corner of Franklin and Bench you will see the Catholic Convent School, built in 1859 and designed by the region's first Catholic priest, Samuel Mazzuchelli. **16.** Proceed south to the 1854 Union Baptist Church. This is a transition building with a Romanesque Revival doorway and an Italianate bracketed roof line. **17.** On the northeast corner of Perry and Bench is the fine Ryan-Taylor house. This building, erected in 1855, has a Corinthian-columned front portico, a Queen Anne southern bay window, and rear ell with two-story porch, another example of the southern influence found here and there in Galena. **18.** On the west side of Bench is the Wilcox Italianate house, built in 1885. It was designed by architect Edward Copps. **19.** At 120 North Bench is a house built by Nicholas Dowling in the early 1850s. **20.** Go east a bit on Perry to the Amos Farrar house, which dates from 1832. **21.** Back on Bench Street on the west side is the Greek Revival house built about 1838 by James Strode. It has a two-story portico and second-story front balcony. **22.** Next is the fine 1854 Greek Revival brick house with prominent limestone capping on the entrance doorway and windows. Wide limestone steps with wrought-iron railings lead from the street to the recessed entrance. Prominent on the north and south ends are Federal-style double-chimneyed gables. **23.** Near the northwest corner of Hill and Bench is the Romanesque Revival First Presbyterian Church, erected in 1838. The fine white steeple is copied from Boston's Old South Church. **24.** Across the street on the east side of Bench is the Greek Revival Bradner Smith house, built in 1855. The bay window is an 1868 addition. **25.** On the southeast side of Hill and Bench is the William A. Jordon house. This oak-and-walnut frame house was built in 1838. **26.** Across the street is the 1940 limestone-faced firehouse with bright red trim. **27.** Turner Hall, next door, was built in 1874 by the Galena Sociale Turner Gemeinde. **28.** Henry Fricke built the Italianate house next door in 1878. It has a portico entrance topped by an ironwork balustrade. **29.** The First Methodist Church next door, built in 1857, was attended by U.S. Grant. **30.** At 209 South High, on the northeast corner of Washington and High, is the Strobe house, built in 1852. Its front section is Greek Revival. The additions come from later periods. **31.** At Washington and High Streets is the Old City Cemetery. **32.** The red brick Romanesque Revival St. Matthew Lutheran Church was dedicated in 1854. Like other Galena churches, it has a prominent white steeple. **33.** Farther east is the red brick Italianate Herman house, with a fine bracketed roof line and a columned white front porch with balustrade, giving the second story an open porch. Its original ornamental iron front fence is in good repair. **34.** At 121

South High is the modest red brick Greek Revival house U.S. Grant rented in 1860. It has a wide front porch, and its doorway includes a transom and side windows. **35.** Take High Street to Washington and turn north on Prospect. At the corner of Prospect and Hill is the Gothic Revival Grace Episcopal Church, built in 1848. Now turn east on Hill and follow it to Commerce Street. Turn north one half block and you will be back at Market House Square.

SOUTH TOUR

Parking is available at Washington and Water Streets. **1.** At Commerce, Green, and Water Streets is the Renaissance Revival U.S. Custom House–Post Office, built in 1857 and designed by architect Ammi B. Young. **2.** Walk west on Green to Main, where you will find the Frederick Stahl Italianate store designed by architect Oliver Marble in 1854. **3.** Across the street is the Greek Revival Stephen Thrasher store, built about 1839. **4.** A little south on the block is the 1851 Italianate Alexander C. Davis store, which is reputed to have the earliest cast-iron window lintels in Galena. **5.** The Davis and Schirmer Greek Revival block of five stores on the other side of Main was built in 1846. The original facade is still in place on 304 Main; 310 Main has been restored. **6.** On the other side of Main is the Italianate N. and H. Corwith Bank of Galena, built in 1853. **7.** Farther south and on the other side of Main is the Philip Byrne Italianate house, built in 1854 and designed by Telford, Williams, and Co. **8.** Next is the R.P. Guyard Greek Revival store, built about 1848. **9.** Erected next door in 1845 is the Greek Revival Charles Peck warehouse. **10.** At the corner of Water Street you can see the floodgates and the levee built in 1949. At this point you should pause and look carefully at Main Street. This narrow street is bordered by commercial buildings dating from the mid-nineteenth century. It is sometimes called "the wall" because the buildings have common walls and are mostly two and three stories high with an occasional fourth story. As in most nineteenth-century business districts, the interesting architectural features are preserved on the second- and third-story facades. Here and there are bay windows and balconies, elaborate window treatments, and ornate cornices, frequently supported by heavy brackets. **11.** Farther along Main Street is the War Memorial, honoring veterans of World War I and II as well as the Korean and Vietnam wars. **12.** Next door is the frame Phineas Block warehouse, built in 1827. **13.** Around the corner on Bench is the Daniel S. Harris & Co. Greek Revival building, erected in 1842. **14.** Across Bench at 611 is the handsome Italianate 1851 William Hempstead house with elegant window hoods and a fine entrance portico. The front decorative-iron railing is still in good shape. **15.** Walk a little west up the alley labeled Magazine and

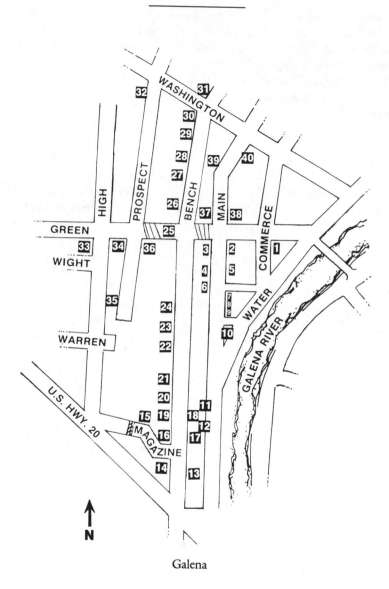

Galena

you will find Lolly's Doll and Toy Museum housed in a simple red brick Federal-style building. **16.** Back on Bench at 605 is the 1827 D.R. Davis house. This simple frame Greek Revival house has dormers and a portico added later. **17.** Across Bench is the earlier Greek Revival William Hempstead house, built in 1843. Of note are the eyebrow windows in its frieze. **18.** The 1837 Federal-style George W. Fuller house is one of Galena's first brick houses. **19.** On the other side of the street is 603 Bench, the Frederick Stahl house. This brick Greek Revival structure has a fine entrance with fanlight transom, side windows, and eyebrow windows ventilating the attic. **20.** Next at 601 is the limestone Classical Revival Galena Public Library, built in 1907. Claude & Stark designed this building, which has a handsome Corinthian-columned portico. **21.** At 525 Bench is the Stillman-Brush house, built in 1837. The influence of New Orleans architecture is seen in the decorative cast-iron work added sometime between 1844 and 1852. **22.** The Greek Revival Westminster United Presbyterian Church, built in 1848, was designed by builders William B. Smith, Andrew Dodds, and W.B. Willie. **23.** The Greek Revival Jacob Frysinger house was built in 1845. Its distinguishing feature is the north doorway's egg-and-dart molding. **24.** Feehan Hall, a Romanesque Revival hall built in 1886, was designed by architect J. Keenan of Dubuque, Iowa. **25.** As you approach the intersection of Main and Green, on the left, or west, notice Green Street. It is so vertical that it can handle only foot traffic. **26.** Cross Green Street and you will find the 1848 Italianate Horatio Newhall house at 235 Bench. This fine house has a belvedere on the roof, which is bracketed. A wide front porch is supported by columns and decorated by a rooftop balustrade. **27.** The Queen Anne-style St. Michael's Catholic Rectory, designed by builder J.B. Ginn, was built in 1896. **28.** St. Michael's Roman Catholic Church is an 1857 replacement for the 1842 church. The Romanesque Revival church, designed by its first priest, Father Samuel Mazzuchelli, has twin red brick towers on either side. **29.** The Galena–Jo Daviess County History Museum is housed in the 1858 Daniel A. Barrows Italianate homestead. It has hooded windows, a pediment, and heavily bracketed eaves. The architect was William Dennison, who also designed the U.S. Grant house (East Tour, 12). **30.** The 1838 Philip Schirmer house is near the intersection of Bench and Washington. The apartments across Bench Street are the upper floors of Main Street buildings and are entered from Bench Street by bridges from the sidewalk. **31.** The 1851 firehouse across Washington, renovated by the Galena Historical Society, includes the 1855 fire "masheen," which was pulled up hill by the firemen on foot. **32.** Travel west up the hill near the old Washington Street steps to Prospect, then turn left. Of particular note are the Second Em-

pire house at 215 Prospect and its more modest neighbor to the south.
33. Go one block west on Washington to High Street and then one
block south on High, noting the view of the town below. On the west
side of High is the Augustus Estey house. This fine red brick Italianate house has a bracketed third-floor dormer with round window and
eaves with eyebrow windows. A wide columned porch stretches
across the front; its balustrade becomes a second-story porch.
34. Return to Green Street and go east one block to 235 Prospect
Street, an Italianate red brick house. Limestone steps lead from the
street to a two-story half-porch. **35.** The Romanesque Revival Central High School is located at 411 South Prospect. The clock tower is a
local landmark. **36.** Turn around and go north on Prospect. On the
southeast corner is a fine high Victorian Italianate brick house with
bracketed eaves and square third-floor tower. Above the first-floor
front bay window is a second-story balcony complete with sheltering
roof. A columned porch stretches across half the front. **37.** Walk east
down the Green Street steps to Main and go north. On the west side
of the street is the George Ferguson building, housing the General
Store Museum, an excellent reproduction of a nineteenth-century
store. **38.** The Italianate DeSoto house at Main and Green Streets,
completed in 1853, was the Grant campaign headquarters in his 1868
presidential race. **39.** A little north on the other side of Main is the
1892 J.G. Schmohl Italianate store, with cast-iron front. **40.** Across
Main is the 1874 Italianate Steward Crawford–W.R. Rowley store.

EAST TOUR

To tour the east side of the river you can either leave your car on the
west side and take the footbridge across or take U.S. 20 (Spring
Street) across the highway bridge and turn left onto Park Avenue to
the southwest corner of Bouthillier and Park, where there is parking
around the old station. **1.** The Illinois Central depot was built in 1857.
This Italianate brick building has interesting window treatment and
two cupolas. It now houses the Galena–Jo Daviess Area Chamber of
Commerce. **2.** The East Galena Town Hall, built in 1872, is a small
one-story white Greek Revival building with pediment and front
portico. **3.** Grant Park contains a statue of the General and a memorial to the Civil War dead as well as cannon from the Civil, Spanish-
American, and World Wars. **4.** At 600 North Park Avenue is the
imposing Italianate Orrin Smith house. It has a columned two-story
porch on the front and an enclosed cupola and widow's walk on the
top. **5.** The small one-and-one-half-story Greek Revival house at 512
Park was built by Joseph Hoge in 1845. The entrance is protected
by a pediment and a Doric-columned portico. **6.** The house at 506

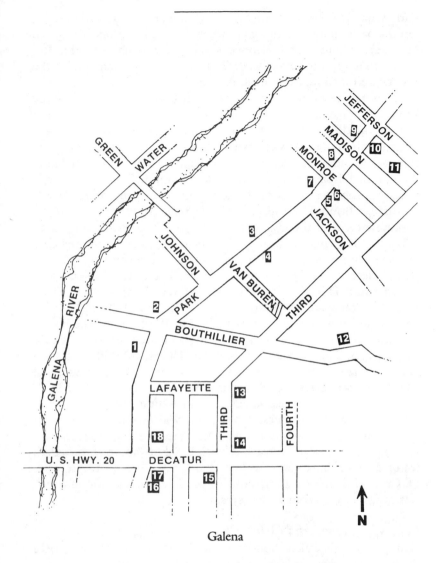

Galena

Park is mainly Italianate, with bracketed roof and porticoed entrance, but the bay windows, although bracketed, are a forerunner of Queen Anne, and the carpenter's lacework gable is a touch of Gothic Revival. **7.** Across the street is the Telford house, an example of the French Second Empire style. **8.** At 401 Park is Union House, originally built as a tavern. **9.** The house at 305 Park Avenue was built by William R. Rowley. **10.** The Raco house at 310 Park is a Greek Revival building built in 1870, late for this style. It has a columned front porch and a rear wing with a two-story side porch. **11.** Turn right at the end of the block and right again on Third Street and note the 1845 rock house built into the side of the hill. This Federal-style house has an entrance door with side lights and a transom. **12.** As you go east on Bouthillier and pass Third Street on your left, look for parking areas near the U.S. Grant house, built in 1859 in the Italian villa style. The entrance front porch, the white lintels, and the heavy brackets supporting the roof are nice details. It is furnished in 1865–85 period pieces and is open to the public. **13.** The Cyrus Aldrich house at 900 South Third Street was built as a Greek Revival house about 1846. The Italianate details are later additions. **14.** At Decatur (U.S. 20) and Third is the 1852 house of Elihu B. Washburne. The house, now a state historic site, has a grand pediment and portico. **15.** A little south at 1009 Third Street is the house of Thomas Melville, the uncle of *Moby Dick*'s author. **16.** At 1008 Park Avenue is the grandest of all Galena houses, a restored Victorian Belvedere, built in 1857 by J. Russell Jones. Note its elaborate facade, including a two-story porch, two second-story balconies, cupola, and widow's walk. It is open to the public as a museum June–October, 10:00 A.M.–4:00 P.M. **17.** The 1826 Classical Revival red brick Hunkins house at 1004 Park features Doric pillars on the first floor and Ionic on the second. **18.** Cross U.S. 20 on Park Avenue to 908, the Soulard house, which was built as a log cabin in the 1830s.

Festivals, Tours, and Other Places of Interest

Tours of historic Galena houses are held twice a year. The first, held the second weekend in June, is conducted by the Galena–Jo Daviess County Historical Society, 211 South Bench, Galena, IL 61036, 815–777–9129. The second is sponsored by the Guild of the First Presbyterian Church on the last weekend in September. Guided tours are provided by: Countryside Tours, 815–777–1670; Galena Historical Society (groups only), 211 South Bench, Galena, IL 61036, 815–777–9129; Galena Tours, 815–777–1248; Historic Galena Foundation, Inc., 525 Bouthillier, Galena, IL 61036, 815–777–1060; Historic Galena Guided Tours, 815–777–0035 or 2364. The Belvedere (East Tour, 16), open June–October, 1008 Park Avenue, Galena, IL 61036, 815–777–0747. Dowling House (North Tour, 12), open June–November, Main and Diagonal Streets, Galena, IL 61036, 815–777–1250. Galena–Jo Daviess County History Museum (South Tour, 29), 211 South Bench, Galena, IL 61036, 815–777–9129.

Historical Information

Galena–Jo Daviess County Historical Society, 211 South Bench, Galena, IL 61036, 815–777–9129. Galena–Jo Daviess Chamber of Commerce, Bouthillier and Park Avenue, Galena, IL 61036, 815–777–0203, 800–892–9299 (Illinois), 800–874–9377 (outside Illinois). Galena Public Library has a fine collection of genealogical information, 601 Bench Street, Galena, IL 61036, 815–777–0200.

Lodging

Aldrich Guest House, 900 Third Street, 815–777–3323.

Bedford House, U.S. 20 west, 815–777–2043.

Chestnut Mountain Resort, 8700 West Chestnut, 800–892–0738 (Illinois) or 800–435–2914 (out of state), and 312–456–1161 (Chicago office).

Colonial Guest House, 1004 Park Avenue, 815–777–0336.

DeSoto Hotel, 230 South Main Street, 815–777–9208.

Eagle Ridge Inn and Golf Course, U.S. 20 east at Galena Territory, 815–777–2444.

Fricke House, 119 South Bench Street, 815–777–9430.

Harris House, 713 South Bench Street, 815–777–1611.

Hellman House, 318 Hill Street, 815–777–3638.

Lafayette Guest House, 911 Third Street, 815–777–1160 or 2760.

Log Cabin Guest House, 1161 West Chetlain Lane, 815–777–2845.

Palace Motel, U.S. 20 west, 815–777–2043.

Ryan Mansion Guest House, U.S. 20 west, 815–777–2043.

Spring Street Guest House, 414 Spring Street, 815–777–0354.

Stillman's Inn, 513 Bouthillier Street, 815–777–0557 or 0580.

Stillwater's Inn, 7211 West Buckhill Road, 815–777–0223 or 312–528–6313.

Timmerman's Motor Lodge, U.S. 20, East Dubuque, IL 61025, 815–747–3181.

Triangle Motel, U.S. 20 west, 815–777–2897.

Victorian Mansion, 301 South High Street, 815–777–0657.

Restaurants

Baker's Oven and Tea Room, 200 North Main Street, 815–777–9105.

Benjamin's, 103 North Main Street, 815–777–0467.
Clark's Restaurant, 129 South Main, 815–777–0499.
Kathleen's, 200 South Main, 815–777–0551.
Kingston Inn, 300 North Main, 815–777–0451.
Market House Tavern, 204 Perry Street, 815–777–0690.
McCormick's, 515 South Main, 815–777–3330 or 3773.
Silver Annie's, 124 North Commerce Street, 815–777–3131.

VII:4
Dubuque
DUBUQUE COUNTY
Iowa

To a flatlander, Dubuque is startlingly hilly. Streets rise straight up from the old part of town at the river's edge in the manner of a Duluth or a mini-Pittsburgh. Lead first brought settlers to hilly Dubuque, and when lead declined, this town, like Mineral Point and Galena, witnessed an exodus to California's gold fields. Next came lumber, shipbuilding, flour milling, and the railroad. Today the city boasts heavy construction machinery factories and furniture plants and still nurtures its excellent river location.

One of the early business tycoons, living on lofty Fenelon Place and working far below, built himself a funicular so that he could go home more quickly for lunch. The Fourth Street elevator, as it is now called, still operates daily. All day it takes people up the tracks in a tiny car to view the wonderful sweep of the Mississippi River and the tidy 1850s mansions at the top. Then it brings them down again to browse in the shops housed in the old buildings in Cable Car Square.

About four miles north stands the Ham House Museum near Eagle Point Park. It is a fine old house filled with museum-quality furniture in well-re-created 1850s rooms. The surroundings are spectacular. The park, on the very edge of a high bluff, looks down on the General Zebulon Pike Lock and Dam, the rapids, and the Wisconsin-Illinois shore. The paths and the restored pavilions are perched so close to the precipice that only a sturdy chain link fence stands between the viewer and eternity.

Directions

Dubuque would be a delightful place to spend a weekend. It is about a six-hour drive from Chicago. With enough time, you would be able to take a cruise on the river as well as a leisurely tour of the town. If you skip the river cruise, you might be able to visit both Dubuque and Galena. From Chicago take Interstate 90 to Rockford, then change to U.S. 20 into Dubuque. It becomes Dodge Street after

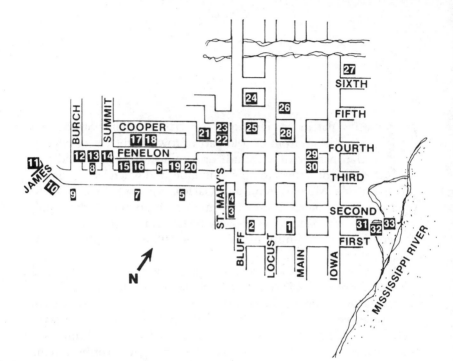

Dubuque

you cross the Mississippi. To reach the historic area, turn right from Dodge onto Main Street, then north to First Street.

ARCHITECTURAL TOURS
SOUTH DUBUQUE

The area roughly from Iowa Street on the east to Bluff Street on the west and from First to Seventh Street is the site of the first permanent settlement. The port, called the Ice or Second Street Harbor and known as the boat landing or the Port of Dubuque, is here; so are the Catholic cathedral, the county courthouse and jail, numerous commercial and residential buildings, and the Fenelon Place elevator. If you walk the area, it will probably take about an hour, including a ride on the elevator. A combination of walking and driving would shorten the time, but don't omit the elevator ride, amazing in itself and for the spectacular view of the town and the river from the top. **1.** The Italianate storefronts at 169–85 Main Street have bracketed eaves and ornate window hoods. These buildings, dating from the 1860s, are typical of the commercial buildings of this period. **2.** A triplex Queen Anne multifamily structure, designed by architect F.D. Hyde, was built in the 1880s by Bishop Hennessy. It has third-floor dormers, a variety of window styles, a bay with conical roof, and cupolas. **3.** Across Bluff Street at the end of Cathedral Square is St. Raphael's Cathedral, built in 1857–59. It replaces an earlier church designed by Father Mazzuchelli. The architect was John Mullaney. The Gothic tower and the traceried windows are its most prominent features. **4.** Adjacent to the cathedral at 231 Bluff is the rectory or parish house, built in 1863 by Bishop Smyth. This three-story Italianate structure has a porticoed entrance, bracketed roof, and hooded windows reminiscent of the earlier Italianate style. The second and the third floors have two ironwork balconies apiece. **5.** Turn left at West Third. In mid-block on the south side of the street at 440–42 is a vernacular Federal-style double house whose facade is divided by pilasters. Topped by a plain cornice, its windowsills are limestone. **6.** Across the street at 541 and obscured from view is the Steil house, built in the 1870s. This large Italian villa has a prominent off-center three-story tower, bracketed eaves, and rounded windows. **7.** On the south side of Third is a wooded lot known as Kelly's Bluff, reputed site of buried wealth. **8.** On the north side of Third Street between Summit and Burch is 757, the Barmeier house. This Second Empire limestone house was built in 1850. Only the center portion remains of the two-story veranda that once stretched the width of the house. **9.** The east part of the McCarthy house at 804 West Third was built in 1861 and the western section was added in the 1890s. This late Italianate house has bracketed eaves, but also bay windows, a pediment, and an

Eastlake wraparound porch. **10.** On the corner of James and Third at 890 West Third is the Spahn house, built in the late 1870s. The original veranda has been replaced by a porticoed entrance, but the two-story bay on the east and the bullseye window in the attic remain. The facade has been restored. **11.** On the other corner of James Street is 900 West Third, the Bissell house. Designed by local architect F.D. Hyde, this Queen Anne house has dormers protruding from the roof and from the gables, a small second-story porch, and a wraparound front porch. **12.** Go east to Fenelon Place. The Hattie Scott house at 788 is Second Empire, built in 1880; it has a mansard roof, two-story bay, bracketed cornice, and hooded second-story windows. **13.** The Georgian Revival–Italianate Scott house at 732 Fenelon Place was built in the late 1860s. Its handsomely carved front door is flanked by side lights and capped by a transom. Heavy brackets support its eaves. The original cast-iron fence, complete with gate, remains. **14.** At 710 Fenelon is the Georgian Revival Cox house. This solid two-story house has stained-glass side lights flanking its front door. **15.** Across Summit on Fenelon is the 1865 Cunningham house at 690. It is another example of Georgian Revival. **16.** Charles Markle's house at 572 Fenelon is a "Dubuque German"-style house built in 1860. Its exterior is original. The windows have limestone lintels and sills. **17.** The Tredway house at 565 Fenelon is a Queen Anne-style house with three-story tower and wraparound front porch. **18.** The J. Seippel residence at 541 Fenelon is a late Queen Anne house with gables, porches, and bay windows. **19.** On the south side of Fenelon at 514 is a vernacular house built in 1910 by Fay O. Farwell. The house has gables with three-part windows in the third story and a half front porch. **20.** The Trewin house at 512 Fenelon is an 1890s "modern" style, designed by local architect Thomas Carkeek. It has a gambrel roof, dormers, and a long side porch. **21.** The Fenelon Place elevator was built by J.K. Graves, who lived at 541 Fenelon. Traveling up and down a 65-degree grade, the car traverses 289 feet. **22.** The cable-car shops on West Fourth Street have been renovated into commercial space and apartments. **23.** The Romanesque Revival apartment at the southwest corner of Fifth and Bluff Streets was built at the turn of the century. It is called "Redstone" and also has some Queen Anne touches such as the two-story bay, two three-story corner towers, gables, and dormers. **24.** On the northeast corner of Fifth and Bluff is the house built in 1894 by D.A. Sullivan. This large Richardsonian Romanesque house has a front porch stretching between two towers, heavy cornices, and a front gable with a double window on the third floor. **25.** A little east at 304 West Fifth Street is the Thedinga house, one of the oldest surviving brick homes in the city. Built in 1855, this Federal-style building has stepped end walls and six-over-six windows as well as a side-lighted and transomed entrance doorway. **26.** The Dubuque town clock dates from 1872. **27.** The gold-domed Richardson Romanesque–Beaux-Arts Dubuque County courthouse was completed in 1893. Atop the building is a handsome gold-domed clock tower topped by a fourteen-foot statue of Justice. The adjacent 1858 Egyptian Revival jail now houses the Dubuque Museum of Art. Tours of these two buildings are provided by the Art Association daily at 2:00 P.M. **28.** On the northwest corner of Fourth and Main is the Five Flags Theatre, built in 1910. The architects were C.W. and George L. Rapp, who went on to become leading theater designers in the 1920s. This Flemish Renaissance-style building has a heavily decorated facade. **29.** The Classical Revival commercial building at 372 South Main was built in 1910 for Henry H. Melhop. **30.** The Neoclassical Silver Dollar building at 342 South Main was built for the German Bank in 1902. The facade is divided by four large Corinthian columns which support the cornice. You have been looking at the oldest part of Dubuque. Certainly no visit to this area is complete without a look at Ice Harbor, the port of Dubuque. Here you will find reminders of Dubuque's days as a great river port. **31.** Take Third Street east across Iowa and Central to the Riverboat Museum at Second Street and the Harbor. **32.** Adjacent is the *William M. Black*, a moored steamboat that now serves as a museum. **33.** Adjacent is the riverboat-excursion quay where the *Spirit of Dubuque*, a modern stern-wheeler, is moored.

DOWNTOWN

This district, centering around Locust between Tenth and Loras, is principally an area of imposing mid-nineteenth-century houses and churches. The commercial area is farther east toward the river. The downtown is an area that you might well want to walk, as it is only about five blocks long and on every block there is a building of architectural significance. You might park in the vicinity of Twelfth and Locust and walk in either direction. **1.** On the southwest corner of Locust and Tenth is a series of row houses built after the Civil War in the Italianate style. The entrance doors are hooded, and the roof is supported by heavy brackets. Each has a three-story bay. All have English basements, so the entry is on the second floor. **2.** Catercorner across Tenth Street is the First Congregational Church. Designed by architect David Jones and built in 1857, this Gothic Revival church has a four-story bell tower and a rose window over the entrance. **3.** The Eclectic house at 1005 Locust has a two-story front porch and a two-story south and east bay, and each third-floor dormer is different. It was built in the 1880s by James Guthrie. **4.** At 1025–37 Locust is a group of Second Empire row houses with a cornice, mansard roof,

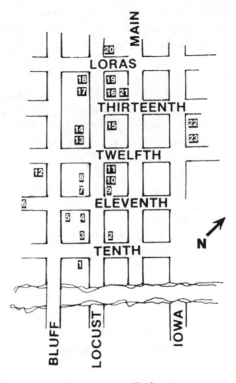

Downtown, Dubuque

and fancy hooded dormers. The replacement of the original entrance steps detracts from the buildings' charm. **5.** The Carnegie-Stout Library at the southeast corner of Bluff and Eleventh Streets was designed by the Chicago architectural firm of Williamson and Spencer in 1901. This Neoclassical Revival building has an entrance portico modeled after the Roman Pantheon. A balustrade is mounted along the roof line. This is the best example of the style in Iowa and hence is on the National Register. **6.** At the west end of Eleventh Street is all that remains of another elevator, built in 1887. **7.** The Richardsonian Romanesque house at 1105 Locust Street was built in 1890 by F.D. Stout. This monumental Minnesota-sandstone structure has a tower, dormers, two-story bay, and front porch topped by a second-floor balcony. **8.** The lively Queen Anne house at 1145 Locust was built in 1892 by H.L. Stout. The most amazing feature of this elaborate house is the three-story Byzantine tower. The wraparound stone porch has a frieze. A second-floor porch above the entrance is topped by another smaller one on the third floor. The same tier of porches is repeated on the south side. The architect was Fridolin Heer, the designer of the courthouse(South Dubuque, 27). **9.** The 1856 row houses at 1100–34 Locust Street are Federal-style with stepped end walls. They are individual units with a common wall and individually styled entrances. Three of them have identical roof lines; the fourth has a more elaborate cornice. **10.** The house at 1182 Locust Street was built by Alfred Tredway in the 1880s. Designed by courthouse architect Fridolin Heer, it is Second Empire with a two-story bay on the front and a Greek Revival entry. **11.** The Italian villa at 1192 Locust was built in 1855 for Fred Weigel. The front porch extends around the west side and a cupola sits atop the roof. **12.** Around the corner high above Twelfth Street is 1207 Grove Terrace. This Gothic Revival house was built by B.M. Harger in 1890. The original facade has not been changed. The wide front porch wraps around both sides. A lace bargeboard decorates the roof line; a small porticoed balcony above the entrance and third-floor dormers are decorative touches. **13.** At 1243 Locust Street is the Goodrich-Wilson-Ryan home. This Eclectic house has a Greek Revival entry. **14.** The Italianate-style house at 1257 Locust was built in 1846 as the Westminster Presbyterian Church manse. **15.** Across Locust is the William L. Bradley house at 1268. This two-and-one-half-story Italianate structure has a two-story bay on the south side, bracketed eaves, and decorated gables. A front porch has a pediment entrance. **16.** On the northeast corner of Thirteenth and Locust is the Queen Anne Ezekiel Woodworth home, built in 1881. This red brick house has a Stick-style front porch and decorative third-floor gable. **17.** On the west side of Locust, 1375 was built by William Andrews in 1873, designed by Chicago Palmer

House architect, Van Osdel, and called the Ryan house after a later owner. This Second Empire–Italianate structure is one of Dubuque's most elaborate houses. The enclosed porch, first-floor bay, and roof-top belvedere are highly decorated. **18.** Next door is another William Andrews house, also designed by Van Osdel. This grand house has a mansard roof and is topped by a four-story tower. **19.** The Cooley house at 1394 Locust has been greatly altered. **20.** As you approach the alley between Locust and Main, look back and you can just see "Fort Rittenhouse," built in 1846 by a stone mason of the same name. **21.** One block south on Main is 1337, a Queen Anne house built by C.H. Eighmey. The house has a pediment, a two-tiered front porch, and a three-story tower. **22.** Go one block east to Thirteenth and Iowa where on the southeast corner you will find City Hall. Designed by midwestern architect John Francis Rague in 1857, it is modeled after Boston's Faneuil Hall. A fancy cupola was removed in the 1950s, but otherwise this National Register building's facade is unchanged. **23.** A little farther south on Iowa Street are 1256 and 1236, commercial buildings. Both have been restored and look much as they did at the turn of the century.

JACKSON PARK

The area from Loras Boulevard to Seventeenth and from West Locust to Iowa Street is residential. Most of the opulent houses here were built at the end of the nineteenth century and are little changed. The area is approximately three blocks by three blocks, and it can be comfortably walked in less than an hour. If you feel strong you might walk up the Montrose steps to get a better sense of the nineteenth-century town. Parking is permitted on Iowa between Loras Boulevard and Fifteenth Street. **1.** On the northeast corner of Main and Loras at 1410 Main is St. John's Episcopal Church. This English Gothic Revival structure, built in 1878, has five Louis Tiffany windows, a vaulted ceiling, and a rose window over its entrance. A short tower with battlements is featured prominently. **2.** Across the street on the northwest corner of Loras and Main is a remarkable Queen Anne house designed by Fridolin Heer, the courthouse architect, for Nicholas Schrup in 1909. This substantial house has a stone wrap-around porch, three-story hexagonal tower, gable with Palladian window, bay windows, fancy brickwork, and a third-floor balcony; the grand facade remains. **3.** Another house designed by Fridolin Heer is at 1433 Main. This Italianate house was built for David B. Henderson. The home has twin bays topped by balustrades with a semicircular front porch in between. The second-story windows have heavy dripstone hoods. **4.** Another Italianate-style house is next door at 1455 Main. The front part was built in the 1860s and the rear in

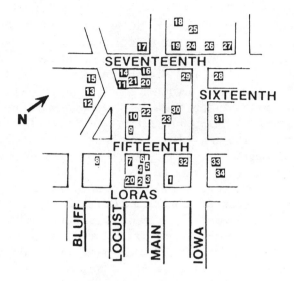

Jackson Park, Dubuque

1856. A wide front porch is trimmed by a frieze. **5.** Still another example of Fridolin Heer's work is the large, plain Italianate house at 1471 Main. Its only decoration other than austere window hoods is the frieze along the roof line. It was built in 1881 for Alonzo J. Van Duzee. **6.** The Second Empire house at 1491 Main was built by Alexander Young. The house's elaborate facade boasts twin two-story bays, a bracketed cornice between the second and third stories, and highly decorated third-floor dormers. A metal canopy stretching to the curb is an addition. **7.** Go west on Fifteenth to 1492 Locust, erected in 1882 for Benjamin B. Richards and designed by F.D. Hyde. This Stick-style house has decorated gables, two-story bay windows, and second- and third-floor balconies over the small entrance porch. **8.** A block west are the Montrose steps between 1461 Locust and 91 Bluff leading to the street above. This is one of twenty-five public stairways through or around the bluff. **9.** The Queen Anne duplex house at 1552–54 was built for Horace Poole. The house has a wide front porch and center gable flanked by dormers. **10.** Another duplex at 1590–92 was built in 1870 for Edward C. Peaslee. A porch stretches across the front. **11.** At 315 West Locust is the house built in 1888 by C.J. Lesure. This Queen Anne house has leaded windows, bays, a pediment over the entrance porch decorated by a modern eagle, dormers, and decorated eaves. **12.** Across West Locust, 324–26, is an Italianate duplex townhouse, home of William Ruston. This handsome house has matching two-story bays, bracketed eaves, and entrance porch. **13.** A little farther north is 346–48, a Queen Anne duplex with a gambrel roof, dormers, and an unusual two-story porch. **14.** On the east side of West Locust is the 1902 Classical Revival Albert Jaeggi house. It has a brick frieze, quoins, twin second-story bays, and a columned front porch. **15.** On the southwest corner of Seventeenth and West Locust is the John Mullaney house, built in 1880. This vernacular house has a prominent attic dormer and decorative Stick-style entrance porch. **16.** The Queen Anne–Italianate row houses at 252 West Seventeenth Street have been renovated. An added attraction is the rear courtyards. **17.** Duplex houses are scattered throughout the district. The Queen Anne at 265–67 West Seventeenth Street has dormers, a large front gable, and an interesting entrance. The iron fence along the sidewalk is original. **18.** Go a bit north on Main to the Madison Street steps, built in 1918 and leading to Madison Park above. **19.** On the northeast corner of Main and Seventeenth at 195 West Seventeenth is a late Queen Anne house. Built by J.F. Stampfer, it has a gambrel roof with a Palladian window, bays, a tower with conical roof, and a stone-pillared front porch. **20.** South on Main there are four Second Empire houses, each somewhat different from the others. At 1655 Main is the first. The rear portion was built in 1860, and twenty years later the front section was added. In 1913 the porch and bay window were added. The third-floor dormers are particularly ornate, and the second-story windows have plain but elegant hoods. **21.** The simplest of the four houses is the double Mulligan residence at 1631–33, with its twin two-story bays connected by an entrance porch. The third story may have been added, for its shingles contrast with the brick of the building. It was erected in 1870. **22.** At 1611 Main is a fancier example of this style. It was designed in 1875 by the courthouse architect Fridolin Heer for John Olinger. The third-floor dormers are ornate, the second-floor window hoods tastefully restrained, and the columned porches elegant. **23.** On the east side of Main is 1640, another Fridolin Heer house. Ornate ironwork crowns the roof line, and the third-floor windows include bullseyes and dormers. The windows on the two lower floors have fancy hoods and sills. A columned entrance porch reflects the same elegance. It was built in 1878 for Frank Robinson. **24.** Now return to Seventeenth Street and proceed east. A combination Queen Anne–Italianate house, built in 1880 by James Cushing, is at 175 West Seventeenth. The front porch terminates in a gazebo and the windows are hooded. **25.** Look above the preceding house and you will see perched high on the cliff I.J. Cushing's house. It was originally connected to 175 by a catwalk and was also accessible from a road atop the bluff. This 1894 Queen Anne house has a wide front porch and corner tower with conical roof, but metal siding conceals some of its decoration. **26.** At 135 West Seventeenth Street is a rather plain Queen Anne house built by Richard Bonson. The prominent gables have windows, and a wide porch stretches across the front. **27.** On the next corner at 75 West Seventeenth is a large Gothic Revival building with two four-story towers and a Classical Revival entrance portico. Its facade is divided by pilasters. The original building was erected as the first female seminary west of Chicago. **28.** At the southeast corner of Iowa and Seventeenth is the First Presbyterian Church, a Victorian Gothic building erected in 1896. It has a large tower with a steeple, stained-glass windows, and decorated gables. **29.** On the west side of Iowa Street is the former German Methodist Church, a simple Stick-style building. **30.** You might walk into Jackson Park, the site of the early town cemetery. **31.** On the east side of Iowa, facing the park, is 1560–68, designed by local architect Albert Ney in 1898. It has twin two-story bays and a limestone veneer facade. **32.** On the southwest corner of Fifteenth and Iowa is St. Patrick's Church. Designed by local architect John Keenan in 1878, it is patterned after French Gothic architecture of the twelfth century. Its most prominent feature is the 180-foot tower. **33.** At 1454 Iowa Street is an Art Deco building in sharp contrast to its nineteenth-century neighbors. **34.** The Second Empire house at 1450 Iowa was built by Richard Schroeder.

Festivals, Tours, and Other Places of Interest

Three self-guided walking tours of approximately half an hour have been designed by the Dubuque County Historical Society, P.O. Box 305, Dubuque, IA 52001, 319–557–9545. Escorted tours can be arranged through the Dubuque County Historical Society, 319–557–9545 or the Chamber of Commerce, 319–557–9200. Tours of the newly restored Dubuque County courthouse, 319–557–1851 (or group, 319–582–9856) are conducted by members of the Dubuque County Fine Arts Society daily at 2:00 P.M. Special tours can be arranged. The home of Frank D. Stout (Downtown, 7) is open for tours Friday, Saturday, and Sunday, noon–3:00 P.M., late May–late October, and is operated by the Dubuque Historical Improvement Company, 1105 Locust, Dubuque, IA 52001, 319–582–1894. *William M. Black* Museum (South Dubuque, 32) is in the last of the steam-powered sidewheeler ships, open May 1–October 31, 10:00 A.M.–6:30 P.M., Second Street Harbor, Dubuque, IA 52001, 319–557–9545. Five Flags Theatre (South Dubuque, 28), open noon–4:00 P.M., Wednesday–Sunday, Memorial Day–Labor Day, Fourth and Main, Dubuque, IA 52001, 319–556–4369. Ham House Museum, open May 1–October 31, daily 10:00 A.M.–5:30 P.M., also Sundays in December, 2241 Lincoln next to Eagle Point Park, Dubuque, IA 52001, 319–583–2812. Riverboat Museum (South Dubuque, 31), open daily 10:00 A.M.–6:30 P.M., May 1–October 31, Second Street Harbor, Dubuque, IA 52001, 319–557–9545, handicapped accessible. Sightseeing cruises aboard the *Spirit of Dubuque*, Second Street Harbor, daily at 2:00 P.M. and 4:00 P.M., May 1–October 31, Roberts River Rides, 62 Locust Street, Dubuque, IA 52001, 319–583–5379 or 1761. Fenelon Place Elevator (South Dubuque, 21), open April–November 30, 319–582–6496. Eagle Point Park is a 162-acre area atop a bluff overlooking the Mississippi and the General Zebulon Pike Lock and Dam; unique shelter buildings were designed by Alfred Caldwell, a student of Frank Lloyd Wright, 319–582–1849. Carriage rides available from the Dubuque Livery Company, 319–582–8927.

Historical Information

Dubuque's Cathedral District: An Architectural Overview (1985) by the Dubuque Historic Preservation Commission. Dubuque County Historical Society, P.O. Box 305, Dubuque, IA 52001, 319–557–9545. Greater Dubuque Chamber of Commerce, Marilee Harrmann, 880 Locust Street, Dubuque, IA 52001, 319–557–9200.

Lodging

Canfield Motel, 36 West Fourth Street, 319–556–4331.
Chateau Motel, 3750 Central, 319–556–2120.
Corral Motel, 1280 Dodge, 319–556–1551.
Dodge House Motel, 701 Dodge, 319–556–2231.
Dubuque Inn, 3434 Dodge, 319–556–7760.
Fulton Motor Court, 2565 Central, 319–556–4445.
Holiday Inn, 1111 Dodge, 319–556–3340.
Julien Motor Inn, 200 Main Street, 319–556–4200.
Midway Motor Lodge, 3100 Dodge, 319–557–8000.
Redstone Inn, Fifth and Bluff, 319–582–1894.
Regal 8 Inn, 2680 Dodge, 319–556–0880.
Stout House, 1105 Locust Avenue, 319–582–1894.

Restaurants

Alte Glocke Grille, 200 Main, 319–556–4200, handicapped accessible.
Bridge Restaurant, 31 Locust, 319–557–7280.
Demetri's Restaurant, 665 Dodge, 319–557–9460.
Iron Kettle Deli, 1256 Iowa, 319–556–8051.
Koster Maria Cafe, 340 West Fifth, 319–556–9495.
Redstone Inn, Fifth and Bluff, 319–582–1894, handicapped accessible.
Ryan House, 1375 Locust Street, 319–556–9900.
Sfikas, 401 Central, 319–582–8140.
Shot Tower Inn, Fourth and Locust, 319–556–1061.
Yen Ching, 926 Main, 319–556–2574, handicapped accessible.

VIII:1

Wabash

WABASH COUNTY
Indiana

IN 1826 two important treaties were signed here with the Potawatomi and Miami Indian tribes. One opened the Indiana and south Michigan territory to settlement, and the other made provision for a canal or road to be built across Indian land.

The settlement of Wabash began to develop quickly as Irish workers moved in to work on the famous Wabash-Erie canal, begun at Fort Wayne in 1832. This canal, the longest in North America, linked Lake Erie with the Ohio River. Located at the confluence of four rivers and designated one of the main ports of this famous canal, the town of Wabash has always been a transportation center.

One "first" of which Wabash is justly proud is the 1880 experiment which placed four carbon lamps atop the courthouse tower. This made Wabash the first town in the country to have public lighting. Another and continuing source of local pride is Mark Honeywell, whose plumbing and heating business produced the thermostat. Honeywell's business merged with the Minneapolis Regulator Company and is now the giant Minneapolis Honeywell Company. The Honeywell family has been generous to the town of Mark Honeywell's birth. One of the family's many gifts is the splendid Honeywell Center.

Although hard times set in with the decline of the canal and the railroads, Wabash's significant Victorian architecture merely aged. It was not replaced. Here you can find a wide variety of buildings which give a vivid picture of the town as it was at the turn of the century.

Directions

A leisurely weekend trip would include a visit to Wabash and Fort Wayne. From Chicago take Interstates 80 and 90 to State Route 15 and go south to Wabash.

ARCHITECTURAL TOUR

It is strongly recommended that you start your tour with a visit to the Honeywell Center, where there is a slide show depicting the architecture of Wabash and a tour of the splendid Art Deco Honeywell Center. The map included in this text combines both the Marketplace (Canal to Hill Streets) and the Old Wabash (north of Hill Street) Historic Districts. You will notice that our numbers are different from those on the map you can obtain from the Honeywell Center. However, the latter's numbers are given in the text, labeled, for example, 16H. Start at the Honeywell Center. There is parking across Market Street. **1.** The handsome Art Deco Honeywell Center, 275 West Market, was begun in the early 1940s and finished in 1952 (2H). **2.** The commercial buildings are mainly interesting for their second-story detail. At 102 West Canal is a combination Italianate–Victorian Gothic commercial building with decorative window treatment and interesting cornice (6H). **3.** The Italianate commercial building at 49 West Canal was built around 1880. Its elaborate cornice features eyebrow windows. **4.** The Second Empire commercial building at 68 West Canal was erected about 1880 (5H). **5.** Another Italianate commercial building at 46 West Canal dates from the 1880s (9H). **6.** At 20 East Canal, built in 1882, is an example of the combination of Victorian Italianate and Gothic (16H). **7.** The Bedford building, 231–37 South Wabash, was constructed in 1901. This example of Richardsonian Romanesque Revival has a balustrade along the roof line, a heavy stone front facade, and arched windows of various sizes (22H). **8.** The Neoclassical building at 55 West Market Street was erected about 1915. It retains some of its grandeur despite the addition of a sign marring its facade (12H). **9.** The Richardsonian Romanesque Revival building with some Neoclassical features at 84 West Market Street is a commercial example of the style and was built in 1898. It has three large arched windows and an imposing cornice (11H). **10.** Another example of Second Empire is 2–8 West Market, built in 1876. Notice the cornice and mansard roof (19H). **11.** The historic building at 144 South Wabash Street, the site of the M.C. Honeywell Heating and Plumbing Company, is another Romanesque Revival building dating from the 1890s (26H). **12.** The gingerbread Victorian Romanesque City Hall at 101 South Wabash was built in 1883. The front gable and cornice are elaborately decorated, and complementary arches outline the first floor (24H). **13.** Scheerer's Market, 102 South Wabash, is a Second Empire commercial building, erected in 1883. Notice the mansard roof, the cornice, and the window treatment (25H). **14.** Just west is the Italianate former sheriff's office and jail, built in 1880. **15.** The north side of Main Street and adjoining Wabash Street are dominated by 30 South Wabash, the courthouse, built in the Italianate style in 1879. The architectural firm of B.V. Enos and Sons designed the building, which is an outstanding example of a public building in this style (21H). **16.** *Lincoln of the People*

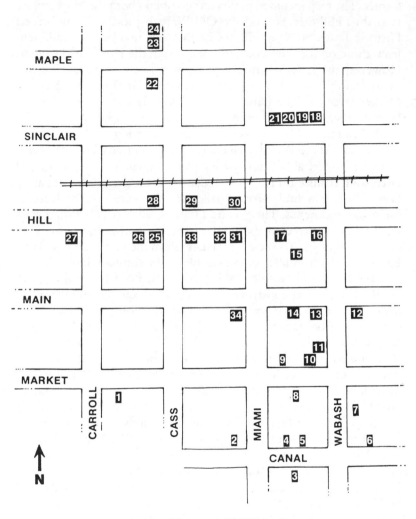

Market Place and Old Wabash
Historic Districts

by sculptor Charles Keck, was erected in 1932. **17.** A block west at 89 West Hill, the Memorial Hall–Wabash County Historical Museum, a Romanesque Revival building, was erected in 1897. Its east and west corners are towers, and the arched entrance is supported by two small towers. The architect was J.C. Gault (23H). **18.** Go north to the northwest corner of Sinclair and Wabash Streets to 40 West Sinclair, an example of a Jacobean Revival house built around 1870. This red brick house has a two-story front bay, bullseye window in the front gable, and arched entrance porch. **19.** On the same side of the street is 44 West Sinclair, a Stick-style house of outstanding quality built about 1890. **20.** The Italianate Calvin Cowgill house at 56 West Sinclair was built around 1850. Heavy hoods top all its windows, and apparently there are roof vents. **21.** At the northeast corner of Sinclair and Miami is 88 West Sinclair, an example of Queen Anne–Stick style built around 1880. The wraparound porch has intricate woodwork. A second story tower ends in a conical roof. The west gable is ornately trimmed, and the roof is decorated by a balustrade. **22.** A block and a half west is 192 North Cass Street, a Queen Anne-style house built about 1890. **23.** A little north is 204 North Cass Street, a Carpenter–Builder house erected about 1890. **24.** The Colonial Revival house at 240 North Cass Street was built around 1900. The wide front porch has delicate columns, and a dormer protrudes from the attic. **25.** The impressive Richardsonian Romanesque-style structure at 209 West Hill, the southwest corner of Cass and Hill, was built in 1894. The former Wabash high school has a dominant center tower and impressive three-arched entrance. **26.** Next door at 261 West Hill is a house in the same style. Called the Wolfe house, it was built in 1895. A prominent oriel window topped by decorative ironwork and a third-floor dormer are its interesting features. **27.** Go west and in the next block you will see 313 West Hill Street, the Clarkson Wessner house, a Queen Anne built about 1885. This remarkable house has porches on both the first and second floors, dormers, and a variety of window styles (1H). **28.** The Second Empire McNamee house at 200 West Hill was built around 1870. Its corner pavilion has a third-floor dormer; the cornice has eyebrow windows; a small portico shields its entrance; and a side porch is nicely decorated (4H). **29.** The Beaux-Art–Neoclassical Carnegie Public Library is at 188 West Hill. It was built in 1903 and added to in 1972. **30.** The Wabash Christian church and educational building located at 110 West Hill Street is a Romanesque Revival structure erected in 1866. The architect was James Ford of Wabash. A handsome central tower dominates its facade, and two tall arched windows flank its doorway (20H). **31.** Across the street on the south side of West Hill is the Gothic Revival Presbyterian church and educational building. This handsome church was built in 1880. A large segmented-wheel window and arched, pedimented entrance decorate its facade. **32.** Another Queen Anne-style house, at 161 West Hill, was built about 1890 (14H). **33.** The Italianate house at 177 West Hill was designed by James Ford in 1841 as his home. In 1913 it was remodeled (10H). **34.** Go south two blocks to the southwest corner of Main and Miami. At 110 South Miami Street is the Neoclassical post office, designed by John Knox Taylor and built in 1911. Among its prominent features are its recessed entrance with large Doric columns, pediment with bullseye window, and rooftop balustrade (17H).

Festivals, Tours, and Other Places of Interest
Honeywell Center, 275 West Market Street, Wabash, IN 46992, 219–563–1102.

Historical Information
Honeywell Center, 275 West Market Street, Wabash, IN 46992, 219–563–1102. Wabash County Historical Museum, 89 West Hill Street, Wabash, IN 46992, 219–563–5058. Wabash Carnegie Library, 188 West Hill Street, Wabash, IN 46992, 219–563–2972.

Lodging
Scottish Inns, Wabash, Junction of State Route 13 and U.S. 24, 219–563–2195 or 1–800–251–1962.
Wabash Inn, 1950 South Wabash Street, 219–563–7451.

Restaurants
ABC Curb-A-Terio, 500 West Manchester, 219–563–1574.
Bill-Mar Food Service, Honeywell Center, 275 West Market Street, 219–563–1102.
Clark Cafeteria, 1146 North Cass Street, 219–563–2425.

VIII:2

Fort Wayne

ALLEN COUNTY
Indiana

ORT Wayne is a pleasant town that cares about preserving
the glory of the past. Its old buildings are protected by a
facade grant program. A walk through the Allen County
courthouse with its gleaming tile floors, faux marble columns, and a sparkling rotunda fresco ceiling will reveal some of the
beauty that Fort Wayne is trying to preserve.

Among its claims to fame, Fort Wayne was the birthplace of night
baseball in 1883 when two local teams played under seventeen arc
lights. Their brilliance was equal to 4,857 gas burners.

Directions

On a weekend trip to eastern Indiana, you might combine visits to
Fort Wayne and Wabash. From Chicago take Interstates 80 and 90
east to exit 49. Turn south onto State Route 49 to Valparaiso, then
east onto U.S. 30 into Fort Wayne. Or, if you prefer the fast route,
travel east on Interstate 80 to exit 144 and turn south onto Interstate
69 into Fort Wayne.

ARCHITECTURAL TOUR

The area just west of downtown began to be settled in the 1820s.
Architectural styles run the gamut from Greek Revival to Prairie. A
mixture of sizes is evident from the small workingman's cottage of
mid-century to the grand Queen Anne mansions. You can take a
leisurely walk along West Wayne and West Berry Streets in less than
an hour. Drive to the 700 block of West Wayne and park on the street
near the church or in the parking garage on the north side of West
Wayne near St. Joseph's Hospital. **1.** At 701–11 West Wayne is the
handsome limestone Victorian Gothic Revival Broadway Christian
Church, with two asymmetrical towers, a slate roof, parapeted gables,
and Gothic windows. **2.** The Richardsonian Romanesque house at
721 West Wayne, designed by Wing and Mahurin, has a corner tower
with cone-shaped slate roof and end gable connected by an arched

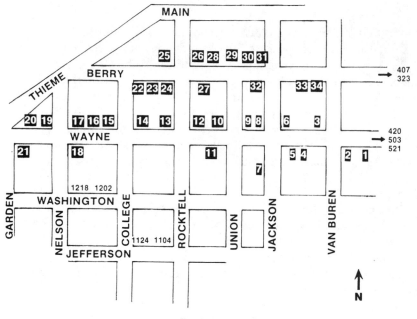

Fort Wayne

porch. The facade is of granite rubble, and the columns are of contrasting polished granite. It was built for L.O. Hull. **3.** At 802 West Wayne is an elegant Italianate house built in 1870. It has heavily bracketed eaves and a front gable that is similarly supported. The windows are hooded. The front porch is probably an early addition but not out of keeping with the original design. **4.** Across the street at 805 West Wayne is an 1890 brick Queen Anne house. A two-story tower with conical roof dominates the facade. A solid front porch shields the entrance. **5.** Another more elaborate Queen Anne house, built in the same year, is at 825–27 West Wayne. The facade is original except for the 1920s porch, which is not obtrusive. The front corners each have a tower, one square and the other conical. The window hoods are varied, and there is a third-floor multiwindowed dormer. **6.** Across the street at 832 West Wayne is an even fancier Queen Anne house also dating from 1890. It, too, has a conical three-story tower. The front gables are decorated, and the arched entry protects the door. **7.** A short detour south on Jackson will give you a view of yet another Italianate house. This rather austere structure was built in 1860 for Johan Matsch. The facade is broken by a front gable and a three-bay front porch protecting the entrance. **8.** At 902 West Wayne is a 1920 Prairie-style house. Its horizontal emphasis is in sharp contrast to the Queen Anne soaring towers, turrets, and gables of some of its neighbors. **9.** The Neo-Jacobean–Queen Anne house at 924 West Wayne seems elaborate because of its many decorated gables. Ronald McDonald commissioned Wing and Mahurin to design this house in 1887. **10.** Across Union is 1010 West Wayne, a worker's cottage built around 1880. This vernacular structure has basic Greek Revival lines, with Italianate window hoods and an enclosed porch addition modifying the style. Finding a small cottage among larger houses is typical of mid- and late-nineteenth-century land use. **11.** On the other side of West Wayne is 1011, a combination Queen Anne–Colonial Revival house. It has the classical cornices of the Colonial period and the Queen Anne square tower, decorated eaves and gables, and two-story bay. **12.** The brick Queen Anne house at 1030 West Wayne is a grand house, marred by the addition of the enclosed front porch. The three-story tower is its most prominent feature, but notice also the third-story dormer and second-story front bay. **13.** Another wooden Queen Anne is at 1104 West Wayne. A multisided tower with a slate roof dominates the facade. The wide front gable is decorated with medallions, and an original columned porch protects the entrance. **14.** The 1886 Van Arman home's version of Queen Anne was popular in Fort Wayne. The brick house at 1128 West Wayne has an overpowering three-story tower. Although the front porch is an addition, it is not objectionable. **15.** The Richardsonian Romanesque house at 1202

West Wayne was designed in 1905–6 by architects Wing and Mahurin for Paul Mossman. Borrowed from Queen Anne is the three-story tower, but its stone-rubble facade bespeaks a different style. The first-floor porch has been reduced to a terrace which lets more light into the first floor. **16.** The 1910 house at 1210 West Wayne is Eclectic. It has the horizontal planes of the Prairie style in the roof and porch and also has a terracotta tile roof. It was built for Arthur Perfect. **17.** Yet a later style is the 1920 Bungalow at 1220 West Wayne. **18.** The row of houses at 1225–37 West Wayne, built in 1890, are compatible but different. All are two-story with attic and all have front porches. **19.** The Eclectic shingled house at 1314 West Wayne is a one-and-one-half-story Bungalow with bracketed eaves. The off-center entrance porch is characteristic of the craftsman details common to this style. **20.** A bit west at 1316 West Wayne is a 1910 Dutch Colonial Revival house. It has the gambrel roof of this style, leaded-glass windows, and the original facade including a porch. **21.** A favorite style of the early twentieth century is represented in the Georgian Revival house at 1337 West Wayne, built in 1910. This elegant house has a classical entrance porch with balustrade, third-floor dormer with Palladian window, corner pilasters, bracketed eaves, and flat arches decorating the tops of its windows. The facade is original. **22.** Go north one block to West Berry Street and turn east. The 1890 Stick-style house at 1127 West Berry is a variation of late Victorian Queen Anne. The ornamentation on the front gable, the porch pediments, and the elaborate spindlework on the porch are good examples of this style. **23.** At 1115 West Berry is another rather similar 1894 house. It has checkerboard millwork on the gables and cornice to contrast with its clapboard siding, and decorated pediments protect its entrances. **24.** In sharp contrast is 1107–9 West Berry, a Prairie-style house built in 1920. The heavily bracketed overhanging roof and wide, substantial front porch are good examples of this style. **25.** The Greek Revival 1860 house at 1102 West Berry is a good example of this style. Particularly interesting is the classic cornice with dentils and arched attic window. A small entablature lintel supported by columns shields the entry, and the windows have blinds as well as decorative hoods. **26.** The Colonial Revival building at 1026 West Berry should be considered as two buildings: the original front, and the rear addition, a two-and-one-half-story clapboard structure built in 1900 with steep gables, a recessed brick porch, and unlikely rear turret. **27.** The simple Italianate house at 1021 West Berry was moved to this location in 1981. It was originally Greek Revival in style but was later remodeled to the popular Italianate while retaining its original entrance doorway and porch. **28.** The Prairie-style house at 1012 West Berry was built in 1920. Except for turning the attached garage into a room, the facade is original. The house is symmetrical, with the wide entrance door topped by a three-window bay and a dormer. Two three-window bays are on either side of the entrance door, and two windows flank the large middle second-story window. **29.** The apartment block at 932–26 West Berry was built in 1925. This elegant Eclectic four-story building has a facade decorated with shallow wrought-iron and terracotta balconies, an unusual brick cornice, and a courtyard. **30.** The Greek Revival house at 922 West Berry was built in 1840. The facade is original except for the two-story porch, which matches the classic lines. The original six-over-six windows, the entrance portico, the roof line, and fan-shaped attic window are typical of this style. **31.** The Prairie-style house at 910 West Berry was extensively remodeled in 1920 from its earlier Italianate appearance. The roof overhang, large windows, and wide porch are characteristic, but the central entrance with its transom and side lights are reminiscent of an earlier style. **32.** At 903 West Berry is a gem of a Queen Anne house. The three-story tower is matched by a second-story gable with porch. The facade is original, including the decorative woodwork, fish-scale shingles, fancy gables, and wraparound Stick-style front porch. **33.** Another somewhat different Queen Anne house is at 835 West Berry. This house has a prominent fish-scale-decorated front gable, stained-glass windows, a wide wooden porch, and original siding. **34.** A different version of the Queen Anne style is at 801 West Berry. The 1880 two-and-one-half-story house has a porte-cochere, columned front porch, and decorated gables. You are now one block north and one block west of your parking place in the 700 block of West Wayne.

Festivals, Tours, and Other Places of Interest

Group tours are available of historic homes and buildings from ARCH, Inc., P.O. Box 11383, Fort Wayne, IN 46857, 219–426–5117. Horse Around Town offers a carriage sightseeing tour of downtown Fort Wayne or the West Central historic district, 1004 West Cass Street, Fort Wayne, IN 46857, 219–422–8018.

Historical Information

Allen County–Fort Wayne Historical Society, Michael Hawfield, president and CEO, 302 East Berry Street, Fort Wayne, IN 46802, 219–426–2882. ARCH Inc., Gretchen Wiegel, executive director, P.O. Box 11383, Fort Wayne, IN 46857, 219–426–5117. City of Fort Wayne, Department of Community Development and Planning, Richard La Rowe, City-County Building, One Main Street, Fort Wayne, IN 46802, 219–427–1140. The Greater Fort Wayne

Chamber of Commerce, 826 Ewing Street, Fort Wayne, IN 46802, 219–424–1435.

Lodging

Fort Wayne Hilton, 1011 South Calhoun, 219–426–7769.

Holiday Inn Downtown, 300 East Washington Boulevard, 219–484–7711.

Restaurants

Blue Mountain Coffee Company, 122 West Columbia, the Landing, 219–426–1142, handicapped accessible.

Columbia Street West, 135 West Columbia Street, the Landing, 219–422–5055.

Downtown, 110 West Columbia Street, the Landing, 219–426–8220.

Eating Place and Wok, 818 South Calhoun, 219–422–6854, handicapped accessible.

Figaro's, 613 South Harrison Street, the Landing, 219–424–0690.

Henry's, 535 West Main Street, 219–424–9246.

VIII:3
Kokomo

HOWARD COUNTY
Indiana

I T seems that all approaches to Kokomo lead through the lush flatlands and corn fields of central Indiana, so it is a surprise to find rolling hills throughout the city. Kokomo is blessed with a well-restored nineteenth-century "Old Silk Stocking District." Stained-glass windows and door panels can be seen throughout the district, most of them produced by the Kokomo Opalescent Glass Company, which is still producing art, cathedral, and stained glass of Tiffany quality.

Kokomo, established in 1844 as the county seat of Howard County, grew slowly until the discovery of natural gas in 1887. This brought a period of rapid industrial growth due to the promises of abundant energy. The city's architectural treasures date from this period. Among them is the fine Victorian mansion built by Monroe Seiberling, one of the city's many investors.

Directions

You could spend a pleasant fall or spring weekend visiting Kokomo and Anderson. From Chicago take Interstates 80 and 90 to Interstate 65 to Lafayette. Turn east onto State Route 26 to U.S. 31, and take it north into Kokomo.

ARCHITECTURAL TOUR

The Old Silk Stocking neighborhood is just west of downtown. It was home to financiers, entrepreneurs, and industrialists at the turn of the century. Many of the grand old houses remain and are currently being renovated. You can drive and park, for the buildings of architectural interest are scattered. Although of National Register quality, they are not listed there because the inhabitants prefer local regulation. **1.** The Colonial Revival house with a grand two-story portico at 316 Kingston was built in 1940 by Walter Kemp. Evenly spaced windows, an arched entry, and three third-story dormers decorate its facade. **2.** A block north at 1030 West Maple is the Greek Revival

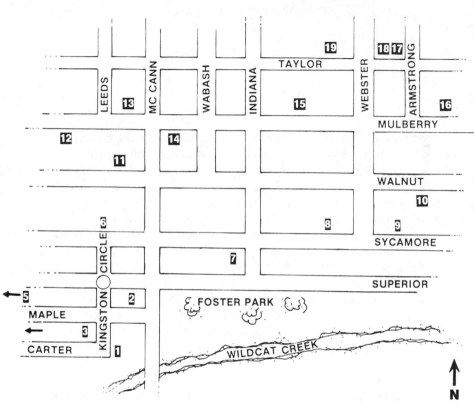

Old Silk Stocking Historic District

Deno house. The two-story front porch may well be an addition.
3. At 1107 West Maple is a combination Bungalow–Stick-style house built early in the twentieth century. It was remodeled in the late 1970s.
4. West at 1223 West Superior is the Russell house, a small one-and-one-half-story Greek Revival cottage with a modest entrance portico.
5. Also west is 1235 West Superior, the Norman Revival Harper house. **6.** The grand Seiberling Mansion at 1200 West Sycamore Street is Neo-Jacobean–Romanesque Revival in style. It is now the site of the Howard County Historical Museum. It was designed by Arthur LaBelle of Marion. This elaborate mansion was begun in 1889 and finished in 1891. There is a wealth of detail in both the interior and the facade. Prominent among its features are a large, round center tower with conical roof and a wide wraparound columned front porch with pedimented entrance. **7.** The Krebs house at 809 Sycamore Street was probably built in the early twentieth century. It has a Greek Revival entrance and Italianate roof brackets and attic dormers. **8.** The Classical Revival Bolinger house at 600 West Sycamore was built in the early twentieth century. It has Greek columns supporting the entrance and the windows on the two wings as well as a tile roof. **9.** The Second Empire Duncan house at 542 West Sycamore has the traditional mansard roof and dormers and the central pavilion protruding from the second and third floors. A Queen Anne-type balustrade atop the first floor and fancy glass in the front windows are also marks of this style. **10.** A Victorian Classical Revival home stands at 417 West Walnut. It has a spacious wraparound porch across the front; the porch roof is apparently accessible from the second floor. This well-preserved house was built in 1894 for W.E. Blacklidge.
11. The building at 1020 West Walnut is the Norman Revival Bourff house. **12.** One block north at 1105 West Mulberry we find a combination Classical Revival and Shingle-style house. It is a two-and-one-half-story building. **13.** Across the street is 1002 West Mulberry, the Art Nouveau home designed in 1910 by architect Frank B. Hunter, who also designed the governor's mansion in Indianapolis. **14.** There is an intricate example of Shingle-style architecture at 905 West Mulberry, the Victorian Saban house. It has attractive roof details and Stick-style porches at the front and side entrances. **15.** The brick Carpenter–Builder cottage at 606 West Mulberry was built in 1871 by Daniel Harris. **16.** One and one half blocks east is 414 West Mulberry, the Wray house, which has a two-story entrance porch and pediment with a fanlight. The porch on the first floor is flanked by terraces. **17.** A block north is 508 Taylor, a Classical Revival house. The small entry porch appears to be a recent addition, but the two-story bay and the third-floor dormers are original. **18.** At 522 West Taylor is the Cottage-style Ferries home. It has an ornate wraparound porch and

protruding bay on the east side. **19.** The Carpenter Gothic-style house at 614 West Taylor was probably built in 1889. This one-and-one-half-story house has stained-glass windows and fancy woodwork in the gables.

Festivals, Tours, and Other Places of Interest

Greentown Glass Museum, open Tuesday–Saturday, 1:00 P.M.–4:00 P.M., Sunday, 1:00 P.M.–5:00 P.M., 112 North Meridan, Greentown, IN 46936, 317–628–7718. Haynes Museum, open Tuesday–Sunday, 1:00 P.M.–4:00 P.M., 1915 South Webster, Kokomo, IN 46901, 317–452–3471. Howard County Historical Museum, open Tuesday–Sunday, 1:00 P.M.–4:00 P.M., 1200 West Sycamore, Kokomo, IN 46901, 317–452–4314.

Historical Information

Howard County Historical Museum, 1200 Sycamore, Kokomo, IN 46901, 317–452–4314. Old Silk Stocking Neighborhood Association, Toni Fox, 1104 West Walnut, Kokomo, IN 46901, 317–456–3019.

Lodging

Howard Johnson's Motor Lodge, U.S. 31 Bypass South, 317–457–8211.

Ramada Inn, 1709 East Lincoln, 317–459–8001.

Red Carpet Motel, R.R., Sharpsville, 317–963–2727.

Restaurants

Gold Rush Restaurant, 3201 South Lafountain, 317–455–1280, handicapped accessible.

VIII:4
Anderson
MADISON COUNTY
Indiana

T HE earliest inhabitants of Anderson were Indian mound builders, traces of whose work can be found throughout the county and all of which must predate 1827, when Anderson became the Madison County seat.

The railroad came in 1851, and in 1887 natural gas was discovered. Local industry underwent a boom and Anderson was known as the "Queen City of the Gas Belt." Its grand houses date from this period.

By 1897 the Union Traction Company, the first area interurban railway, was expanding to connect the leading gas belt cities with the state capital, Indianapolis. With the dawn of the automobile age, the railways declined, but Anderson prospered as the manufacturer of thirteen different makes of automobiles.

Directions
You might think about spending a weekend in central Indiana visiting Kokomo and Anderson. Take Interstates 80 and 90 from Chicago to Interstate 65 east of Gary. Go south to Indianapolis. Take Interstate 465 east to Interstate 69 and leave it at the Anderson exit.

ARCHITECTURAL TOURS
WEST EIGHTH STREET HISTORIC DISTRICT
Just west of the central business district is the West Eighth Street historic district, which is within the village limits established in the John Berry plat of 1823. Its boundaries are Seventh Street on the north, Madison on the west, Ninth on the south, and Brown-Delaware Street on the east. In 1976 the district was placed on the National Register because of its collection of late Victorian Queen Anne, Gothic Revival, and Italianate homes. Parking is available on the east side of John Street between Eighth and Ninth. 1. The Patrick Skehan house at 406 West Eighth Street was built in 1893 in the Italianate style. A decorative balustraded deck tops the roof, and a wide porch with off-center entrance protects the front. 2. The Free Classic

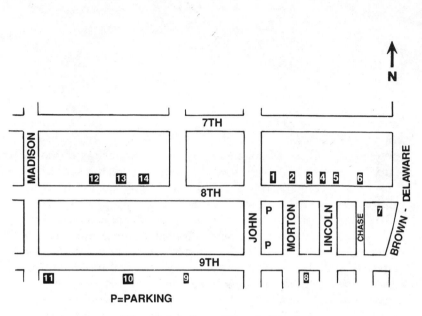

West Eighth Street Historic District

Daniel Mustard house at 338 West Eighth was built in 1904. A wide columned porch stretches across the front, with a pediment at the entrance. The two-story house has a dormer in the attic. **3.** Next door is 334 West Eighth, the Goodykoontz Carpenter–Builder house, erected in 1864 and remodeled in 1895 and again in 1960. **4.** At 322 West Eighth is the Jeffrey Ferris Queen Anne house. It has an imposing semicircular entrance portico terminating in a second-story balcony and a round turret on the third floor with windows on three sides. It is currently painted pink with white trim. **5.** Next door at 310 West Eighth is an Italianate–Free Classic house built between 1880 and 1910. Note the gable on the third floor above the entrance, which is topped by a fancy lightning rod. **6.** The Free Classic-style house at 212 West Eighth was home to John H. Terhune. It was built in 1886. A rooftop pediment and large columned porch running across the front are its distinguishing features. **7.** Back west a few blocks is 215 West Eighth, the Queen Anne Johnson house, built in 1902. **8.** One block south and two blocks west is 431 West Ninth, the Gothic Revival Van Pelt house, built about 1860. **9.** Two blocks west on Ninth Street is 711, a Queen Anne house, built around 1890. It is architecturally outstanding; note the third-floor tower with conical roof, column-supported front porch, variously decorated windows, and sunburst third-story gable. **10.** On the southeast corner of Madison and Ninth is the Jacobean Revival Otterbein United Methodist Church, built about 1900. **11.** At 926 West Ninth is the Queen Anne Connelly house, built in 1892. **12.** The Colonial Revival Lynch house at 920 West Eighth was built in 1920. Note its tile roof and side portico entrance. **13.** The Queen Anne Wynant house at 834 West Eighth was built in 1895. It has a wide wraparound front porch terminating in a balcony across the second story. **14.** Slightly east on the same side of the street is 830 West Eighth, the Queen Anne Walker house, built in 1895. **15.** The three-story Charles Van DeVinter Queen Anne house at 824 West Eighth was built in 1904. It has a wide arched front porch supported by slender columns.

WEST CENTRAL HISTORIC DISTRICT

This district is directly south of the Eighth Street district. Most of the houses were built between 1895 and 1910. They are mostly Queen Anne and Carpenter–Builder. The district is also listed on the National Register. There is a parking area on the southeast corner of Tenth and Brown-Delaware and another at the northeast corner of Brown-Delaware and Twelfth. **1.** At 1015 Brown-Delaware is the fine Free Classic Jones house built in 1908. It has a second-floor balcony over the first-floor porch and limestone lintels and quoins decorating the facade. **2.** The Arts and Crafts house at 1019 Brown-

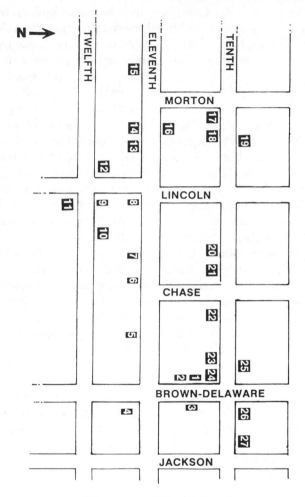

West Central Historic District

Delaware was built by Miron G. Reynolds. It has red brick on the first floor and stucco and half-timbers on the second and many gables. Large concrete urns flank the porch entrance. 3. On the other side of the street at 1030 Brown-Delaware is the Gothic Revival Trinity Episcopal Church, built in 1910. 4. The Stephen Markt house at 129 West Eleventh was built in 1875. It is a two-story frame Italianate with a wide front porch. All the windows have decorative hoods. Both interior and facade are original. 5. Proceed west half a block to 219 West Eleventh, built by Charles L. Henry. It has a wraparound porch with fluted Ionic columns and several stained-glass windows. 6. The Bungalow at 301 West Eleventh was built by Edward Lyst in the 1920s. Its facade is stucco with brick-trimmed porch and windowsills. 7. The house at 311 West Eleventh was built in 1875 by Charles T. Doxey. The style is Italianate with wide, overhanging bracketed eaves. 8. In 1928 the apartments at 1106 Lincoln were built by William Surbaugh. The Colonial Revival apartments have a prominent two-story porch supported by brick piers. 9. Another multifamily unit at 330 West Twelfth, the Bonsor or Lincolnshire apartments, were built in 1927 in the Tudor Revival style. 10. A little east at 322 West Twelfth is the Free Classic house built in 1903 by Herbert Berg. The inside and outside of the house are original. 11. One of the largest houses in the area, 321 West Twelfth, was built by Harry Canaday in 1903. The house has a wraparound front porch supported by fluted Ionic columns and a square balustrade. Other details are a sunburst dormer on the north side, a classical entrance flanked by side lights, and a round window in the front gable. 12. On the north side of the street is 408 West Twelfth, an American four-square, or saltbox, built sometime between 1895 and 1925. It was the home of Bernard Lavelle. 13. The Queen Anne house at 411 West Eleventh was the home of George W. Wright. 14. The Queen Anne–Stick-style house at 415 West Eleventh was built in 1890. The gables have fish-scale shingles and the wraparound front porch has classical columns and a balustrade. 15. Proceed along the street to 435 West Eleventh, a Stick-style house built in 1898. It has a variety of window styles and a corner front porch. 16. The Queen Anne house at 420 West Eleventh was built around 1891. The aluminum siding on the first floor is the only change in its facade. The second story has fish-scale shingles, and there are a variety of window styles. As you proceed north along Morton Street, take a good look at the original brick-paved street. 17. The cottage at 431 West Tenth is a Bungalow-style house built in 1910. It has cornice brackets over the doorway and along the roof line. 18. A little east is 429 West Tenth, a clapboard Carpenter–Builder house erected for Patrick McLaughlin in 1912. It has a full front porch and is an excellent example of this style. 19. On the north side of the street is 424 West

Tenth, a two-story brick Colonial Revival house built for Neel Mc-Cullough around 1915. **20.** A block farther east is 309 West Tenth, a Classical Revival apartment house built around 1915. **21.** Still farther east is 301 West Tenth, a Queen Anne house built around 1900. **22.** In the next block east at 231 West Tenth is the Romanesque Revival Hope Congregational Church, built about 1895. The facade is decorated with Roman arches and windows. A short square tower anchors one end. **23.** Proceed east to 221 West Tenth, the Shingle-style Stilwell house built in 1895. It has an interesting oval entrance and two matching bays with Palladian windows on the second story. **24.** Alfred Makepeace built 203 West Tenth, a Queen Anne–Colonial Revival house, around 1905. The house has a colonnaded wraparound front porch, fish-scale gables, a stained-glass window on the first floor, and an eyebrow window on the east. **25.** The Italianate-style house at 212 West Tenth was built between 1875 and 1915. The facade includes limestone window lintels, a two-story bay, classical columned front porch, and porte-cochere. **26.** In the next block on the north side of the street is 120 West Tenth, the Delaware Court apartments, built in 1927 in the Colonial Revival style. This three-story building with third-floor dormers is brick with white trim. It was designed by local architect E.F. Miller and built around an interior court. **27.** The cornerstone for 923 Jackson, the Central Christian Church, designed by J.W. Brown of Cincinnati, was laid in 1899. The church is a large rock-faced building with an irregular floor plan, numerous windows of various shapes, and an arched entrance with heavy paneled door.

Historical Information

Madison County Historical Society, Gruenewald Home, 626 Main, Anderson, IN 46016. Planning Department, City of Anderson, 120 East Eighth Street, P.O. Box 2100, Anderson, IN 46018, 317–646–9690. Anderson Public Library, 111 West Twelfth Street, Anderson, IN 46016.

Lodging

Holiday Inn, 5920 Scatterfield Road, 317–644–2581.
Lee's Inns of America, 2114 East Fifty-ninth Street, 317–649–2500.
Motel 6, 5810 Scatterfield Road, 317–642–3333.
Sheraton Inn, 5901 Scatterfield Road, 317–649–0451.

Restaurants

Chef Mu's Magic Wok, 817 State Road 9 South, 317–643–7000, handicapped accessible.

Jim Dandy's, 1900 East Fifty-third, 317–642–0773, handicapped accessible.

Bob Evans' Farms, 5555 Scatterfield Road, 317–643–0064, handicapped accessible.

MCL Cafeteria, Mounds Mall, 317–643–2682, handicapped accessible.

Mr. Steak, 840 State Road, 317–644–3404, handicapped accessible.

Pelican, 3300 South Main, 317–644–2828, handicapped accessible.

Spa, 3 Jackson, 317–644–9678.

VIII:5
Lafayette

TIPPECANOE COUNTY
Indiana

THE county and its extraordinary courthouse are named "Tippecanoe" after William Henry Harrison's victory over the Indians at the river of the same name. It was his moniker in his later successful presidential campaign when his backers proclaimed "Tippecanoe and Tyler too."

William Digby founded Lafayette and named it for his idol, the French general Lafayette, who helped the American colonies to defeat the British.

The founding of Purdue University in 1865 has had long-lasting favorable effects for the greater Lafayette area. John Purdue, a sucessful businessman, persuaded the state legislature to build its land grant college not more than two and a half miles from the Lafayette courthouse, placing the university in present-day West Lafayette. Mr. Purdue sweetened the deal by giving the new university 100 acres of land and $150,000. Building started in 1871; the first students graduated four years later, and the university began to grow.

Directions

A trip to Lafayette is best done on a weekend when you will have time to tour the districts leisurely. It could be combined with a trip to Kokomo or Wabash. From Chicago take Interstates 80 and 94 east to Interstate 65 and south to the State Route 26 exit into Lafayette, which becomes South Street. When you come to Fourth Street, turn right, where there is a city parking lot.

ARCHITECTURAL TOURS

The architectural treasures date mainly from the period of urban expansion between 1873 and 1920. Styles are predominantly Italianate, with some representation of the Second Empire, Art Deco, and Neoclassical schools. The tours include downtown, the Centennial district north of the center, and the Ellsworth district to the south.

The latter two are residential and all are National Register Historic Districts.

DOWNTOWN LAFAYETTE HISTORIC DISTRICT
We shall concentrate on the sides of the public square facing the courthouse; this is the center of commerce. Buildings generally date from the last quarter of the nineteenth century. As usual, we recommend walking the area. At a slow pace this tour will take a maximum of half an hour. 1. Walk north two blocks to the northwest corner of Fourth and Ferry Streets, where you will find 324–26 Ferry, an Italianate commercial building erected in 1880. Known as the Kettelhut building, it is a two-story brick with bracketed eaves and cornice. 2. A little west at 310 Ferry Street is an 1869 Federal-style two-story commercial building. Notice the brick arches over the windows. 3. Across the street is the 1931 Neoclassical–Art Deco Federal building and U.S. Post Office. It is a large structure, encompassing half a block, with entrances on Third, Fourth, and Ferry Streets. This two-story limestone edifice was designed by prominent Midwest architect Walter Scholer, Sr. 4. On the northeast corner of Ferry and Third is the Kirby Risk building, erected in 1882. This three-story vernacular-style commercial building has arched windows and a hip roof. 5. The Woolworth Building is at the northwest corner of Third and Main Streets. In 1885 it was an Italianate building, but the facade has been altered to Art Deco. 6. Walk south on Third Street, noticing the dominance of the courthouse. At the northwest corner of Third and Columbia Streets is the Italianate River City Market building, erected in 1860. It is really three buildings, the most conspicuous of which is the Emerson block with its three stories and three bays. A large bracketed metal cornice decorates the south and west roof line of this Italianate structure. The Queen City and Hub buildings are in the same style, but are two-story with bay windows. 7. Catercorner on the southeast corner of Columbia and Third Streets is 301 Columbia, the Stallard and Schuh building. Erected in 1870, this Italianate structure has heavily bracketed eaves, and its facade is divided into three sections. The main entrance has a double pediment and bronze doors and is supported by stone columns. 8. Walk east along Columbia Street to number 331, the Italianate Cooke and Bache building, erected in 1880. This four-story building has wide eaves supported by large stone brackets. 9. Next door at 337 is the Lafayette National Bank building, designed by Walter Scholer, Sr. This 1926 Neoclassical limestone structure has large Doric columns and parapet with entablature. 10. Dominating the square is Lafayette's most remarkable building, the Tippecanoe County courthouse, designed by James Alexander and completed in 1884. Entrances to this amazing edifice

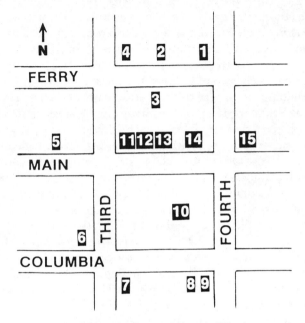

Downtown Lafayette Historic District

are from all four sides of the square. It rises two stories to a mansard roof and a dome topped with a statue of Justice. While predominantly a Second Empire building, it has much Classical Revival decoration. Walk around the building and notice particularly the fountain on the southwest corner dedicated to the pioneer founders, Union veterans, and the city's namesake, General Lafayette, whose statue crowns the fountain. **11.** The Lafayette Life building at 300–306 Main Street is the tallest building on the square, rising ten stories. This Neoclassical structure was designed by the courthouse architect, James Alexander, in 1919. Of note is the break in design that gives the upper floors a more decorative facade. **12.** Walk east to the Ross building at 308 Main. It is a Gothic Revival structure erected in 1918. Its terracotta facade is resplendent with arches and stained glass. Two gnome statuettes holding chains decorate the base of the second story. **13.** At 316 Main is the startling Classical Revival First Merchants National Bank, erected in 1918. The facade resembles a Roman triumphal arch and is lavishly decorated by a small statue of General Lafayette over the entrance, flanked by flying Victories. **14.** Farther east is the Italianate Perrin building, erected in 1877, the only remaining example of cast-iron architecture left in the city. The four-story structure has arched windows on the second and fourth stories and flatter or segmented arches on the third, in addition to geometric and floral ornaments. It is crowned by a cornice, bracketed eaves, and a crested inscription plaque with the building's name, date, and street number. **15.** Across Fourth Street on the northeast corner is the Oppenheimer building. This three-story structure, erected in 1870 and remodeled in 1914, has a decorated terracotta facade. You are now one block from your parking place. You might want to go east on Main Street to the corner of Fifth and Main, where you can look south, or right, toward the Farmers' Market.

CENTENNIAL HISTORIC DISTRICT
The district is just north of the Downtown district and runs roughly from Ferry to Union and Third to Ninth Street. By 1841 the city's boundaries were north of the district. A tour of the district gives you a good idea of the design of a centralized railroad town, dependent on pedestrian movement. We advise that you travel this extensive district by car. You might want to park on Ferry Street between Sixth and Eighth Streets, as there are a number of houses worth viewing on the north side of the street. Unless you linger, this tour can be completed in half an hour. **1.** The Haywood building at 300 North Fifth Street is a good example of an early twentieth-century industrial building. This 1914 structure has a reinforced-concrete frame to support the machinery used in printing. **2.** Go east one block to Sixth Street. On

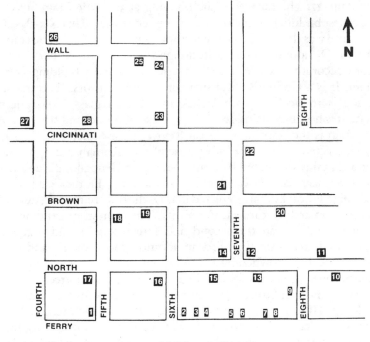

Centennial Historic District

the northeast corner at 315 Sixth Street you will find Lafayette's oldest church building, St. John's Episcopal Church, built in 1857. The architect of this Gothic Revival building was William Tinsley, the designer of many midwest churches and academic edifices. In 1978 it was individually listed on the National Register. 3. Next door at 608 Ferry Street is the Federal 1844 Samuel Johnson house, the oldest residence in Lafayette. Its doorway is framed by transom and side lights, and the first floor windows are nine-over-nine and the second floor's are six-over-six. 4. At 612–14 Ferry is a large Italianate house built in 1874 with bracketed eaves, window hoods, and limestone sills. On the second floor an oriel window looks west. 5. The elaborate Italianate house at 620 Ferry Street has a three-story tower. The remainder of this 1865 house is two-story with a heavily bracketed roof and varied window hoods. 6. The 1878 Italianate house at 622 Ferry Street is an elegant two-story house with two-story front bay and pedimented entrance. It has a side porch and entrance, window hoods, and bracketed eaves. 7. At 636 Ferry is an 1850s Greek Revival house with limestone lintels and sills. 8. The house at 640 Ferry is in sharp contrast with the preceding one. This 1892 Stick-style house contains a variety of materials. The first floor is masonry, the second fish-scale shingles, and the third clapboard. 9. Turn left at Eighth Street and you will see 316 North Eighth Street on your left. This Dutch Colonial house was built in 1910. It is a masonry house with gambrel roof and limestone lintels and sills. 10. Continue on to North Street and then right, or east, to see St. Boniface Catholic Church and rectory, built in the Gothic Revival style. The church was erected in 1865 and the rectory ten years later. The former has a gable roof, tower, and spire. Next door to the west is the church school, a Romanesque Revival structure dating from 1908. 11. On the other side of North Street note the 1870 two-story Italianate house with projecting brick cornice, limestone lintels and sills, pilasters, and pointed arch entrance. 12. Continue east on North Street to 411 North Seventh Street, located on the northeast corner. There you will find the First Baptist Church, built in 1872. This Romanesque Revival structure has towers of uneven height, and arches define the main entrance. 13. Across North Street is 705, a 1920s Bungalow that contrasts with its nineteenth-century neighbors. 14. On the other side of North Street on the northwest corner with Seventh is the Wells Memorial library, a Neoclassical structure erected in 1927. Its facade is decorated in Beaux-Arts fashion with columns and pilasters. The building was designed by Walter Scholer, Sr., the architect of a number of commercial buildings in the downtown area. 15. On the south side of North Street at 615 is the Marian apartment complex, an example of an early-twentieth-century multifamily building. 16. Go west to Sixth, and on the southwest corner you will see the Trinity United Methodist Church. Built in 1869, this Gothic Revival church has a heavily decorated facade that includes four towers, two rectangular and two polygonal and all with spires. Over the entrance arch in the front gable is a wheel window. **17.** One block west on the southwest corner of Fifth Street is the Monon depot. This Neoclassical station, built in 1901, is topped by a parapet and has roundels over the two entrance doors and an uncharacteristic bay window in the middle. **18.** Railroad tracks ran along Fifth Street and the river banks, and the adjacent area was primarily industrial. Workers typically lived close to their work, as urban public transportation was nonexistent. Typical of some of the workers' houses built in the district's western section are the Italianate brick row houses at 417–27 North Fifth Street. The facades are modestly decorated with simple cornice and pilasters. Later additions include the porches and awnings. **19.** Proceed east on Brown Street to 517. This Jacobean house is a variation on the Queen Anne style. Built in 1886, this two-story house has gables with dormers, a decorative cornice, and limestone lintels and sills. **20.** A block and a half farther east is the Eclectic Armstrong house at 711 Brown Street. As its style implies, it has a variety of decorations, including gables with dormers, a frieze, and a two-story portico supported by Tuscan and Ionic columns. **21.** Return to Seventh Street, and turn right, or north. At 514 is a fancy example of the Dutch Colonial style. This 1916 house has a Palladian window in the end of the gambrel roof, with a bay window projecting from its clapboard first floor and a shingled second story. **22.** North on the southeast corner with Cincinnati is 525 North Seventh, a two-story Stick-style house built in 1880. It has gable roofs over both the projecting bay and the porch and fish-scale siding midway between floors. **23.** Return to Sixth Street and turn north, or right. On your left at 604 is the locally significant Queen Anne Oppenheimer house, built about 1860. Originally in the simpler Italianate style, it now has gables with dormers, stick and shingle siding, and an arched entrance-door transom. **24.** At the southwest corner of Sixth and Wall at 634 North Sixth is a good 1863 example of the Second Empire style with Ionic columns supporting the cornice and upper porches. **25.** Go west on Wall Street to 511, a working-class Gothic Revival one-and-one-half-story cottage with bargeboard-decorated gable and a bay window. **26.** Continue west a block on Wall and on the northeast corner with Fourth Street you will see 713–15 North Fourth Street, a Greek Revival house dating from 1850. This house has a fanlight in the front gable, limestone lintels and sills, and a two-story bay. **27.** Go south one block to Cincinnati Street. On the northwest corner is the modern 1920 Indiana Gas Company office, which is very different from the older buildings surrounding it. **28.** Go east one block to Fifth and on the northwest corner you will see 602 North Fifth, another early house built before the railroad tracks were laid. This 1845 one-story frame Greek Revival structure is known as the DeHart house. Its entrance is supported by columns and pilasters and flanked by a transom and side lights. Window hoods and pilastered corners complete the facade decoration.

ELLSWORTH HISTORIC DISTRICT

The district is south of and adjacent to downtown, roughly bounded by Fifth Street on the west, Columbia Street on the north, and the Norfolk and Western railroad alignment on the southeast. The district was settled between 1840 and 1870. The lots are small and land use diverse, typical of the pedestrian town of the mid-nineteenth century. The architectural styles vary from Greek Revival to Gothic Revival cottages inspired by Andrew Jackson Dowling's pattern books, as well as Italianate, Second Empire, and Romanesque. Buildings of note are scattered, so we recommend you tour by car. In general, the more modest houses are in the western section and the grander ones are against the hills in the east. The trip will take about half an hour. **1.** From downtown take Sixth Street to South Street. Turn left, or east, to 620–22 South Street. This house was built for Lew Falley in 1872. **2–4.** The next three row houses were inspired by similar houses in Boston. Ira G. Howe built them in 1851. These two-story brick Italianate buildings have two-story bays called "Boston swell fronts," elaborate second-story window hoods, and fancy entrance doors with etched-glass panels in floral designs. **5.** A more elaborate brick Italianate house, 630 South Street, was built in 1852 by Moses Fowler. It is also two-story with wood bracketed cornice, low hipped roof, and decorated limestone lintels. **6.** Go south one block to Alabama and turn right, or west, to 609. This two-story frame building with brick porch was built for Lewis Kimmel in 1868. **7.** Go south to 206 South Sixth Street, a house built in 1868 by John Connally. The house is a stuccoed Greek Revival structure with wooden cornice and pediment. **8.** The house at 211 South Sixth is another example of the influence of Andrew Jackson Dowling's pattern books. This Gothic Revival two-story house has elaborately decorated gable eaves. **9.** Turn right onto New York to see another example of the Dowling influence at 511. This one-and-one-half-story Gothic Revival house has gables with bargeboard trim. The front porch has fancy wood columns, which may not be original. **10.** Turn around and cross Sixth Street to 601 New York, a two-story stucco Italianate villa with a third-story tower. This house was built for James B. Falley in 1862–64. **11.** The house at 617 New York is a

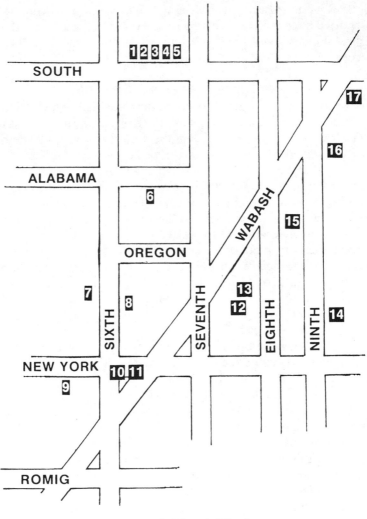

Ellsworth Historic District

one-and-one-half-story Queen Anne, built in 1889. This clapboard house has a front porch and an octagonal dormer. **12.** Continue east to Eighth Street and turn left to 221 South Seventh Street. This two-story Greek Revival house, decorated with four pilasters, was built for Peter Ball. The tower is a later addition. **13.** The original owner of 213 South Seventh Street was Robert C. Gregory. The two-story Greek Revival house, built in 1843, has four brick pilasters and a recessed doorway. **14.** Retrace your steps to New York Street, proceed east to Ninth Street, and turn left, or north, to the Samuel Moore house at 203. This Queen Anne home, built in 1891, has third-floor gables with windows and a prominent three-story tower with pyramidal roof atop a second-story bay. The upper stories are fish-scale shingle, and the first is yellow masonry. A wraparound front porch sports a pedimented entrance. **15.** Go north on Ninth to the grand Cyrus Ball house at 402. This Italianate–Second Empire building was erected in the late 1860s. The columned entrance is matched on the second floor by a porticoed window. Above that is a tower with mansard roof in which is implanted a bullseye window; crowning all is an ironwork balustrade. **16.** Continue north on Ninth to 917, the Perrin Seawright house, built in 1868. The Italianate trim was added later and was copied from ironwork in New Orleans. **17.** Proceed north on Ninth to Wabash. Take Wabash northeast to South Street. At the southeast corner of Wabash and South Streets is 909, the house built in 1851–52 by Moses Fowler. This two-story stucco English Gothic Revival cottage has gables decorated with elaborate bargeboard, fancy bay windows with balustrades, and a recessed porch. It is a copy of a cottage that appears in one of Andrew Jackson Dowling's pattern books, entitled "A Villa in the Pointed Style." In 1940 the Tippecanoe Historical Society purchased the home and turned it into a museum.

Festivals, Tours, and Other Places of Interest

Tippecanoe County Historical Society Museum, 909 South Street, Lafayette, IN 47902, 317–742–8411.

Historical Information

David Parrish's book *Historical Architecture of Lafayette, Indiana*, 1978, Purdue Research Foundation, has 22 excellent pictures of some of the city's architectural treasures along with descriptive material. Tippecanoe County Historical Museum, 909 South Street, Lafayette, IN 47902, 317–742–8411. Wetherill Historical Resource Center, 1001 South Street, Lafayette, IN 47902, 317–742–8411. Greater Lafayette Chamber of Commerce, 322 Main Street, P.O. Box 348, Lafayette, IN 47902-0348, 317–742–4041. Ramona Lawson, Redevelopment Commission, City of Lafayette, 324 Ferry Street, Lafayette, IN 47902, 317–742–1145.

Lodging
Lahr House, 115 North Fifth Street, 317–742–4055.

Restaurants
Chinese Village, 528 Main Street, 317–742–4966.
Downtowner, 501 Main Street, 317–742–8955.
Heart's Delight, 525 Main Street, 317–742–8180.
Sarge Oak, 721 Main Street, 317–742–9442.
Sergeant Preston's of the North, 6 North Second Street, 317–742–7378.

Indianapolis

MARION COUNTY
Indiana

INDIANAPOLIS was founded in 1820 as the state capital and has since grown into a city with over one million inhabitants. This city has made a firm commitment to preserving its historic past. The historic commission is restoring the old canal bed through the center of the city. Union Station has been delightfully renovated into a mall, and the adjoining train shed now houses a motel. The city is justly proud of the "Indy" 500 race track, which is on the National Register. But most interesting are the two widely different restored sections. Lockerbie Square was originally a working- and middle-class neighborhood, whereas the Old Northside area's once grand homes housed wealthy industrialists and President Benjamin Harrison.

Directions

Indianapolis is well worth a weekend. Not only are its historic districts of interest, but the city offers a rejuvenated downtown and a variety of entertainment. From Chicago take Interstates 90 and 80 east to Interstate 65, then southeast to Indianapolis. Approaching the city, take Interstate 65 right into the Old Northside area, exiting at Pennsylvania Avenue. To get to Lockerbie Square, go south on Pennsylvania to Vermont, then east to East Street and south one half block to Lockerbie Street.

ARCHITECTURAL TOURS

Lockerbie Square and Old Northside are the two most renovated historic districts.

LOCKERBIE SQUARE

To reach Lockerbie Square from Monument Circle in downtown Indianapolis, drive north on Meridian Street three blocks to Vermont Street. Turn right and go east five blocks to East Street. Turn right, or south, one half block to Lockerbie Street; turn left, or east, and your

Lockerbie Square

first stop is on your left. It is best to park your car and tour Lockerbie Square on foot since there are so many one-way streets. **1.** The Nickum-Holstein house, 528 Lockerbie, was the residence of James Whitcomb Riley from 1893 to 1916. The 1872 brick Italianate house has a columned side portico, a bracketed cornice with frieze windows, and round arch window hoods. It is now a museum honoring the Hoosier poet James Whitcomb Riley. **2.** Across the street, 527 Lockerbie was built in 1855 by Mary Foote. The porch, gable, and trim were added in the 1890s. **3.** Built in 1856, 517 Lockerbie is an example of the early vernacular cottage. **4.** Around the corner, 337–35 North East Street is a combination late Federal/Italianate-style double residence, built in 1866–67. **5.** The house at 333–31 North East Street, built about 1876, is one of the best examples of an Italianate residence in Lockerbie Square. This two-story house, with heavy bracketed cornice and decorative window trim, was built by William H. Keely. **6.** In the next block south, 315–13 North East Street, a double residence built between 1887 and 1889, has an interesting front facade with twin front porches and third-floor gables. **7.** Built in 1882, 237 North East Street is the site of the Lockerbie Square United Methodist Church, designed by prominent German-born architect Diedrich A. Bohlen. The multicolored brickwork is unusual. **8.** The house at 520 New York Avenue was built about 1895. Its semicircular tower and front-porch balustrade are unique in Lockerbie Square but typical of the Queen Anne style. **9.** The Gothic Revival cottage at 536 East New York was moved to this site in 1976. It was built in 1872–73 and has notable window detail and a small entrance porch. **10.** The simplified Queen Anne house at 540 East New York Avenue has a remarkable facade featuring horizontal clapboards, vertical boarding and shingles, ornamental lintels, and carved moldings beneath the windows. **11.** This typical one-and-one-half-story cottage at 314 North Park Avenue dates from 1864. The elaborately decorated facade includes decorative bargeboard outlining the front gable and a front porch enlivened by carpenter's lace. Its first owner was Alfred Foster. **12.** The George Holler house at 324 North Park Avenue, built in 1863, is another example of the popular cottage. The facade is only slightly decorated. **13.** Built in 1888, 605 Lockerbie with its bay window and staggered front porch is a good example of the architecture of the period. **14.** John Treiter built 609 Lockerbie Street in 1867. This two-story Italianate house has had its original cornice removed and the shingled gable added late in the nineteenth century. The small front stoop was added still later. **15.** Oliver Keely built 615–17 Lockerbie Street in 1880. This brick Italianate residence with a wide front porch is a double residence. **16.** The house at 320 North College Avenue is another Oliver Keely enterprise, built in 1865. It is a typical one-and-one-half-story cottage. **17.** Asa Holland built 316 North College Avenue in 1865. The two-story clapboard house with wraparound porch retains its original facade. **18.** The commercial structure at 330 North College Avenue was built in two stages, the west portion in the 1860s and the east in the 1870s. This Italianate building has facade details including elaborate metal window moldings, a cornice supported by heavy brackets, and small horizontal frieze with eyebrow windows. **19.** The brick house at 338–40 North College Avenue was built about 1859 by Herman Koch as a double house. The front porch with its spindle decoration was added later. **20.** The two-story house at 342 North College Avenue was built about 1859 by Joseph Staub. It is late Federal-style with a recessed second-floor porch on the south side, the type of porch popular in warm climates. The Historic Landmarks Foundation of Indiana restored it. **21.** The three-story 417–19 North College Avenue building is a double house built about 1905 by Michael Mode. The Indianapolis Historic Preservation Commission restored its exterior. **22.** Built in the 1860s and remodeled and enlarged to present appearance and size in the 1890s, 425–27 North College is a double house. **23.** Across the street is 426 North College Avenue, a brick house built in 1862 by Christian F. Schrader. **24.** On the east side of the street is 429 North College, a Greek Revival cottage built about 1855. The present porch was added sometime between 1898 and 1913. **25.** Herman Lieber built 407 North Park Avenue, a Chalet-style cottage, around 1860. **26.** At 519 Vermont Street is a vernacular cottage built around 1885 by David Wiley. It is a good example of a Stick-style cottage. **27.** Another Wiley building, 523 East Vermont Street, is a Stick-style two-story house with its original facade. **28.** At the southeast corner of Park and Vermont is 353 Park Street, a Federal-style brick house built by Frederick Thoms. It has a recessed second-story side porch reminiscent of southern houses. **29.** The Henry Runge house at 542 Lockerbie Street was built in 1894–95 and retains its original architectural details, including the wide front porch and gauged clapboard siding. **30.** Next door at 538 Lockerbie Street is a one-and-one-half-story brick cottage with tall four-over-four windows on the first floor, typical of many such buildings in the area. It dates from 1863.

OLD NORTHSIDE

Instead of approaching Old Northside from the Pennsylvania exit off Interstate 65, you can go north from Monument Circle on Meridian to St. Clair Street. Take it east to Delaware and go north about four blocks to your first stop. This large area, which extends from Twelfth to Sixteenth Street and from Pennsylvania to College Street, is best explored by car. The trip can take from twenty minutes to an hour.

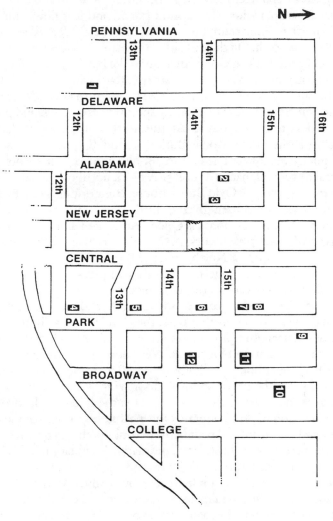

N →

PENNSYLVANIA

DELAWARE

ALABAMA

NEW JERSEY

CENTRAL

PARK

BROADWAY

COLLEGE

Old Northside

1. Benjamin Harrison built this house at 1230 North Delaware. It was designed by architect Herman T. Brandt in 1874–75. It is a fine brick Italianate with a wide wraparound porch, and it is now a museum. 2. Go north to Fourteenth Street, then east one block to Alabama, and turn left, or north. On the east side of the street is a pocket park called Shawn Grove Park. 3. Go north around the block to 1416 New Jersey where you will find a simple one-story cottage which has been moved to the site. Its front porch is decorated with carpenter's lacework. 4. Go south two blocks to Twelfth and turn east, or left, and proceed two blocks to Park Avenue. At the northwest corner of Park and Twelfth is the grand Morris-Butler Second Empire house at 1204. Designed by architect Diedrich A. Bohlen in 1864, it has a dominant central tower and mansard roof. 5. A block north on the same side of the street is 1306, the Ovid Butler house. Built originally in the Greek Revival style, it has been given a third story and some Queen Anne features. The carriage house is Queen Anne with asymmetrical elevations and detailed plasterwork. 6. One block farther north on the same side of the street is 1428 North Park, the Bross-Cline-Hilenberg house, built in 1905. This late Queen Anne house displays none of the fanciful embellishments of earlier houses of this style. It has a columned porch with pedimented entrance, second-story bay, and third-story dormer. 7. On the next corner north is 1504, the Von Hake-Rau house, one of the finest Queen Anne houses in the community. Much of the original terracotta decoration remains. 8. Next door at 1514 is the Italianate John B. Conner house, built about 1883. The second story retains its original style; the porch and first-floor windows are later revisions. 9. Across the street at 1553 North Park is the house built in 1888 by Alfred W. Coffin. This elaborate Queen Anne house with onion dome tower and a wraparound pedimented front porch was restored under the auspices of the Historic Landmarks Foundation of Indiana. 10. Proceed north to Sixteenth Street and east to Broadway. Go south a bit to 1531 Broadway, built in 1875 by Samuel Merrill. This fine Italianate house still retains its elegant iron-grille gate. 11. The fine Stick-style house at 1508 Broadway was built by Ovid Butler in 1876. Of particular note are the fancy third-floor bargeboard gable details, the first-floor bay window, and the nicely crafted front porch. 12. The Victorian Gothic house at 1422 North Broadway was built by Patrick H. Jameson in 1876. The tripartite porch and the griffins on the rooftop are plainly visible.

Festivals, Tours, and Other Places of Interest

The Historic Landmarks Foundation conducts customized tours, including a downtown walking tour, a highlights bus tour, and a bicycle tour, Kemper House, 1028 North Delaware Street, Indianapolis, IN; for information on the regularly scheduled tours and to discuss and make reservations call 317–639–4646. James Whitcomb Riley Lockerbie Street Home, open Tuesday–Saturday, 10:00 A.M.–4:00 P.M., Sunday noon–3:30 P.M., 528 Lockerbie, Indianapolis, IN, 317–631–5885. Indianapolis Museum of Art, open Tuesday–Sunday, 11:00 A.M.–5:00 P.M., Thirty-eighth and Michigan Road, Indianapolis, IN, 317–923–1331. Das Deutsch Haus-Athenaeum, a superb example of German Renaissance Revival architecture, designed by the Indianapolis architectural firm of Vonnegut and Bohn, 401 West Michigan, Indianapolis, IN, 317–636–0390. Indiana Historical Society, open Monday–Friday, 8:30 A.M.–5:00 P.M., Saturday 8:30 A.M.–4:00 P.M., 3315 West Ohio Street, Indianapolis, IN. Benjamin Harrison house, open Monday–Saturday, 10:00 A.M.–4:00 P.M., Sunday, 12:30 P.M.–4:00 P.M., 1230 North Delaware Street, Indianapolis, IN. Schnull-Rauch House, home of the Junior League, a house museum filled with original furnishings, building designed by Vonnegut and Bohn, 3060 North Meridian Street, Indianapolis, IN.

Historical Information

Historic Landmarks Foundation of Indiana, Kemper House, 1028 North Delaware Street, Indianapolis, IN 46202, 317–639–4646. City Center, 46 Monument Circle, Indianapolis, IN, 317–267–2960. Indianapolis Historic Preservation Commission, 1821 City-County Building, Delaware, Washington, and Alabama Streets, Indianapolis, IN 46204, 317–236–4406.

IX:I

Centerville

WAYNE COUNTY
Indiana

ENTERVILLE was platted in 1814. It was located on the National Road which brought prosperity through the 1850s. Centerville was home to future governors, statesmen, abolitionists, and writers, and thus gained an important role in the state and national life. Governor Oliver Morton, who kept Indiana on the Union side of the Civil War and was considered by some as second only to Lincoln as the savior of the Union, lived here, as did author Lew Wallace of *Ben Hur* fame.

Here among the antique shops you can see more Federal homes and townhouses than in most midwestern towns. Antique collectors will find Centerville a treasure trove.

Directions

You could spend a pleasant weekend in fall or spring visiting the east-central Indiana towns of Brookville, Metamora, Oldenburg, and Centerville. From Chicago go east on Interstates 80 and 90 to Interstate 65 south to Indianapolis. Take Interstate 70 east from Indianapolis to the Centerville exit. Go south into Centerville. From Richmond, U.S. 40, the old National Road, leads directly to Centerville. It is the latter's main street.

ARCHITECTURAL TOUR

If you are approaching from the Interstate exit, you would turn east, or left, onto Main Street at the stoplight, the only one in town. Proceed one and a half blocks to Mansion House. From Richmond on the old National Road, Mansion House would be on your right soon after entering the town. 1. Mansion House, 214 East Main Street, was a tavern and inn serving travelers on the National Road. The present building was built in 1840 by Henry Rowan. It is a Federal–Greek Revival four-story building. Mansion House is owned by and serves as the headquarters for Historic Centerville.

2. On the same side of the street in an unprepossessing building is the City Hall. **3.** Proceed westward through the traffic-light intersection and pause just beyond the northwest corner of Main and Morton. Look southeast toward 107 South Morton and its companion row houses. These Federal-style houses were probably built in early 1840. **4.** Across Main Street on the southwest corner of Main and Morton is the American house, a three-story Greek Revival building erected in 1837. **5.** At 119 West Main on the south side of the street west of the American house is the Dill-Donnelly house, a two-story white brick terrace house. **6.** The Raridan tenement at 118 West Main was constructed in 1835 and was the first Centerville house to be renovated, in 1963. It is a Federal-style house. **7.** The Pritchett house at 122 West Main is a Federal-style house. The handsome Grecian entry leads to the central hall, flanked by double parlors. **8.** The Bloomfield-Franz house, next door, was built about 1835. This Federal-style house has a nice fanlight over the front door which was installed when the house was renovated about 1978. **9.** Across Main Street from the Pritchett house is the Morris-Gregg-Wheeler house. It has a fine Grecian doorway with transom and side lights dating from 1835. The original facade remains intact. **10.** Next door at 137 West Main is the Julian-Hamilton house. The door and the paneled doorjamb outlining the entry are original refinements. **11.** On the southwest corner of Spruce and Main, the Woods-Hohenstein house is Federal-style with a fine six-over-six window sash on the second story. **12.** On the northwest corner of Spruce and Main across from the previous house is the Gentry house. It is Federal-style with a restored facade. **13.** The second house west is the Gentry-Eichorn house. The original building is the gable end facing the street. The ell to the west is a recent addition. **14.** Farther west is 214 West Main. This Greek Revival townhouse is divided into two parts connected by a spanner arch. It has an excellent Grecian Doric cornice and paneled door entry. The easternmost building was built by Samuel Abrahams in 1825. **15.** Next door the Swain-Jones home is another Federal-style house. **16.** Across the intersection on the southwest corner of Main and Ash is a one-and-one-half-story Pennsylvania Dutch-type house built about 1835, a style that was rarely built in the Middle West in this period. Its dormer windows appear to be the originals. **17.** At the end of the block is the O.P. Morton house at 313 West Main Street. Its facade is intact. The Greek Revival house was built by Jacob Julian in 1847. The yellow brick house seems to have its original facade. **18.** The Jacob Julian house at 116 East Plum was completed in 1857. The house is a combination of Federal and Italianate styles. **19.** The Old Cemetery is north of the railroad tracks between Spruce and Morton.

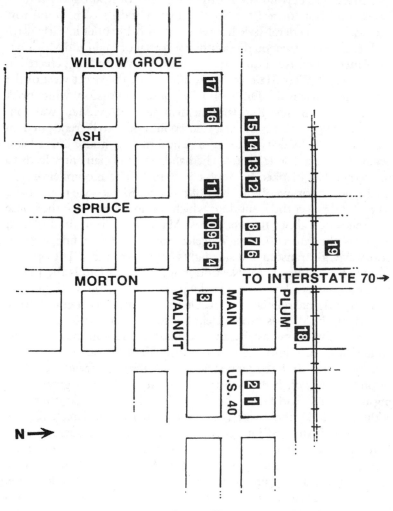

Centerville

Historical Information

Historic Centerville, provides a map and information, P.O. Box 73, Centerville, IN 47330, 317–855–3014. Gertrude Ward, Box 14, Centerville, IN 47330, 317–855–2621. Inezetta Stiver, 116 East Plum Street, Centerville, IN 47330, 317–855–5387. The Public Library, on the south side of Main just west of the intersection with Morton, also distributes the Historic Centerville map along with a booklet compiled by Stephen D. Jones describing the historic buildings.

Lodging

A & H Motel, National Road, Centerville, 317–966–6907.

Budget Motel, Centerville Road North and Interstate 70, 317–855–7039.

City View Motel, National Road, 317–962–2943.

Richmond Motel, National Road, 317–855–5616.

IX:2

Brookville

FRANKLIN COUNTY
Indiana

ANY historic small towns grow, but Brookville did not. In fact, its population has decreased amazingly. In the 1820s Brookville was the cultural, political, and social center of the new state and had a population of 10,000. Today this recreational center for water sports and hunting has only 3,000 inhabitants.

Evidence of mound builders has been found here. These mounds, predating the Indians, were spaced so that the builders could send smoke signals up and down the Whitewater valley.

Directions

You might spend a delightful weekend visiting Centerville, Brookville, Metamora, and Oldenburg. You can reach Brookville via U.S. 52 eight miles east of Metamora or U.S. 27 south from Richmond to State Route 101.

ARCHITECTURAL TOUR

1. The Old Cemetery dates from 1855. **2.** The Governor James B. Ray house was built in 1821. Located on the south side of Tenth Street between Franklin and Short, it is of clapboard construction and is currently painted gray. **3.** At 911 Main Street is a fine Classical Revival house with an impressive circular columned porch on the front. **4.** Next door at the corner of Ninth, at 901 Main, is the Tyner house. It has an elaborate Corinthian column entrance and a two-story wraparound porch. **5.** At Main just north of Eighth Street on the east side is the dignified Greek Revival brick Goodwin house. **6.** Across the street at 814 is a brick Italianate house with white trim. It has small porches on the north and south sides and bay windows on the first and second floors. **7.** The Franklin County Seminary, built between 1828 and 1831, is on Fifth Street just east of Mill Street. It is Federal-style with Greek Revival doors. **8.** On High Street as it bends eastward south of Third Street is the white clapboard two-story

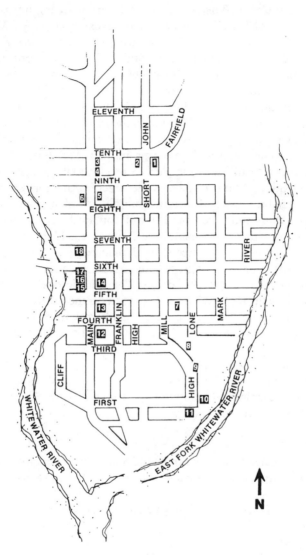

Brookville

Carpenter–Builder house in which Lew Wallace, author of *Ben Hur*, was born in 1827. **9.** The Noble family home at 353 High was built in 1831. It is a brick Italianate house. **10.** Next door is St. Michael's Catholic Church, a Gothic Revival structure built in 1862. **11.** Across High on the southwest corner we find St. Michael's Convent, a fine brick structure that is almost completely obscured by stately old trees. **12.** At the southeast corner of Fourth and Main Streets is a fine Second Empire brick building. **13.** On Main between Fourth and Fifth Streets on the east side stands the elaborate Classical Revival Franklin County courthouse. Its recessed entrance is highlighted by two-story Ionic columns. It has a prominent clock tower. **14.** At the northeast corner of Main and Fifth Streets is a three-story Georgian Revival bank building. **15.** Across the street on the northwest corner is the Franklin County Insurance building, which has a limestone front on Main and a red brick facade on Fifth. It has touches of Italianate and also of Romanesque Revival. **16.** North on the same side of Main is a gray three-story Italianate commercial building. **17.** The next three buildings, 528–560 Main, are additional examples of commercial Italianate buildings. The middle one has an ornate white pediment. **18.** At Main and Seventh on the southwest corner is another Italianate commercial brick building with an elaborate cornice and pediment as well as interesting window treatment.

Historical Information

Historic Hoosier Hills, P.O. Box 407, Versailles, IN 47042, 812–689–6456. Chamber of Commerce, Fifth and Court Streets, Brookville, IN 47012, 317–647–3177.

Lodging

Inn of Connersville, 37th Street and State Route 1, Connersville, IN 47331, 317–825–7531, 800–322–9764 (Indiana), 800–826–2573 (elsewhere).

Willhite's Tourist Home, 1049 Main Street, 317–647–6690.

Restaurants

Hertel's Restaurant, 370 Main, 317–647–4711, handicapped accessible.

Thies Restaurant, U.S. 52 south of Brookville, 317–647–7911, handicapped accessible.

IX:3

Metamora

FRANKLIN COUNTY
Indiana

THIS town, which was founded in 1811, is not known for its old buildings. The attraction here is the reconstructed canal and its buildings. The Whitewater canal connected Hagerstown via Metamora with Lawrenceburg on the Ohio River. This seventy-six-mile engineering feat dropped about 470 feet and included fifty-six locks, seven feeder dams, and twelve aqueducts or flumes. Metamora has a duplicate of the original 1836 "Benjamin Franklin" which carries the modern traveler the old way—with two horses on the towpath pulling the boat. The canal crosses Duck Creek on a covered aqueduct. The children will love this well-re-created boat ride. You can combine it with a trip on a steam train from Connersville.

Directions

You can combine a trip to Metamora with a visit to the quaint German village of Oldenburg. Metamora is reached by U.S. 52 southeast from Indianapolis and by State Route 229 north from Oldenburg to U.S. 52. Take the latter one mile east to Metamora.

ARCHITECTURAL TOUR

Turn south off U.S. 52 on either Columbus Street, the easternmost approach, or Clayborn Street, the westernmost. Parking can be found off Clayborn, or you can proceed to the canal on Columbus Street. The tour will take you along the canal, and, if you desire, two blocks north of it. The architectural tour includes all the buildings of architectural merit. 1. The grist mill, located between Main Street and the canal, was built in 1845 by Jonathan Banes. 2. Jonathan Banes' home is a two-story brick Federal-style house. It was built about 1840. 3. The Odd Fellows Lodge, the only three-story building in Metamora, was built in 1853. 4. The two-story frame Federal-style commercial building next door dates from 1848. 5. The structure now housing the Mill Street Gallery was built in the 1880s. 6. On the southwest

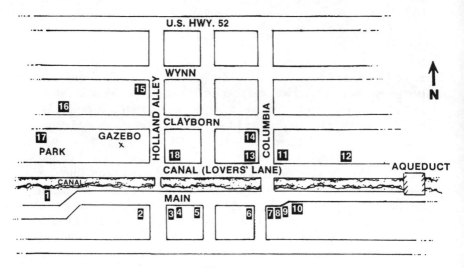

Metamora

corner of Columbia and Main is another nineteenth-century functional commercial building. This one has a heavily bracketed cornice and was built in 1885 by Alfred Blacklidge. **7.** Across the street on the southeast corner is the Greek Revival Masonic Lodge, built in the 1870s. **8.** Van Camp's drugstore, an Italianate commercial building, dates from the 1850s. **9.** Martindale Confectionery is an Italianate commercial building that was constructed in the 1850s. **10.** Martindale Hotel, a Federal-style structure, was built in 1838 by Ezekial Tyner and expanded to the west in the 1870s. **11.** The old Faulkner-Pierce drugstore was constructed in 1840. The front part of the Italianate building is the older part; the back half was built after 1865. **12.** The Greek Revival Metamora Christian Church was built in 1871. Its most prominent feature is the square tower. **13.** On the northwest corner of Lovers' Lane and Columbia across from the Canal House is the old cobbler's house and shop, built in the Federal style about 1850. **14.** At the southwest corner of Columbia and Clayborn Streets is the old blacksmith's shop. **15.** At the southwest corner of Wynn Street and Holland Alley is the Greek Revival Methodist Episcopal Church, built in 1853 and remodeled in 1886. **16.** The Walker Brothers distillery warehouse was built in the 1850s on Clayborn west of Holland Alley. **17.** A little west and across Clayborn is a pink Victorian Italianate–Queen Anne-style house, built in the early 1870s by Monroe Allison. Its nine rooms are on six different levels. Seven different carpenter's lace patterns, all from different railroad stations, decorate its eaves. It is crowned by an enclosed cupola. **18.** Cut across the park to Canal Street, where you will find the renovated Farmers Bank. You can recross the park and walk across the bridge to the mill where you started.

Festivals, Tours, and Other Places of Interest

Whitewater Valley Railroad runs weekends, May–early November and on Memorial Day, Independence Day, Labor Day, from Connersville to Metamora via Laurel and returns, P.O. Box 406, Connersville, IN 47331, 317–825–2054. The canal boat, a duplicate of the 1836 "Benjamin Franklin," is boarded from Lovers' Lane just east of Columbia Street, Metamora, IN 47030.

Historical Information

Historic Hoosier Hills, P.O. Box 407, Versailles, IN 47042, 812–689–6456. Merchants Association of Metamora, P.O. Box 117, Metamora, IN 47030. Whitewater Canal, State Historic Site, P.O. Box 88, Metamora, IN 47030, 317–647–6512.

Lodging

Publick House, corner of Columbia and Clayborn Streets, 317–647–3415.

Thorpe House, Clayborn Street one block north of the canal foot bridge, 317–647–5425 or 317–932–2365.

Restaurants

Hearthstone, U.S. 52 and the Millville Locks, 317–647–5204.

Thorpe House, Clayborn Street, 317–647–5425 or 317–932–2365.

IX:4
Oldenburg
FRANKLIN COUNTY
Indiana

THE wonderfully varied background of early mid-America comes vividly alive to the Oldenburg visitor. The town is a piece of old Germany and its tidy look is enhanced by brick sidewalks, colorful flower boxes, hand-tooled tin facades, and hilly tree-shaded streets.

The Convent of the Immaculate Conception stands guard over the town, and the gentle Franciscan nuns welcome a chance to show visitors their handsome chapel, by appointment.

Directions

You could spend a most pleasant weekend touring Oldenburg and Metamora. From Indianapolis take Interstate 74 southeast to State Route 229 at Batesville and proceed north for about two miles. Another route from Metamora: take U.S. 52 west a mile to State Route 229 and go south on it to Oldenburg. This is the scenic approach.

ARCHITECTURAL TOUR

Note that there are no street numbers and the buildings are not open to the public. The tour, which takes about an hour, begins at the Holy Family School playground which provides parking when school is not in session. 1. The Italianate Peter Benz house, just east of the parking lot on the south side of the street, was built in the 1880s. 2. Proceed east, skipping the next house to the third house, which was built about 1865 by Phillip Dickman. The facade is original. 3. Proceed east across Washington Street, or Washington Strasse. Still on the south side of Main, the third house from the corner is a plain brick one, built about 1860, whose facade is original. 4. Next door is the Kellerman house, built in 1860; the second story and gambrel roof were added in 1902. 5. Across the street on the north side of Main, the second house east of Washington belonged to Joseph Brink. This long, narrow brick house was built about 1870. 6. Next door, on

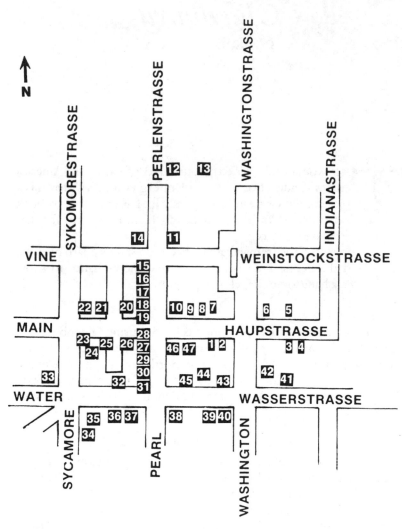

Oldenburg

the northeast corner of Main and Washington, is the Kessing Post Office. **7.** On the north side of Main across Washington is the Convent and Academy of the Immaculate Conception. This large Victorian Romanesque structure, designed by Oscar Bohlen, was built between 1899 and 1901. **8.** Next door is the Convent Chapel, designed by D.A. Bohlen of Indianapolis. The facade, except for the front doors, is original. **9.** Adjacent is the Bunnemeyer house, built about 1860. **10.** On the northeast corner of Pearl and Main is Scheper Store—Farmers and Merchants Bank, built about 1855. It has pressed-metal ornamentation by Casper Gaupel. Currently it is the headquarters of the Oldenburg Preservation Association. **11.** At the northeast corner of Pearl and Vine are the remains of the convent wall through which one can see the convent grounds. **12.** Farther out on Pearl are the Holy Family Cemetery and Chapel. **13.** The Convent Cemetery and Mortuary Chapel was built in 1900 by Oscar Bohlen, who designed the Convent and Academy about the same time. The Fatima Shrine was donated by the Henry Wolfrum family in 1950. **14.** On the northwest corner of Pearl and Vine is the Ortman cottage, built about 1870. It has an ornate porch and saltbox roof. **15.** Across the street on the southwest corner of Vine and Pearl is the Herman House, built about 1870. It has an ornate, pressed-metal cornice and tile roof on its "summer kitchen" behind the house. **16.** Next door, on the west side of Pearl Street, is the Drees house, built about 1870, which has an original facade. **17.** Next is the town park, which was platted as a public square in 1837. **18.** The adjacent building is the Hackman store barn, which dates from the 1880s. **19.** On the northwest corner of Main and Pearl stands the Hackman-Munchel store, built in 1851–62. This red brick Italianate commercial building is the largest secular structure in the town. The elaborate white-painted metal ornamental work on the first-floor and second-story windows was designed by master tinsmith Caspel Gaupel in 1890 and has a Germanic flavor. Notice the three bay windows on the second story. In 1897 a house was added at the west end and in 1910 a porch. **20.** On the northeast corner of St. Joseph and Main you will see a double house, built about 1860 and known as the Sellmeyer-Burdick-Heppner house. **21.** Across St. Joseph on the northwest corner is the Sellmeyer-Burdick-Wagner building. This Italianate building has an ornate cornice and pediment and cast-iron first-floor facade. **22.** Next we find the Heppner house, built in the 1850s; its facade was remodeled in 1900. **23.** Across Main on the south side is the Stone house, built of local limestone in the 1850s. The brick addition on the east dates from the 1890s. **24.** The adjacent barn was built about 1900 by Joseph Freihage. **25.** On the southwest corner of Main and St. Joseph was the 1870s tinsmith shop of Gaupel and Schmidt which produced so much of the ornamentation for the town's buildings. Its original ornate pressed-metal facade has been removed. **26.** Continue east on the south side of Main. The Dahmus Hoelker house, built about 1860, was remodeled in 1900 with the addition of the Classical porch and second story. **27.** Next to it is the brick Peine carriage house which sports an ornate Gaupel cornice. This building dates from 1890. **28.** The Fette-Peine house on the southwest corner of Main and Pearl, facing Pearl, was built between 1850 and 1855. The facade was changed in 1882 to the present simple frame with elaborate porch entry. **29.** South on the west side of Pearl Street lies the Francis Hohman saloon, now called King's Tavern, built about 1850. The Gaupel cornice, window hoods, and embossed sign were added in the 1890s. **30.** The Town Hall and Fire Station is an Italianate building with prominent bell tower. The original building dates from 1878. **31.** On the northwest corner of Pearl and Water we find one of the town's earliest extant buildings, the Joseph Huegel house, built in 1845. It is the largest stone house in town. **32.** West on Water Street on the north side there still exists a wattle-and-daub-walled house dating from the 1840s. It is called the Moorman house. **33.** West on the northwest corner of Water and Sycamore is the Clem Fischer blacksmith shop, built in 1908. **34.** South of Water on Sycamore on the east side is the Kamp-Blank house, built in the 1850s. The older west residential wing is of limestone and the newer wing is of brick. **35.** North of the latter a paved creek bed was built about 1860 to restrain the brook. **36.** Proceeding east on the south side of Water Street is Stuerwald's general store and tavern, which has a shallow front porch. **37.** Next door is the Conrad Huerman house, a timber-frame building dating from the 1840s. It has a saltbox roof and two front doors. **38.** The famed tinsmith Caspel Gaupel's house is located on the southeast corner of Pearl and Water Streets. When built in 1850, it was on the north side of Water Street. **39.** The sixth house east on the south side of Water is the Henry Kleinmeyer house, built about 1840. **40.** Next door is Eberhard Waechter's cradle shop, built in 1845 of timber frame with wattle-and-daub walls. It now houses a museum. **41.** East of the Washington intersection on Water is the Water Street stone bridge, a limestone structure with a perfect barrel vault, built about 1880. **42.** The Kuntz-Kellerman store at the northeast corner of Washington and Water and facing Washington was built about 1840. It is a simple Federal-style building with an 1895 addition whose ornate cornice spells out "Kellerman" on the embossed pediment. **43.** Across Washington on the northwest corner of Water and Washington is the Waechter-Schmidt-Hoelker house, built in 1864. This simple Federal-style house originally had a two-story Greek Revival porch. The gabled Queen Anne eastern section was added around 1900. **44.** The Dickman-Knights' building, farther west on Water, was built around 1870. The facade is original. **45.** Next door is the former Horst blacksmith shop, built around 1870. **46.** On the southeast corner of Main and Pearl is the Holy Family Church, built in 1862. The stained-glass windows were added in 1919, and the spire was enlarged and heightened in 1890. There have been some interior changes, but the fine Gothic altars are original. It is similar to many other German Catholic churches in southern Indiana because of its Gothic Revival style in red brick. **47.** Holy Family School, just east on Main, is a Jacobean Revival building erected in 1932 and designed by Werking and Sons of Richmond, Indiana.

Festivals, Tours, and Other Places of Interest
Convent and Academy of the Immaculate Conception, tours can be arranged by appointment, Main and Washington, Oldenburg, IN 47036, 812–934–2475.

Historical Information
Oldenburg Preservation Association provides a walking-tour map with text by William Selm, Indiana Farmers and Merchants State Bank Building, northeast corner of Main and Pearl Streets, Oldenburg, IN 47036.

Restaurants
Koch's Brau Haus, Wasser Strasse, 812–934–4840.

IX:5
Madison

JEFFERSON COUNTY
Indiana

ADISON was established early in the 1800s, and its prime location on the Ohio River made it a bustling port through the middle of the nineteenth century. Some years ago, however, the small and no longer prosperous town faced up to a question that confronts many towns. Should it opt for development or put its energy and resources into preservation? Madison chose to restore. The credit for sparking this revival goes to John Windle, who came to Madison in 1948 and founded Historic Madison, Inc., in 1960. Looking at Madison you see that one person can make a difference.

Located halfway between Cincinnati, Ohio, and Louisville, Kentucky, this small town contains one of the finest collections of nineteenth-century American architecture to be found in the Midwest. It is a town restored to museum quality, but it does not exist as a mere exhibit, for most of the buildings are in use. The town boasts grand houses like the splendid Lanier mansion and the handsome Sullivan and Shrewsbury homes as well as more modest residential and commercial buildings.

Directions
This town is well worth a weekend. If you can spare more time, you will enjoy seeing the other southeastern Indiana towns of Rising Sun, Aurora, and Lawrenceburg. Madison is a five-and-one-half-hour trip from Chicago via Interstates 80 and 90 east to south Interstate 65 to Columbus and then southeast on State Route 7. You may also continue on Interstate 65 to Scottsburg and meander east on State Route 56. Either way you will get a good view of the southern Indiana countryside.

ARCHITECTURAL TOURS
The walking tour of the town is divided into two two-hour tours: west and east. The city has converted almost every corner in town to a

ramp for ease in touring by wheelchair. Madison is a treasure. Keep your eyes open, for we note only the outstanding examples of its remarkable architecture. The streetscape in many blocks presents a beautifully preserved view of Federal and Greek Revival townhouses, and along Main Street, particularly above the first floor, the fanciful commercial architecture of the mid- and late-nineteenth century. Unless otherwise specified, buildings are not open to the public.

WEST TOUR

This tour begins in the city parking lot on West Main and Poplar Streets. 1. The Jeremiah Sullivan house, 304 West Second Street, was Madison's first mansion. The brick house was built in 1818 and is unchanged architecturally. Note the fine fanlight over the entrance. Considered one of the best examples of the Federal style in the Northwest Territory, it is open to the public. 2. The Schofield house at 217 West Second, built in 1817, is another fine Federal-style home. It, too, is open to the public. 3. Another Federal-style building is the Talbott-Hyatt house at 301 West Second, built about 1820. This handsome white-painted brick house, owned by Historic Madison, Inc., has gardens and outbuildings restored to their original design. It is open to the public. 4. Farther south on Poplar and First Streets is the Shrewsbury house, designed in 1846–49 by Francis Costigan in the Regency style. Costigan studied with America's most highly educated architect, Benjamin Henry Latrobe, who established Greek Revival architecture in this country. This grand house has a famous freestanding spiral staircase and handsomely proportioned rooms. Today, it is a museum open to the public. 5. West on the north side of First Street is the white Classical Revival Presbyterian Church, built in 1846. Its bell tower is reminiscent of Christopher Wren's style. 6. North on Elm and Second, one block away, is the Colonial Inn. 7. Still farther west at 511 West First Street is the grandest of Madison's homes, the James F.D. Lanier Memorial, a Francis Costigan masterpiece in the Classical Revival style. Built at the height of Madison's prosperity, 1840–44, it not only has a handsome interior and exterior but also has splendid landscaping which features an extensive lawn rolling down to the river. The house is open to the public. 8. The octagonal building on First Street, which can be seen from the Lanier garden, was the Pennsylvania Railroad's third passenger station. Its unique shape is repeated in the second-story cupola. 9. The Trolley barn, two blocks north on Main at 715, housed trolley cars that ran the length of Main Street on rails in the nineteenth century. Immediately west is an example of facade preservation through Historic Madison. 10. Directly across Main Street at 718 is the Greek Revival Holstein-Whitsitt house, designed in 1840 by Francis Cos-

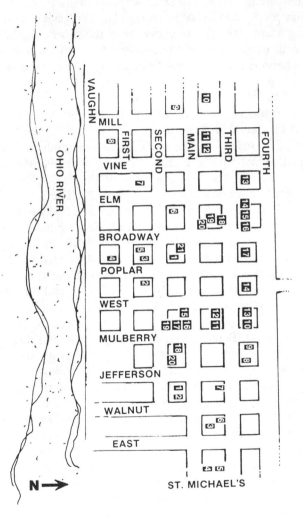

Madison

tigan. The house is reminiscent of the New England townhouses found in Salem, Portsmouth, and Kennebunk which were designed by Costigan's contemporaries Bullfinch and McIntyre. **11.** Farther east on the north side of Main Street at 620 is a fine red brick Italianate villa, remarkable for the iron lacework on its front and the iron fence enclosing the lawn. Note also the heavy brackets holding up the roof. **12.** The house at 610 Main was the home of Abraham Lincoln's half-sister, Mrs. Helms, during the Civil War. The house is less grand than its neighbor, with which it shares the front fence. It has a modest porticoed entrance, limestone lintels, and a beaded white cornice. **13.** In the next block east at 408 Third Street is the home of the famous architect Francis Costigan, who designed numerous homes, churches, and commercial buildings in southeastern Indiana. His own home was built in 1849. In its facade there are three large six-over-six windows and a prominent Corinthian-columned portico. **14.** In the next block east at 312 West Third Street is the house of Jesse Bright. It has been remodeled. **15.** Built in 1837, 310 West Third Street has maintained its original design. **16.** The houses on the west side of Broadway north of Third Street are excellent examples of Madison architecture in the 1830s. **17.** East of Broadway on Third is an early Methodist Chapel named for Bishop Roberts. **18.** The Baltimore-style house of John Paul's wife, built in 1837, is located at 419 Broadway. **19.** In the mid-block south on Broadway is the Trinity Methodist Church, a Norman–Gothic building dating from 1873. **20.** The ornate fountain in the middle of Broadway in front of the Methodist church was presented by the French Republic in 1876 to the Philadelphia Centennial Exposition. **21.** The iron storefronts in the Italianate style dating from the 1850s give Madison's Main Street commerical area an architecture reminiscent of the heyday of the steamboat.

EAST TOUR

This walking tour starts in the city parking lot at Jefferson and Second Streets. As you walk north on Jefferson, note that there are early commercial buildings on both sides of the street, and there is an English archer tower on top of the Knights of Pythias building at 314 Jefferson. **1.** The Jefferson County courthouse, built in 1854–55, is a fine example of the Greek Revival style. Look west across Main Street and note the fine four-story Second Empire Masonic building. **2.** The three-story Italianate building at 325 East Main has a dark cornice and white-painted brick facade. The window hoods are distinctive. **3.** The Madison Volunteer "Fair Play" Fire House was built in the 1880s in the style of Italianate Renaissance towers. It has an 1850s hand-drawn fire engine and the remarkable "Little Jimmy" weathervane. **4.** St.

Michael's Catholic Church, designed by Costigan and built in stages
from 1838 to 1839, is north of Main Street on St. Michael's Street. This
Romanesque Revival church is built of limestone. **5.** St. Michael's
rectory is an adaptation of the Pope's garden house at Villa Lante. It is
made of limestone. **6.** Note the old brick buildings on either side of
Third Street as it approaches Jefferson. **7.** The house with Italianate
cornices at the southeast corner of Jefferson and Third is a good
example of this style. **8.** Turning north on Jefferson, notice the
Federal house at 521, embellished with Classical Revival columns and
Romantic-era ironwork. The rear addition dates from the 1850s.
9. One block over on Mulberry Street is Christ Episcopal Church,
built in 1847–48 in the English Gothic style. Notice the handmade
locks and bricks. **10.** Taking Mulberry Street to Third, you will find
a Romanesque Revival painted brick building, erected about 1832.
11. The 1819 building at 108 Third Street shows the influence of
settlers from the southern states. **12.** Fine examples of the Federal
style are at 104 and 106 Third Street. **13.** The auditorium at the corner
of Third and West was built in 1835 as the Second Presbyterian
Church. This Greek Revival building was designed by Edwin J. Peck
and is now the headquarters of Historic Madison, Inc., the institution
that has sparked the renovation of the town. Its fine pediment and
columned portico across the front give it noble proportions. **14.** A
half block west on Third Street is the William Hutchings office and
hospital. This small Federal-style building, restored by Historic Madison, Inc., is open to the public. **15.** Note storefronts on Main Street
with fluted-iron columns dating from the 1850s. **16.** More cast-iron
storefronts on Main and Mulberry Streets, carved to resemble stone,
show the popularity of the Italianate style in the 1850s. **17.** Turn south
onto Mulberry Street and walk on the east side of the street to get the
best view of the buildings, most of which date from the 1830s and are
unaltered. This was the avenue from the river wharf to the center of
town. The first floor was commercial, and the second and third
residential. **18.** The 1850s building at 316 Mulberry has its original
facade. **19.** The Central Hotel at the corner of Mulberry and Second
Streets is Italianate in style.

Festivals, Tours, and Other Places of Interest

Madison Tour of Homes, the last weekend in September every
other year, Friday and Saturday 10:00 A.M.–6:00 P.M., Sunday
noon–6:00 P.M.; for details write to Madison Tour of Homes, Box
273, Madison, IN 47250. Candlelight Tour of Historic Homes, last
weekend in November and first weekend in December; for information contact the Chamber of Commerce, 301 East Main Street,
Madison, IN 47250, 812–265–2956. The *Delta Queen*, the last of

the stern-wheeler boats carrying passengers, makes regular stops at Madison.

Historical Information

River Village: Gateway to the West (1976) by Francis K. Eisan. Historic Madison, Inc., 500 West Street, Madison, IN 47250, 812–265–2967. Madison Area Chamber of Commerce, tour maps available, walking tours east and west, 301 East Main, Madison, IN 47250, 812–265–2956. Historic Hoosier Hills, P.O. Box 407, Versailles, IN 47042, 812–689–6456. Jefferson County Historical Society Museum, open 1:00 P.M.–4:00 P.M., Monday and Friday, Elm Street, Madison, IN 47250.

Lodging

Clifty Inn, Box 387, Clifty Falls State Park, State Routes 56 and 107, 812–265–4135.

Hereford Motor Inn and Lounge, 700 Clifty Drive, 812–273–5151.

Hillside Inn, 831 East Main, 812–265–3221.

President Madison Motel, 906 East First Street, 812–265–2361.

Victoria Inn, 801 East Main, 812–265–2471.

Restaurants

Coach House, Cragmont and Third Streets, 812–265–4026, handicapped accessible.

Key West Shrimp House, 117 Ferry Street, 812–265–2831.

Sirloin Stockade, 746 Clifty Drive, 812–273–5699, handicapped accessible.

Steer, 730 Clifty Drive, 812–273–4386, handicapped accessible.

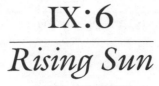

IX:6

Rising Sun

OHIO COUNTY
Indiana

THE first documented white settlement started in 1798 when Samuel Fulton, an uncle of the first steamboat constructor Robert Fulton, and his family arrived. The thriving riverport welcomed steamers and flatboats and had such taverns as "Red Hell" and "Blue Ruin." So prosperous was the riverport that local businessmen did not even consider trying to lure the railroad. Hard times ensued when the river traffic dried up. As a result, Rising Sun's architecture was not replaced. Currently a modest prosperity has returned.

Directions

You could spend a most pleasant weekend visiting the southeastern Indiana river towns of Rising Sun, Aurora, and Lawrenceburg. Or, if time permitted, you could include these towns with a visit to Madison, Indiana. Take Interstates 80 and 90 east to south Interstate 65. Get off I–65 on Interstate 74 eastbound to State Route 1 and go to U.S. 50 south through Lawrenceburg and Aurora. Take State Route 56 south along the Ohio River to Rising Sun. You will be on High Street; turn left toward the river on First Street. At the Riverside Park you will be able to park your car and walk the architectural tour or board the trolley for a view of the town. This is also the Rising Sun Marina and landing point for the *Hoosier Belle*. If you are coming from Madison take State Route 56 east to Vevay, where you can continue the short route via State Route 56 to Rising Sun or take State Route 156, which parallels the river. You will now be on Walnut Street, one block east of High Street. Turn right, or east, on First and proceed to the riverside park.

ARCHITECTURAL TOUR

You might consider taking a trolley ride through the historic district before you walk it. It operates on Saturdays and Sundays. This will give you a feel for the town and make the leisurely hour-long walk more enjoyable. **1.** A good place to start is the Ohio County Historical Society Museum at 216 Walnut. **2.** The combination Greek Revival–Italianate Whitlock house at 301 South Walnut was built in the 1860s. Whereas the porch is obviously an addition, the rest of the facade is original. **3.** Next door at 307 South Walnut is the Carpenter–Builder Whitlock house. Built in 1887, it has many Eastlake details such as the carpenter's lacework decorating the small entrance porch and the front gable. This house has an open "Front Parlor" that displays quilts. **4.** In the next block on the other side of the street at 410 South Walnut is a fine Greek Revival one-story house, built in the 1870s. It has an enclosed cupola atop its bracketed roof. As the house is a late example of this style, it also has an Eastlake porch replete with fine carpenter's lacework. **5.** One block west, or left, is 412 South High Street, an Arts and Crafts-style house built in the 1920s. It is really a simplified Queen Anne with the variety of materials reduced: beautiful red tile roof, plain gables, bay windows, dormers, and a combination porch-terrace across the front. A transition house, it looks simultaneously backward and forward to the Prairie style. **6.** In the middle of the next block north at 310 South High is the Italianate Tumey-Matthews house, built about 1865. It has a bracketed roof and small cupola. The fancy Eastlake porch is an addition. **7.** Proceed north one and a half blocks to 116 South High, a fine Greek Revival house built in the 1860s. **8.** Go west, or right, on Second Street to 133 South Mulberry. On the east side you will find a Federal-style house with a wraparound porch. This clapboard house was built in the 1850s. **9.** A little north is the red brick Federal-style sheriff's house, built in the 1850s. This two-story, tree-shaded house has large three-over-three windows. In 1870 a jail was built on the rear of the house. **10.** Go one block left to 510 Main on the north side of the street. This fine Gothic Revival house has an elegant columned porch across the front, topped by an ironwork balustrade that makes a balcony for the second floor. The front door is topped by a transom and flanked by side windows. **11.** Go east on Main to the Greek Revival courthouse, built in 1845. The two-story portico is topped by a pediment and supported by four heavy columns. Each of the four county offices has outside entrances, for the courthouse has no corridors. Upcoming renovation may alter this, however. It is the oldest courthouse in the state in continuous use. **12.** One block east at 101 High Street at Main Street is a Queen Anne house built in the 1890s. A small Eastlake porch shelters the front door. There are gables and a two-story bay, but the most prominent feature is a three-story tower with a conical dome surmounted by a weathervane. **13.** A little north at 117 High is a fine red brick Italianate house with white trim, built in the 1890s. Its windows have heavy white hoods. Both

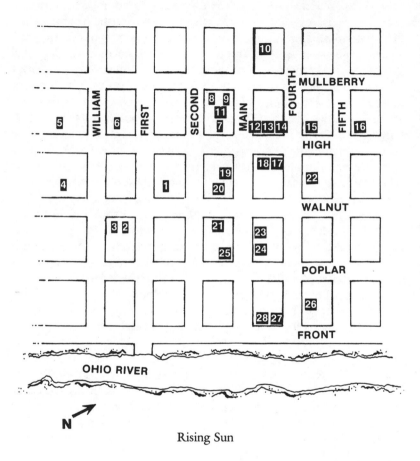

Rising Sun

the roof and the front bay have cornices. The elaborate carpenter's lacework on the small front entrance is repeated on the smaller side porch. **14.** Next door at 121 North High is a Greek Revival house with Italianate touches. The second story and the roof line reflect the original style. The porch across the front is an unfortunate addition. **15.** The Greek Revival house at 201 North High is well preserved. The front portico is supported by four large columns. An iron fence marks the property's boundaries. **16.** Farther north on High near Fifth at 301 North High is a Gothic Revival Church with a large tower from which protrude dormer windows on each side. This is the First United Church of Christ. **17.** Back toward Main on High Street, 112 North High is an Italianate house built in the 1880s. It has a front gable and an ornate front porch, topped by an iron balastrade. An ironwork fence parallels the sidewalk. **18.** Walking toward Main, you will see the 1916 Arts and Crafts-style Carnegie library. The building has an English basement with portico entrance on the second floor. Its large windows admit plenty of daylight. **19.** As you walk toward the river via Main Street, notice 311, a Greek Revival-style house with Italianate touches. Built in the 1860s, it has an Italianate bracketed roof and a recessed doorway and simple windows in the Greek Revival style. **20.** A few yards south of Main Street on Walnut is the 1865 Greek Revival Methodist Episcopal Church. The bracketed cornice is Italianate, but the facade pediment and the small entrance portico are Greek Revival. **21.** Across the street at 109 South Walnut is an Italianate house, built about 1875. This fine house has a bracketed roof, rounded windows, and a small entrance porch. **22.** In the second block north is 308 Fourth Street, a Federalist house built in 1832. The entrance pediment and stair railing have been changed, but otherwise the facade is original. **23.** Return to Main Street where at 220 you will find the Romanesque Revival First Presbyterian Church, begun in 1833 and completed in 1834. The square tower is flanked by protruding dormers. **24.** Also on the same side of the street is the Neoclassical National Bank building, dating from 1910. Four columns hold up its cornice, and a small pediment tops its entrance. **25.** On the southwest corner of Poplar and Main is the Italianate Gibson commercial building. This 1890s structure has a prominent bracketed cornice and hooded second-story windows. **26.** Turn left onto Poplar and go one block to Fourth. Take a right at Fourth and proceed toward the river to 104, a Federal-style house. This 1827 building is one of the oldest remaining structures. **27.** On the corner of Front and Fourth at 133 North Front is another early house, the 1827 Shadrach Hathaway house. This double house still retains its front gable fanlight and vestiges of its original facade, including wooden pegs holding the shutters and an arched carriage entrance. Notice the beautiful flowers and plantings. **28.** Next door is another Federal townhouse from the 1840s which is in better repair. The gem on the block is 127 North Front, built the same year in the same style. It has a transom fanlight with brass eagles and side windows flanking its entrance door. These Front Street townhouses are all that remain of the original part of town.

Festivals, Tours, and Other Places of Interest

Saturday and Sunday a trolley carries passengers through the historic district; see map for boarding places and route. On weekends the *Hoosier Belle*, a forty-eight-passenger ferry operates as a ferry, charter party boat, and dinner and moonlight cruise boat. Open weekends June–October, plying the river between Rising Sun and Rabbit Hash, Kentucky. Periodically the *B.B. Riverboat*, Cincinnati, Ohio, brings passengers from Cincinnati to tour Rising Sun and Rabbit Hash. Rising Sun Marina, Stewart Whitlock Landing, First and Front Street, Rising Sun, IN 47040.

Historical Information

Ohio County Historical Museum, open Sundays, 1:00 P.M.–4:00 P.M., June–October, or by appointment, 216 Walnut Street, Rising Sun, IN 47040. Ohio County Public Library, 100 High Street, Rising Sun, IN 47040. Rising Sun/Ohio County Tourism Bureau, P.O. Box 95, Rising Sun, IN 47040, 812–438–3751.

Lodging

Jelley House Country Inn, 222 Walnut, 812–438–2319.

Restaurants

Jack's Place, 406 Main, 812–438–3922, handicapped accessible.

Aurora

DEARBORN COUNTY
Indiana

AURORA is another river town on the banks of the Ohio. It was platted in 1819 and soon became a shipping center. The *Clinton* was constructed here in 1823–24 and ushered in the steamboat era on the Ohio River. During the Civil War, the enterprising boat builders produced the *Forest Queen*, which was the first steamer regularly to ply the river between Cincinnati and Madison. Many businesses started in the 1800s continue to thrive today, giving the town a nineteenth-century air.

Directions

You could combine a visit to Aurora with Lawrenceburg and Rising Sun and also take a trip on the Ohio River for a pleasant weekend. From Lawrenceburg take U.S. 50 south to Aurora. From Rising Sun take State Route 56 north.

ARCHITECTURAL TOUR

1. The Folbre-Scharf house at 311 Fourth Street is a Federal-style building erected about 1850. The house is raised from the street and entered by a double stairway carved of stone. The entrance porch is a more recent but compatible addition. **2.** The Gothic Revival Gaff-Conwell house at 305 Fourth Street was built about 1860. A wide porch spans the front and the roof line is punctuated by three gables. **3.** One block east at 211 Fourth Street is the United Presbyterian Church. This Greek Revival church was built between 1850 and 1856. It is capped by a plain pediment and a prominent clock tower which ends in a steeple. **4.** St. Mary's Catholic Church, located at 203 Fourth Street, was built between 1863 and 1876. This Gothic Revival church is reminiscent of many built in southeastern Indiana by German-American congregations. Like its counterpart in Oldenburg, it has a high steeple. It is the first of three churches in this style built in Aurora. The others, built in the mid-1870s, are St. John's Lutheran and the First Evangelical United Church of Christ. **5.** The house at

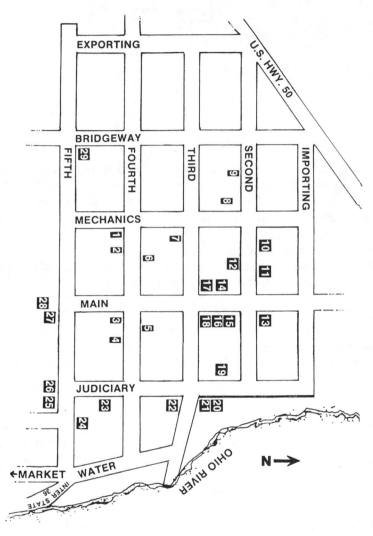

Aurora

220 Fourth Street is unusual for this area. It is an outstanding Queen Anne house with wraparound porch, large attic dormer, and three-story tower, built about 1900. It is known as the Howe-Hoskins-Hastings home. **6.** At 318 Fourth Street is the Gothic Revival First Baptist Church, built in 1938. **7.** The 1870 Dr. Harley Sutton office, now a home, at 315 Third Street is a Second Empire house. This small house has only one dormer protruding from its mansard roof, two large windows, and a recessed doorway on its facade. **8.** St. John's Lutheran Church, located at 214 Mechanic Street, is a Gothic Revival church, built in 1874. **9.** At 413 Second Street stands the Italianate Masonic Hall, built in the 1880s. **10.** At 320 Second Street is a Queen Anne commercial building, erected in 1885. The facade is enlivened by twin two-story bay windows and a balustrade outlining the roof. **11.** The commercial building at 316 Second Street, an example of Second Empire style, was erected about 1870. This three-story structure has four prominent dormers. **12.** Across the street at 321–25 Second Street we find the Levie, Parks, and Stapp Italianate opera house, built around 1875. **13.** At 222 Second Street is the Queen Anne Chambers, Stevens, & Company building, erected in 1900. **14.** The Italianate commercial building at 218–16 Main Street was erected about 1870. The second-story windows are framed by ornamental hoods. Two metal balconies are later additions. **15.** Across the street at 221 Main Street is a Greek Revival–Italianate commercial building, built between 1850 and 1880. **16.** Next door at 229–27 is a commercial building in the same popular style, erected around 1870. **17.** On the northwest corner of Main and Third at 306 Third Street is the Greek Revival First United Methodist Church, built between 1855 and 1862. The three large front windows are subdivided into glass triangles and topped by a fine pediment, from which rise a tower and steeple. **18.** On the northeast corner of Main and Third at 216 Third Street is the Romanesque Revival Aurora City Hall, built about 1890. Two large second-story windows and a pediment proclaiming its use form the facade. **19.** One block east at 214 Judiciary Street is a Federal-style house built in the 1850s. This is one of the few remaining early houses. **20.** On the east side of Judiciary Street north of the parking lot stands a historical marker on the site where the steamboat *Clinton* was built and launched in the years 1823–24. **21.** The 1848 Federal-style building at 203 Judiciary Street became the International Order of Odd Fellows hall. **22.** Across the street at 121 Third Street is the Federal-style Mueller hotel, built about 1845. **23.** At 403 Judiciary is a Gothic Revival–Queen Anne house built between 1870 and 1890. **24.** At 110 Fifth Street we find the Federal-style Stevens-Thatcher house, built in 1849. Its facade is marked by three windows on the second story, two on the first, and a recessed entrance with transom window. **25.** At 113

Fifth Street is the Gothic Revival First Evangelical United Church of Christ, which was built in the mid-1870s. **26.** The Thompson-Dean house at 115 Fifth Street is an example of the combination of Greek Revival and Italianate architecture. Built about 1845, it rises high above the street and has a fine Italianate porch whose roof is supported by columns. **27.** Another early building, the Kastner-McNimery Federal-style house, was built about 1840 at 205 Fifth Street. **28.** At the end of Main is 213 Fifth Street, the grand "Hillforest," built in the Italianate style between 1852 and 1856 by Thomas Gaff. It is the town's architectural gem and commands a magnificent view of the river, valley, and town. **29.** At 412 Fifth Street is the Hurlbert-Stiffler clapboard house, built about 1840. An example of the combination of Italianate and Greek Revival styles, this transitional house has a small Classical entrance portico.

Festivals, Tours, and Other Places of Interest

"Hillforest," open May 1–December 23, daily except Mondays, 1:00 P.M.–5:00 P.M. Eastern Standard Time, 213 Fifth Street, Aurora, IN 47001, 812–926–0087.

Historical Information, Lodging, Restaurants

See Lawrenceburg.

Lawrenceburg

DEARBORN COUNTY
Indiana

SETTLERS began to come down the Ohio River into this area in the 1790s. A steady stream of European settlers came from 1820 to 1870. The Irish came to dig the Whitewater canal. The Germans, who came to avoid military service and religious persecution, were skilled craftsmen. During the Civil War there was considerable upheaval, for citizens were not unanimous in supporting the Union. Confederate sympathizers provided rest and shelter for the foraging Morgan's Raiders. Today the town along the riverfront remains mostly untouched by recent history. It is supported by two large distilleries.

Directions

We suggest that you combine a trip to Lawrenceburg with a weekend visit to the two other nearby towns, Aurora and Rising Sun. From Chicago take Interstates 80 and 90 to Interstate 65 south to Indianapolis, then Interstate 74 southeast to the Saint Leon exit, which is State Route 1. Take it south to Lawrenceburg. Route 1 ends in U.S. 50, which is also Third Street. Take Third to Walnut, turn right to High Street, and turn right.

ARCHITECTURAL TOUR

The town's architecture ranges from Federal to Italianate and Romanesque, with a number of Greek Revival buildings. Although not all of the buildings have been renovated or maintained, this remains a collection of significant nineteenth-century structures. You should allow a little over an hour for a leisurely tour of the district. 1. The 1872 Dearborn County courthouse on High Street is a fine example of a Greek Revival public building. It is the best of architect George H. Kyle's buildings. He was a pupil of Francis Costigan, who built many of nearby Madison, Indiana's, handsome structures. The fluted Corinthian columns of the entrance portico are grand. The building is open from 8:30 A.M. to 4:30 P.M. daily. It is closed on Saturdays,

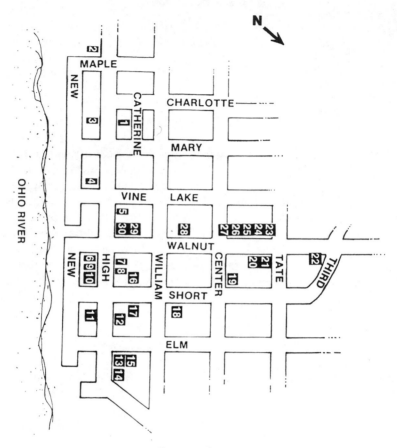

Lawrenceburg

Sundays, and holidays. **2.** Two blocks west at 508 West High Street stands one of the oldest houses in Lawrenceburg. The Federal-style structure was built in 1816 by Samuel C. Vance. **3.** The structure at 226–30 West High Street was built in 1866. It is a fine, sturdy brick building. **4.** The Greek Revival Hamline Chapel Methodist Church at 110 West High Street was erected in 1847. A heavy tower is its most prominent feature. **5.** The small Italianate house at 13 West High Street, built about 1844, has fancy window hoods and a bracketed roof line. **6.** The three-story Hunt House Inn, built in 1818, is at 6 East High Street on the corner of Walnut. **7.** Directly across High Street on the northeast corner is number 3, a Federal-style commercial building erected between 1830 and 1850. **8.** The next building, number 11, another Federal-style commercial building, was built around 1850. **9.** The Romanesque Revival Masonic temple at 12 East High Street was built in 1893. **10.** An 1852 Federal-style building is found at 14 East High Street. **11.** At 124–36 East High are Federal-style row houses dating from the 1830s. **12.** Isaac Dunn built the Federal/Italianate house at 133 East High Street in 1818. It has all sorts of later additions, such as the bay windows and moldings. **13.** Across the street facing Elm Street is the William O'Brien Greek Revival house at 108. It was built in 1840. In its facade you can see touches of the Italian villa style. **14.** The house at 227 East High Street is a large, white brick Federal-style structure, built in 1857–58. **15.** At 128 Elm Street is a small brick Federal house built about 1820 by Benjamin Spooner. **16.** In the middle of the block on the west side at 117 Short Street is the Italianate Carpenters' Union meeting hall, erected about 1860. **17.** Across the street at 124 is the Queen Anne fire station, built in 1885. A prominent bell tower tops its northeast corner. **18.** In the next block at 228 Short we find the Queen Anne 1882 Presbyterian church. The church has a large bell tower, double entrance, and various-sized windows. **19.** The First Southern Baptist Church at 31 East Center Street is a Greek Revival building dating from the 1850s. **20.** The commercial Italianate building at 316–18 Walnut was constructed in 1875. It is one of the many structures that were raised one floor toward the end of the nineteenth century. Such an engineering feat was common; the most celebrated of such activities was the raising of Chicago's Loop while business continued as usual. **21.** The Zion United Church of Christ at 340 Walnut is a Romanesque Revival building constructed in 1867. Unfortunately, the steeple is a modern prefab, but the front gable contains an original large, round window, and the eaves are decorated with dentils. **22.** St. Lawrence Catholic Church is at 548 Walnut Street. The Romanesque Revival building, with triple entrance and large central tower designed by architect Louis Riedinger, was constructed in 1867. **23.** At 331 Walnut stands J.P. Pfalzgraf's saloon, built in 1865. This Italianate commercial building retains its original ambiance. **24.** The small Federal-style house at 325 Walnut was built about 1830 and is one of the town's early structures. **25.** The three-story Italianate commercial building at 321 Walnut proudly proclaims the date of its origin, 1857, on its pediment. **26.** On the same side of the street is 317, a small Second Empire commercial structure with a bracketed cornice, erected in 1880. **27.** The next building, 315 Walnut, is another well-preserved Italianate commercial structure, erected in 1881. Above the first floor the facade is decorated with heavy window hoods, a pediment, and bracketed eaves. **28.** In the middle of the next block is the highly decorated Liedertafel Hall, which was built in 1893. **29.** The three-story Italianate commercial structure at 125 Walnut was built in 1855. **30.** Next door at 119 is a smaller Italianate commercial two-story building decorated with lintels and a nicely bracketed roof.

Historical Information

Chris McHenry, Dearborn County historian, 442 Wilson Creek Road, Aurora, IN 47001, 812–926–2006. The Dearborn County Historical Society museum, Mr. Lynn Slayback, director, open Monday–Friday, 9:30 A.M.–2:30 P.M., located in the courthouse at High and Mary Streets, 812–537–4075. Dearborn County Chamber of Commerce has Chris McHenry's *A Walk Through the Nineteenth Century* as well as *Dearborn County: Interim Report*, which has a good map and a description of all the buildings in the historic district; 213 Eads Parkway, Lawrenceburg, IN 47025, 812–537–0814.

Lodging

Hillcrest, U.S. 50 south of Aurora, 812–926–1991.

Restaurants

Hunt House Inn, 6 East High Street at the corner of Walnut, 812–537–2948.

Tree House, U.S. 50, 812–926–3737, handicapped accessible.

Whiskey's, Front Street, 812–537–4239, handicapped accessible.

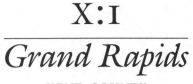

X:I

Grand Rapids

KENT COUNTY
Michigan

GRAND RAPIDS was incorporated in 1838. It soon became a lumber and furniture-making center, and it remains one today. It is the second-largest city in Michigan. Though the architectural tour concentrates on Heritage Hill, a National Register district, do not forget that there are other areas worth exploring, such as Monroe Center downtown and nearby Heartside, a Victorian commercial district.

Downtown Grand Rapids is well worth a visit. The red Calder Mobile in front of city hall and a Calder painting on a half-acre roof viewed from the government building are exceptional. The President Gerald Ford Library and the Ah Hab Awen Park with its superb plantings and picnic tables present a splendid sight along the west bank of the Grand River. Historic Monroe Center, a block away from city hall, with its magnificently restored Amway Grand Hotel and walking street, is in scale and is nicely fitted in between the modern and the stately old.

Directions

In central-western Michigan you might combine visits to Grand Rapids and Muskegon. Interstate 94 east will take you from Chicago to Milburg, Michigan, just north of Benton Harbor. From there switch to Interstate 196, which will take you right into downtown Grand Rapids. At the second ramp immediately after crossing the Grand River, exit right onto College Avenue, then go south five blocks to Fulton Street. Go west one block to Prospect Avenue to begin the north tour.

ARCHITECTURAL TOURS

The area is large, eight blocks by six blocks, so we have divided the walking tour into two parts: from Lyon to the north side of Cherry Street is the north tour, and from the south side of Cherry to Logan Street is the south tour. Each will take more than an hour on foot.

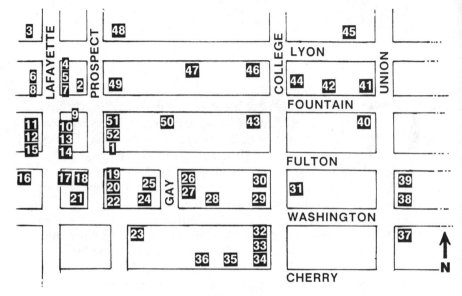

Grand Rapids

NORTH TOUR

1. The Elizabethan Revival house at 427 East Fulton was built in 1907 by T. Stuart White. It was elaborately decorated inside, including living-room murals depicting King Arthur's court and a gold-leaf dining room ceiling by Tiffany. 2. The Victorian Gothic house at 139 Prospect Avenue NE, erected in 1885 for O.E. Brown, has a steep front gable decorated by bargeboard and windows with ornate hoods. 3. At 215 Lafayette Avenue NE is the elaborately decorated Eastlake-style house built for Arthur B. Wykes in 1875. The gables, the windows, the tower with its mansard roof, and the porch with its spindles and carved pediment are decorated. 4. The Classic Revival Loomis-Barnett house at 152 Lafayette Avenue NE was built in 1870. The imposing front portico and the enclosed entranceway with its second-floor balcony are its most important features. 5. The massive American Craftsman house at 148 Lafayette Avenue NE has a pediment decorating its front wraparound porch, gables, dormers, and a second-story oriel window. It was built for James M. Barnett in 1881. 6. At 143 Lafayette Avenue NE is the Tudor Revival house built in 1900 for George G. Briggs. 7. The Classic Revival George Hefferan house at 126 Lafayette Avenue NE was built in 1906. Unusual dormers protrude from its roof, and an entrance portico with balustrade protects its front doorway. An oriel window provides light for the interior staircase. 8. The house at 111 Lafayette Avenue NE is a combination of Eastlake, Gothic Revival, and Italianate. Such a mixture of styles was not uncommon among Victorians. The house was built in 1881 for Gaius W. Perkins. 9. At 230 Fountain NE is the elegant Italianate Shelby-Booth house, erected in 1873. The facade is decorated with a heavily bracketed cornice crowned by a bonneted dormer, a bay, and an oriel window. It also has a pediment supported by Ionic columns. The domed garage was the first building in Grand Rapids expressly erected to house a car. The overhead door appears to be the only change. 10. The Italianate Gallup house, built at 74 Lafayette Avenue NE in 1865, has a pediment supported by Doric columns. The window hoods, bay window, and eaves all are supported by brackets. 11. The second house built by William Shelby in Grand Rapids, at 65 Lafayette Avenue NE, resembles his first at 230 Fountain (9), but it is larger. 12. The Queen Anne house with Eastlake trimmings at 55 Lafayette Avenue NE was built by Thomas D. Gilbert in 1878. The facade is dominated by a third-floor center-front gable and pediment entrance supported by columns, which are part of the front porch. 13. On the east side of the street is 50 Lafayette Avenue NE, built in 1886 by John C. Holt. The glass enclosure of the porch is an addition; otherwise the facade is original. The style is mixed; the Shingle second story is reminiscent of the large

eastern-seaboard cottages and the stone first floor is of Richardsonian Romanesque style. There are also embellishments such as the gambrel roof and Palladian windows from other styles. **14.** Francis B. Gilbert built 40 Lafayette Avenue NE in 1885. **15.** The Frederick house at 35 Lafayette Avenue NE was built in 1885. It presents a combination of styles. The arched windows are Romanesque; the window hoods are from a number of styles; the gables have a Queen Anne flavor; and the portico entrance is Classical. The facade is original. **16.** The Truman Lyon Gothic cottage at 222 East Fulton Street, built in 1845, is one of the oldest houses extant in the area. The main part of the house was constructed of limestone. **17.** The neighboring house at 230 East Fulton was built in 1844. Abram Pike's Greek Revival residence originally stood in Port Sheldon, but he moved it to Grand Rapids. The grand portico with its handsome pediment and Doric columns is flanked by one-story wings. **18.** The Martin Sweet house at 254 East Fulton is a typical grand Italianate residence. Built in 1860, its belvedere commands a view of the river valley below. **19.** The rather austere Italianate house at 18 Prospect Avenue SE was built by Jacob Quintus in 1859. **20.** The house at 26 Prospect Avenue SE was a simple residence when erected in 1880 for Harry K. Dean. Its facade has recently been embellished with a front terrace, fancy doorway hood, and cornice. **21.** At 41 Prospect Avenue SE is an Eclectic house whose most prominent feature is the arched entry porch, which has a cloisterlike appearance. It was built in 1915 for Archibald A. McLeod. **22.** The Queen Anne–Stick-style house at 34 Prospect Avenue SE was built for George R. Mayhew. This highly decorated facade has a wealth of detail around its gables, bay windows, and particularly its carved entrance door. **23.** The Italianate house at 330 Washington Street SE, now an apartment house, was the first residence of Mr. and Mrs. Gerald Ford. Built in 1890 by Loyal E. Knappen, the house has fancy eave brackets and eyebrow windows in the cornice. **24.** The colossal Queen Anne house at 345 Washington Street SE was built in 1887 by Samuel B. Jenks. The facade is embellished by a variety of siding styles, different window types, and a large corner three-story tower with a mansard roof. **25.** Turn north on Gay Avenue SE to 29, an adaptation of the English Georgian country house. Built in 1916 for Henry Idema, it has an intricate Flemish-bond facade and quoins. **26.** The Eclectic house at 400 East Fulton was built in 1902 by Minnie Steketee. A wide front porch and a prominent front gable with Palladian window are important features, as is a second-story oriel window. **27.** Another Georgian-style house was built earlier in 1908, at 20 Gay Avenue SE, for John Duffy. The pedimented entrance sports side lights, fanlight transom, and a larger third-story pediment with a bullseye window. **28.** A throwback to an earlier time is the

Federal-style house built in 1905 for Edward Fitzgerald at 417 Washington Street SE. **29.** A good example of the American Craftsman style is the house at 45 College Avenue SE, built in 1887 by Enos Putman. **30.** The house at 15 College Avenue SE is patterned after the mansions of Dutch patroons in Manhattan. Built in 1904 by Frederick P. Wilcox, it is Grand Rapids' only house of this style. Note the crow's-step roof line. **31.** At 20 College Avenue SE is the Dudley Waters house. This imposing Georgian mansion was a simple two-story frame house until 1930, when it was greatly enlarged and the two-story semicircular portico with galleried terrace was added along with the brick siding and the Palladian entrance. **32.** A bit north is 103 College Avenue SE, another Chateau-style house, built in 1896 by Edward Lowe. **33.** In 1895 Carl A. Voigt built 115 College Avenue SE, an adaptation of the chateau at Chenonceaux. **34.** Turn north on College to the Byrne–Hanchett house at 125 College SE, built in 1891. This copy of an English manor house was embellished by the work of imported Italian artisans and has both oriel and stained-glass second-story windows. **35.** Nearby at 455 Cherry SE is the imposing castle built in 1888 by E. Crofton and Charles Fox. It boasts a tower with battlements, a cast-iron oriel window lighting the staircase, and heavy entrance porch. **36.** Turn left on Cherry to 445 SE, the Greek Revival one-and-one-half-story Damon Hatch house, erected in 1844–45. **37.** Proceed east to 102 Union Avenue SE, an American Craftsman-style house. Built in 1876 for Jeremiah L. Lewis, it has a wide wraparound porch and two-story bay decorated with an Adam garland. **38.** At 62 Union Avenue SE is the Gothic-style clapboard house built in 1885 for Clyde C. McNamara. A wide protective front porch shields the entrance, and a bay window projects to catch the sun and the view. **39.** Another more elaborate 1866 Gothic cottage is at 32 Union Avenue SE. Three sharp bargeboard-decorated gables, a fancy arched front porch, and a large side bay window with stained-glass panels are the most prominent features. **40.** William Williamson built the English-style country cottage at 516 Fountain Street NE in 1913. The original brick walk still leads you into the house. **41.** At 551 Fountain Street NE is the American Craftsman house of Edwin A. Strong. In the 1850s it was a saltbox house, but extensive alterations have made it Eclectic with a dominant second-story Palladian window and Georgian doorway. **42.** The George A. Davis Gothic cottage at 535 Fountain Street NE was built in 1881. It is larger and more elaborate than earlier versions of the style, and its facade, which is original, includes decorated gables and an elaborate front porch reminiscent of the Eastlake and Stick-style decorative trimmings. **43.** The English Tudor Revival house at 432 Fountain Street NE was built in 1879 by William Widdicomb, Sr. **44.** Turn left, or north, on College Avenue to 134 NE, an Eastlake-style house built in 1880. As is common in this style, the front gable is richly decorated, as are the front porch and the bay window. **45.** Walk north to 523 Lyon Street NE, an 1894 Chateau-style building. The four-story tower with tile roof and the different window styles produce a unique facade. **46.** The large Italianate house at 412 Lyon Street NE was recently moved to this location. This house was built in the 1880s by William C. Hopson. **47.** The Italianate house at 324 Lyon Street NE is worth a detour. Built in 1880 by John H. Doornink, it has the usual bracketed cornice, hooded windows, entrance porch, and side portico. **48.** The Prairie-style house at 236 Prospect Avenue NE was designed for Fred W. Rowe in 1910 by a Frank Lloyd Wright protégé, architect Eugene Osgood. The house has the heavy overhang, the ribbon windows, and the horizontal lines of this style. **49.** The imposing Classic Revival Robert Loomis house at 152 Prospect Avenue NE began in 1870 as a simple Greek Revival farmhouse. Later it was remodeled by adding the handsome portico, fanlight, pediment, second-story balcony, Palladian window, and central entrance doorway with side lights and fanlights. **50.** In 1860 Thomas B. Church built 330 Fountain Street NE in the Gothic cottage style. Subsequent owners have changed the facade and the original entrance, which was on Prospect. The only remaining detail from the original facade is the decorative work in the steep front gable. **51.** The Italian Revival house at 64 Prospect Avenue NE was built in 1890 for Elbridge G. Studley. Its windows show the influence of Palladio in their fan-shaped tops, and the roof is tile. This is a rather amazing style to find in Michigan, for it is more common in Florida or the Southwest. **52.** Albert Stickley built the Georgian Revival house at 60 Prospect NE in 1900. This handsome house is dominated by dentillated eaves and pediment supported by six Ionic columns and a fancy cornice and entry. You are now next door to where you started.

SOUTH TOUR

This tour begins at the southeast corner of Cherry Street and College Avenue SE. There is parking here. **1.** The ornate Georgian Revival house at 227 College Avenue SE was built between 1911 and 1913 for Miner S. Keeler. A copy of a house in Rockford, Illinois, this building has a Classical entrance portico and gabled roof with scrolled pediment. **2.** Another Classical Revival house is located at 339 College Avenue SE. Charles Coye built it in 1909. **3.** Return to Cherry Street SE. There you will find 434, an Italianate-style residence built in 1865 for Robert Morris. **4.** The Stick-style Henry F. McCormick house at 222 Madison Avenue SE was built in 1890. The contrasting color of the stick decor, both horizontal and vertical, as well as the Eastlake

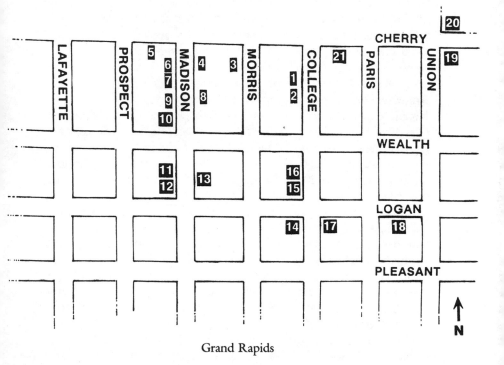

Grand Rapids

decoration on the porch and around the windows, makes this a good example of popular end-of-the-century building. **5.** Back on Cherry Street SE, the Eastlake house at 356 was built in 1885 by Charles Coit. **6.** The Queen Anne–Craftsman Mary Vine house, built in 1900, has a wide front porch topped by a balustrade and a round three-story tower decorated with Adam swag. **7.** The American Craftsman house at 241 Madison Avenue SE was built by Horace A. Lamos in 1892. It has a unique porticoed entrance, second-story bay window, and third-story dormer. **8.** Across the street is 246 Madison Avenue SE, the Classical Revival John Hoult house, built in 1908. One of the unusual features of the house is a third-floor ballroom. **9.** The Queen Anne house at 303 Madison Avenue SE was built in 1883 for Alexander Kennedy. It has a graceful front porch, octagonal tower, and elaborate third-story dormer with a sunburst top. The second-story bay window below has Adam-type scroll decoration. **10.** The Tudor Revival house at 309 Madison Avenue SE was built in 1920 for John S. McDonald. **11.** Isaiah J. Whitfield built the American Craftsman house at 441 Madison Avenue SE in 1897. In addition to its wide front porch the house also has latticed Gothic windows and a large front gable flanked by two third-story dormers. **12.** The American Craftsman house at 455 Madison Avenue SE was built in 1878 for Joseph Penny. **13.** At 450 Madison Avenue SE is the house designed by Frank Lloyd Wright for Meyer S. May. It resembles Wright's Imperial Hotel in Tokyo. **14.** The Prairie-style Frank Lloyd Wright house built for David Amberg at 505 College Avenue SE in 1910 has a prominent front gable and large windows. **15.** Another American Craftsman house, at 455 College Avenue SE, was built for railroad president Charles Heald in 1893. **16.** The Mediterranean-style house at 425 College Avenue SE, built in 1916, is modified to suit its climate by the recessed entrance and heavily overhung tile roof. **17.** James P. Brayton built the imposing Georgian Revival house at 516 College Avenue SE in 1889. Its handsome portico is topped by a gambrel gable and flanked by smaller columned porches. **18.** The modified Georgian-style house at 506 Paris Avenue SE was built in 1906 by Elmer L. Kinsey. Its best feature is its wide columned front porch. **19.** Walk north two blocks to Cherry, and at 600 SE you will see the Chateau-style house built in 1888 by George W. Metz. In addition to its three-story tower it has a decorated gable, heavily decorated windows, a second-story bay, and a porte-cochere. **20.** Across Cherry is 601 SE, a larger and more elaborate Chateau house built in 1892 for Thomas Friant. This house contains glimpses of many styles. The porte-cochere and the towers are Richardsonian Romanesque; the third-floor balcony and oriel window below reflect the Queen Anne; and the sloping shingle roof is a reminder of the Shingle style so popular along the eastern seaboard. **21.** At 540 Cherry SE is the Greek Revival Sanford house, built in 1847. Its grand two-story portico is topped by a pediment with a fan-shaped window. This is the second Greek Revival house dating from the 1840s still standing and in a good state of repair (see North Tour, 17). You have come to the end of the South Tour and are only a few feet from your starting point.

Festivals, Tours, and Other Places of Interest

The Heritage Hill Association conducts an annual open-house tour of the district the first weekend in October and also provides a small brochure outlining two tours of the Heritage Hill district, 126 College SE, Grand Rapids, MI 49503, 616–459–8950. CJ's Tours, escorted tours of historic homes as well as special museum tours, 344 College Avenue SE, Grand Rapids, MI 49503, 616–451–4859. During July and August on Wednesdays between 11:00 A.M. and 3:00 P.M. and the second Sunday of each month you can tour the Voigt House, 115 College Avenue SE (North Tour, 33), Grand Rapids, MI 49503, 616–458–2422.

Historical Information

Grand Rapids Planning Department and Historic Preservation Commission, David Jensen, City Hall, Grand Rapids, MI 49503, 616–456–3031. Heritage Hill, 126 College Avenue SE, Grand Rapids, MI 49503, 616–459–8950.

Lodging

Amway Grand Plaza, Pearl at Monroe, 616–774–2000, 800–323–7500 (worldwide), 800–632–6120 (Michigan).

Bed-and-breakfast accommodations, CJ's Tours, 344 College Avenue SE, 616–451–4859.

Restaurants

A Bit of Europe, 547 Cherry SE at Union, 616–456–6661.
Churchill's, 188 Monroe NW, 616–456–7074.
Cottage Bar and Restaurant, 8 La Grave SE, 616–454–9088.
Gibson's, 1033 Lake Drive, 616–774–8535.
Hong Kong Inn, 121 Monroe Mall, 616–451–3835.

X:2

Muskegon

MUSKEGON COUNTY
Michigan

IN 1890 lumber baron Charles Hackley built a palatial Victorian mansion filled with handcarved woodwork and Tiffany glass windows. His friend and partner, Thomas Hume, built an equally large but less ornate house next door. Both are handsomely restored. The Hackley School, Library, Park, Art Museum, and Hospital were all given to the city by Charles Hackley, who greatly loved his town.

Muskegon, the seat of Muskegon County, has by turns been a lumber and an automobile town. Its fortunes have vacillated, but the town has rebounded with a new emphasis on service and light industries.

Directions

On a trip to western Michigan you could combine a visit to Muskegon and Grand Rapids. From Chicago take Interstate 94 northeast to Milburg, Michigan. Change to Interstate 196 to Holland, Michigan. There you change to U.S. 31, which takes you to Muskegon. Exit on Apple Avenue, State Route 46; go west to First Street and make a right onto Webster Avenue. Proceed to Seventh Street. Turn right, and in two blocks you will see the Union Station. Park there.

ARCHITECTURAL TOUR

The area from Third to Seventh Street and Webster to Western Avenue along the lake is known as Heritage Village. Most of the historic buildings are located here. The structures date from the 1870s to the 1890s. **1.** Union Station, designed by architect S.J. Osgood, opened in 1895. This Renaissance Revival building is dominated by a tower not quite tall enough for the rest of the structure. The facade is original. **2.** Carlson's Grocery has served the neighborhood since the 1890s. Inside you can see the elaborate pressed-tin ceiling so popular with late Victorians. The exterior is decorated by a mural depicting the now-defunct interurban trolley barn, which was located diag-

278

onally across from the grocery. **3.** A block east on Clay between Sixth and Fifth Streets is the reconstructed 1874 Hackley Hose Company number two, now the Firebarn Museum. **4.** On the northwest corner of Clay Avenue and Fourth Street is the Muskegon County Museum. **5.** Now a museum, Charles H. Hackley's Queen Anne mansion at 484 West Webster is a glorious example of late Victorian taste. It was designed by Grand Rapids architect D.S. Hopkins. The highly decorated facade includes a tower, numerous gables, a wraparound front porch and porte-cochere, and a distinctive second-story porch with circular openings. Many of the furnishings date from the 1890s, as do the carved woodwork and the stained-glass windows. Between the Hackley and Hume houses is a three-story barn with stable, jointly used by the two families. It, too, is an elaborate structure with two towers, one with a pyramidal top and the other an onion-shaped one. **6.** Next door at 472 West Webster is the Queen Anne house of Thomas Hume. Built in 1888, it was also designed by architect D.S. Hopkins. Although its facade is highly decorated, it is less flamboyant than the Hackley house. It, too, has a tower, gables, numerous porches, and stained-glass windows. **7.** Next to the Hume house at 462 West Webster is the C.J. Chaddock house. This 1878 Italianate house is the oldest on the block. **8.** The Howden house at 452 West Webster was built by William Rutherford sometime between 1869 and 1881. **9.** On the northwest corner of Webster and Fifth is the John G. Emery Georgian Colonial Revival house, built in 1903. **10.** In 1891 Charles Hackley gave the Romanesque Revival school on Webster Avenue between Fourth and Third Streets to the town. It now houses the Chamber of Commerce. Its most prominent feature is the six-story central tower. **11.** At 315 West Webster stands the stone Queen Anne house of John Torrent, built in 1892. Its facade is replete with towers, dormers, and a wide front porch. The first floor can be viewed between 8:00 A.M. and 5:00 P.M., Monday–Friday. **12.** Across the street is the Prairie-style Hackley Art Museum, built in 1912. **13.** Also across the street from the Torrent house is the Romanesque stone Hackley library. **14.** Hackley Park, the block bounded by Fourth, Clay, Third, and Webster, adds a note of beauty to the town. **15.** On the southeast corner of Clay Avenue and Third Street is St. Paul's Episcopal Church, built in 1893. The English Gothic Revival structure has a glorious rose window which faces west to capture the light of the setting sun. **16.** At the southwest corner of Western and Third is the Frauenthal Center, completed in 1930. The exterior is Art Deco style, and the interior is decorated in an Italian design. **17.** The Amazon building at Western Avenue and Sixth Street, built in the 1890s, has two towers, one of ten stories and the other of six. Otherwise, it is a functional factory. You are now back where you started.

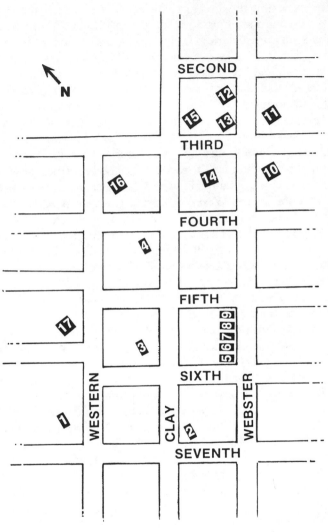

Muskegon

Festivals, Tours, and Other Places of Interest

Firebarn Museum, open Wednesday, Saturday, and Sunday, 2:00 P.M.–4:00 P.M., May 25–Labor Day, 510 West Clay Street, Muskegon, MI 49440. Muskegon County Museum, open Monday–Friday, 9:30 A.M.–4:30 P.M., Saturday and Sunday, 12:30 P.M.–4:30 P.M., 430 West Clay Street, Muskegon, MI 49440.

Historical Information

Romance of Muskegon (1974) by Alice P. Kyes. Muskegon County Conventions and Visitors' Bureau and Muskegon Chamber of Commerce, 349 West Webster Avenue, Muskegon, MI 49441, 616–722–3751 or 616–893–4585. Muskegon Heritage Association, open Monday–Friday, 9:00 A.M.–4:00 P.M., 561 West Western Avenue, Muskegon, MI 49440, 616–722–6520.

Lodging

Alpine Motel, Airline Road at U.S. 31 and Interstate 96, 616–733–1323.

Bel-Aire Motel, 4240 Airline Road, business Interstate 96 and U.S. 31 intersection, 616–733–2196.

Corner House Motor Inn, 3550 Glade Street, 616–733–1037.

Days Inn, 150 Seaway Drive, 616–739–9429.

El Royal Motel, 4620 Airline Road, 616–733–2511.

Motel Haven, 4344 Airline Road, 616–733–1256.

Muskegon Harbor Hilton Hotel, 939 Third Street at Western Avenue, 616–733–0100.

Quality Inn, 2967 Henry Street, 616–733–2651.

Seaway Motel, 631 Norton Avenue at Seaway Drive, business Interstate 96 and U.S. 31 intersection, 616–733–1220.

Restaurants

Bay Cafe, Lumbertown, Muskegon harbor at 1050 Western Avenue, 616–728–7272, handicapped accessible.

Egg Roll House, 110 Muskegon Mall, 616–726–6648.

On the Avenue, 415 Western Avenue, 616–728–7552, handicapped accessible.

Tohado House, 450 West Western, 616–726–4377, handicapped accessible.

X:3
Marshall
CALHOUN COUNTY
Michigan

REAT efforts were made to have Marshall named the state capital, but unexpected legislative opposition prevailed and a small village named Lansing won the honor. However, there are remains of a promotional effort and a governor's mansion in an upper village area still known as "Capitol Hill."

Marshall is another town whose economic downfall led to its emergence, many years later, as a sparkling well-preserved historic district. When historic societies in Marshall began to look around at what they had to work with, the economic potential of preservation became obvious. The project in Marshall, largely organized by Harold C. Brooks, became a success. There are streets of delightfully preserved houses of both the affluent and the railway workers. All the town seems an encapsulated perfectly balanced nineteenth-century community.

Directions
A weekend trip to Marshall could be combined with a tour of Grand Rapids. From Chicago take Interstate 94 northeast to Interstate 69. Marshall is located near the intersection. You can reach the historic district by leaving Interstate 94 at exit 110 and going south to Michigan Avenue and the square, where you will find Honolulu house, or by continuing east to exit 112, which is Michigan Avenue, and taking it west to the square. The other approach is from Interstate 69 south of its intersection with Interstate 94. The exit is marked Michigan Avenue. Take it east to the square.

ARCHITECTURAL TOURS
Much of architectural significance can be viewed in Marshall. Therefore, we have divided the town north of Rice Creek into four districts which can be covered by foot, and one south of the creek which is best explored by car.

SOUTHWEST SECTION

This section covers the area west of Eagle and south of Mansion. Parking is available behind Honolulu house. 1. The Abner Pratt house at 107 North Kalamazoo is known as the Honolulu house. The tropical architecture seems odd in this northern climate. The house has a wide veranda, an entrance hall running the width of the building, and a towered balcony which can be reached via a spiral staircase. It is now the headquarters of the Marshall Historical Society. 2. At 419 Mansion is the Queen Anne-style house built by M.B. Powell in 1893. It has a three-story round tower with conical roof, decorated gables, and a wraparound porch with pedimented entrance. 3. Walk one block west to the McCall house at 523 West Mansion. This small Greek Revival clapboard house with later east and west additions was built for William R. McCall in 1840. The two front bays are later additions, but the porch is either original or similar to it. 4. The Federal–Greek Revival house at 520 West Michigan was built by master carpenter Joseph L. Lord in 1838. The columned entrance and the return gables are Greek Revival touches, while the first-floor windows are Federal. The bay windows were added in 1874. 5. Across the street at 521 West Michigan is an Italianate house built about 1853 by Claudius B. Webster. The clapboard house has heavily bracketed eaves and a wide columned front porch. 6. The Greek Revival Mills house at 514 West Michigan has prominent front first- and second-floor bay windows, added in 1886, but the house was built between 1854 and 1858. 7. One block east at 424 West Michigan Avenue is the Joseph Sibley Federal–Dutch house, built in the 1840s. 8. Across the street is the Federal-style National house, the first brick building in Marshall, erected by Andrew Mann in 1835. 9. Small Westend Park is the site of the Brooks Memorial fountain. 10. The handsome Italianate house at the southeast corner of Westend Park was built by William B. Church in 1873. The arched windows have ornamental hoods, and the cupola repeats the window shapes. Over the years the facade has remained virtually unchanged. 11. Go west a few yards to the Greek Revival stone barn converted into the city's Town Hall in 1930. It was built in 1857–58. 12. Go one block south to Hanover Street, where at 222 you will find the Gothic Revival Watson house. Built in 1864, it is tastefully decorated with bargeboard outlining the front gable and has a Classical Revival porch across the front. 13. A block farther east at 126 West Hanover Street on the north side is an early Queen Anne house, built in 1856 by Loring Johnson. In 1862 the western section and the Stick-style wraparound front porch were added. 14. North one block on Eagle is the octagonal house at 218, built by Increase Pendleton in 1856. The fancy trim, bay windows, cupola, and heavily decorated entrance porch were apparently

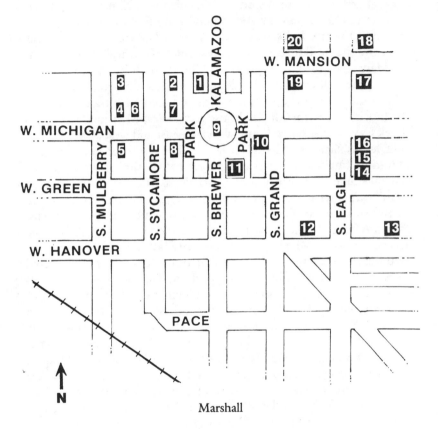

KALAMAZOO

W. MANSION

W. MICHIGAN

W. GREEN

S. MULBERRY

S. SYCAMORE

PARK

S. BREWER

PARK

S. GRAND

S. EAGLE

W. HANOVER

PACE

N

Marshall

added after 1875. **15.** At 216 Eagle Street is a simple wooden Greek Revival house built in the early 1850s. The second-floor casement windows, the wraparound spindle porch, and the first-floor bay window were added in the 1880s. **16.** St. Mary's Roman Catholic Church at 214 South Eagle Street was built in 1891. It is an elaborate Gothic Revival building, a style popular in nineteenth-century midwestern Catholic parishes. **17.** The Greek Revival house at 139 West Mansion was moved to this location in 1868 and remodeled in 1871. **18.** The simple Italianate house at 148 West Mansion was built by O.W.P. Sutton in 1857. The ell is an addition and so are the porch columns, but otherwise the facade is original. **19.** The Van Horn-Perret house at 223 West Mansion was built in 1860. A Gothic Revival-style house, it has arched windows in the gables and a side porch with columns and carpenter's lace trim. The exterior is original. **20.** The Wheeler-Casper house at 222 West Mansion was built in 1893. This Eclectic structure has bay windows, dormers, a large front gable, and a first-floor conservatory or sun room. The facade has not been changed.

NORTHWEST SECTION

This section runs from Eagle on the east to Mulberry on the west and from Mansion Street to North. You may want to cover Eagle and Kalamazoo from Union to North by car or to break your walk in some other pattern, for this is a large district of about thirteen blocks. **1.** The Butler-Porter House at 223 North Eagle Street was built in 1844. The second story with its bracketed roof, bay window, and entrance was added in 1870. **2.** The Charles D. Brewer house across the street at 208 West Prospect Street was built in 1899. It has a wide columned front porch with balustrade, a similar side entrance porch, bay windows on the second story, and dormers on the third. This gracious house has its original facade except for the removal of the front-porch railing. **3.** Although a block out of your way, the remarkable house at 410 North Eagle is well worth the trip. Chauncey M. Brewer built the fine Italianate house in 1858. The house, including its cupola, has remained much as it was built except for the extension of the front porch to the east side. **4.** Return along Eagle to Prospect and turn right, or west. On the north side is 224 West Prospect, the Gothic Revival Taylor-Schuyler house, built about 1843. The house, copied from Andrew Jackson Downing's *Cottage Residences*, was built on a knoll. Even at this early date there was a landscaping plan which showed where the trees and terraces were to be. In 1905 the porch was added and the entrance modified to include side lights. **5.** On the west side of North Grand at 311 is the unusual Gothic Revival Church-Frink house. Andrew Jackson Downing's later pattern book,

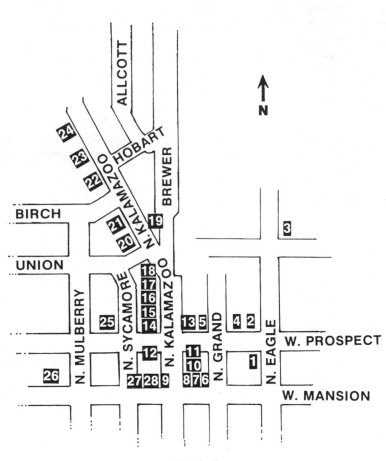

ALLCOTT

HOBART

BREWER

N

24

23

22

N. KALAMAZOO

BIRCH

21

20

19

3

UNION

18
17
16
15
14

N. SYCAMORE

N. KALAMAZOO

N. MULBERRY

25

13 5

N. GRAND

4 2

N. EAGLE

W. PROSPECT

26

12

11
10
8 7 6

1

27 28 9

W. MANSION

Marshall

The Architecture of Country Houses, was apparently followed. Some changes have been made over the years, including a new front porch in the 1880s. The street lamp at the bottom of the stairs leading to the house is the original one installed in the 1880s. **6.** Walk one block south on North Grand and turn right, or west, on West Mansion where on the north side of the street you will see 302, the Allcott-Ingersoll house. This 1838 house was originally a one-and-one-half-story Greek Revival. There have obviously been changes, including the bargeboard trim on the front gable and the front porch, but nonetheless the house is listed on the Historic American Buildings Survey for Michigan. **7.** The Mann house at 314 West Mansion is an 1842 Greek Revival building. There have been no exterior changes in over a hundred years. **8.** At 318 West Mansion is a Gothic Revival house built in 1853. The gables on both the house and carriage house are decorated with bargeboard. A cottage depicted in John Bullock's *American Cottage Builder* of 1854 is similar to this house. **9.** On the northwest corner of Mansion and Kalamazoo at 404 West Mansion is the 1855 Benedict-Haskell-Perret house. This Italianate structure was remodeled in 1878 and again in 1894. **10.** On the east side of Kalamazoo is 210, a simple Queen Anne-style house. It is a clapboard dwelling with fish-scale gables in the attic and on the front-porch pediment. A generous porch stretches across the front. The facade is original. **11.** On the southeast corner of Kalamazoo and Prospect at 224 North Kalamazoo is the outstanding National Register Joy house. The house was built by Nathan Benedict in 1844. In 1854 the prominent three-story tower with bracketed pagoda roof, ornate second- and third-story balconies, and delicately columned front porch were added. This architectural gem is listed in the Historic American Buildings Survey for Michigan **12.** On the southwest corner of Kalamazoo and Prospect is 223 North Kalamazoo, a Queen Anne house built in 1897 by Miles Townsend. The house has a columned wraparound porch with a pediment entrance and a three-story tower with conical roof and weathervane. **13.** At 310 North Kalamazoo Street is the stately Greek Revival Fitch-Gorham-Brooks house, built about 1840. Distinctive features are the five-columned portico, the east and west main entrances, and the sculpture honoring the founders of Michigan's public-school system. In 1921 Kalamazoo architect Howard F. Young renovated the house, and Danish-American landscape architect Jens Jensen planned the grounds. This grand National Register house is on the Historic American Buildings Survey. **14.** Across the street, facing the Fitch house, at 303 North Kalamazoo is the Hays house. These two houses are very similar. The Hays house is of sandstone rather than brick, has one entrance on the east side, and was built two years earlier. The facades of both houses

288 / Weekend Trips

are original. **15.** A bit north on Kalamazoo is the entirely different Bedwell house at 317. This American Four Square-style building was erected in 1900. It is really a combination of the nineteenth-century wide porch, porte-cochere, dormer, bay windows, and stained glass with the horizontal lines of Chicago's Prairie School. **16.** As you walk north you will see 327 North Kalamazoo, the Italianate 1870 Hughes house. A widow's walk graces its heavily bracketed roof. The windows are hooded, and a columned and pedimented porch stretches across the front and south sides. **17.** Next door at 333 North Kalamazoo is the Larkin house, built the same year and in the same style. This house is fancier, with pilasters stretching from the bottom to the bracketed eaves dividing the facade, paired hooded windows, a columned entrance portico topped by a balustrade, and a matching cupola with widow's walk. **18.** Another Italian villa at 337 North Kalamazoo was built in 1868 and is a variation on this popular style. Originally a square house, the Classic porch with balustrade and the southern section were added in the 1890s. Like the Larkin house, it has an enclosed cupola and hooded windows. **19.** Cross Union and on the east side you will see 400 North Kalamazoo, a Gothic Revival house built in 1857 by E.H. Lawrence. It has a porticoed entrance with balustrade and identical front porches on either side. The center front gable has a large arched window, and there are two dormers on either side which are later additions. **20.** On the west side of Kalamazoo is the 1864 Italianate Gilbert house at 403. The Classical entrance porch with balustrade is more recent, as is the bay window. **21.** The Gothic Revival house at 413 North Kalamazoo was built in 1868–69 by George H. Smith. Its steep gables are decorated with fancy bargeboard, or carpenter's lace. The front bay with balustrade is reminiscent of the Italianate style, and the porches are Stick-style. **22.** Proceed north and cross Birch Street. On the west side of the street you will find 513 North Kalamazoo, the Lawrence-Linscott-Van Horn house, a Gothic Revival dwelling built about 1854. The front porch appears to be a later addition, but otherwise the facade, including the small front gable with large hooded window and blinds, is probably original. **23.** Another version of the Gothic Revival style is at 521 North Kalamazoo. The T-form was popular, as were the slightly arched windows with hoods. **24.** Still farther north is the Kardstaedt-Wallace-Cook house at 603 North Kalamazoo. This brick Italianate dwelling was built in 1869. It has an enclosed cupola, second-story bay window, bracketed roof, and a Classical entrance porch, added in 1897. **25.** Go south on Sycamore and turn right, or west, onto Prospect. On the northwest corner of Prospect and Sycamore Streets you will see 504 West Prospect, the Italianate house of William D. Adams. The house has rough stone pillars supporting a Classic-columned wraparound porch and a heavily bracketed bay window; the same hoods cover all the windows. **26.** Continue south on Sycamore one block to Mansion. Turn right to 612 West Mansion, the small Greek Revival 1850s Gilbert-Cleveland house. The wraparound front porch was added at the turn of the century. **27.** S.H. Gorham built the house at 420 West Mansion. It is a Queen Anne house with two-story tower, a half front porch, and projecting second-story bay. In addition, there are gables and a variety of windows. **28.** The J.A. Way Queen Anne house at 414 West Mansion was extensively remodeled in the 1880s when the two-story bay, double front porches, and hipped roof were added. Behind the house is an ornate stable with highly decorated gable, hooded windows, and fancy ironwork roof cresting. You are now back at Honolulu house.

SOUTHEAST SECTION

This section runs from Madison on the west to Gordon on the east, and from Mansion on the north to Green on the south. Parking is available east of Gordon between East Prospect and East Mansion Streets. **1.** At 745 East Mansion is the Gothic Revival 1855 house of Henry A. Tillotson. The H-shaped house has a wide front porch, side-lighted entrance, and prominent front gable with an arched, shuttered window. **2.** The Gothic Revival house at 739 East Mansion has recently been restored. It has bay windows on the south and east and a large arched window in one of the bargeboard-decorated front gables, as well as a half front porch. **3.** Walk west two blocks to Marshall, where at 413 East Mansion you will find the Italianate Wilmarth house, built in 1857–58. It was altered in the 1890s when the porch across the front gabled section was replaced by a small columned entrance shelter and a porch was added to the western section. **4.** The Asa B. Cook house at 405 East Mansion was built in the early 1850s. **5.** At 401 East Mansion is the elaborate Queen Anne house designed by the Detroit architectural firm of Spier and Rohn for Clinton T. Cook. It has a three-story tower with conical roof, pedimented wraparound front porch, gables with half-circle windows, and a variety of other windows. This elaborate house was built in 1886–87. **6.** At 310 East Michigan is the Brooks Rupture Appliance building, a structure built in 1837 and remodeled in 1912 in Italianate style. **7.** On the southwest corner of Mansion and Madison is the Philo Dibble house at 309 East Mansion. This house has Federal symmetry, Italianate heavily bracketed eaves, and a Greek Revival entrance. **8.** The house at the southwest corner of Mansion and High Streets faces the latter. This Greek Revival cottage was built by Daniel Pratt in 1840. The house is unchanged except for some rear additions. It is listed on the National Register and on the Historic American

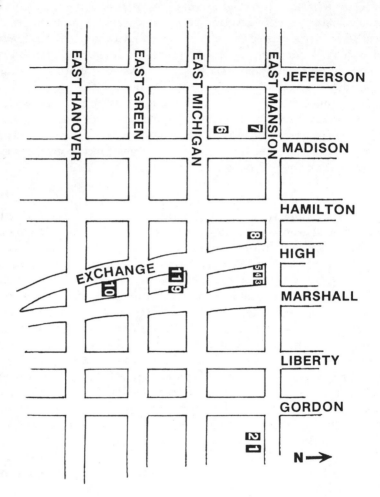

Marshall

Buildings Survey. **9.** One block south on Exchange is all that remains of the once grand Marshall house, built in 1838. Only the west wing survives, and it bears no resemblance to the original three-story building with two-tiered front porch. **10.** The house at 203 South Marshall, built by Oliver C. Comstock in 1849, was originally Greek Revival; in 1856 Gothic Revival touches were added such as the steep gables and the carpenter's lace over the front windows. **11.** At the southeast corner of East Michigan and Exchange is the Grand Army of the Republic hall. **12.** The Samuel F. Dobbins house at 501 East Michigan was built in 1898. The three-story stone and clapboard Queen Anne house has numerous bay windows and gables and a wraparound front porch. You are now two blocks southwest of where you parked.

NORTHEAST SECTION

This section runs from Division to Gordon on the east and from Mansion on the south to the 400 block on the north. **1.** The Greek Revival Gibbs-Sherman house at 606 East Mansion was built about 1842. The only changes in the facade are the hood over the front door and the front bay window. **2.** Take a right onto High Street to see the Gothic Revival Chastian Mann house at 219. This H-shaped house was built in 1861. The eaves are decorated with carpenter's lace, and the facade is original. **3.** The house at 314 East Mansion was built by Henry Haskell in 1859. This Italianate house now has a small pedimented entrance and a wide side porch. **4.** Proceed west to Division Street and turn right, or north. On your left is 221 North Division, the Buck-Gersner house. The house has an unusual tower with a pagoda roof. **5.** The Myers-Lepper house at 224 North Division was built in 1856. In 1864 it acquired its Gothic Revival style. **6.** The house at 306 North Division was built in 1895 by James Dobbins. The Queen Anne house has fan-shaped windows in the third-floor gables, a small second-story porch, a pedimented entrance, and wraparound front porch. **7.** The Queen Anne house at 314 North Division was built in 1886 for Thomas L. Cronin. This structure, with decorated gables, tower, two-story bay windows, conical-roofed conservatory, and Eastlake entrance porch, was designed by Detroit architects Spier and Rohn. **8.** The Greek Revival–Italianate Hall-Edgerton house at 320 North Division was built in 1852. The southern bay window was added in the 1870s; otherwise the facade is original. **9.** The Italianate H.C. Hulett house at 332 North Division, built in 1870, is a pure example of this style with flat bracketed roof, hooded windows and doorways, and Classic veranda. **10.** On the west side of North Division is 331, another version of the Italianate style. The Turner-Merrill house was built in 1853. This house has four sections, a main structure

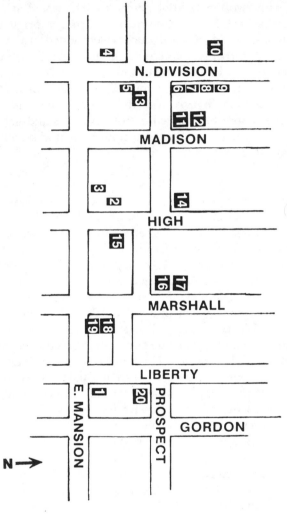

Marshall

with a two-story east wing and a one-story west wing to which a square two-story tower was added. **11.** Return to Prospect Street and proceed one block east to Madison. On the northwest corner is 301 North Madison, the 1881 J.L. Dobbins house. This Italianate house has a two-story bay, bracketed roof, hooded windows, and columned veranda. **12.** The house at 333 North Madison was built in 1857 by Frank Beach. This house is an excellent example of the Gothic Revival style, with elaborately decorated gables and an arched second-story window over the front entrance. **13.** On the south side of East Prospect Street at 201 is the Gothic Revival Bradley house, built in 1859. Its fanciful bargeboard-decorated front gable is its prominent feature. Except for the three-part front window, the facade is original. **14.** Proceed east to High Street and turn left to number 327, the Gibbs-Lacey house. Built in 1847, it is a combination Greek and Gothic Revival structure. It has a recessed columned front porch, bracketed gables and dormers, hooded windows, and board-and-batten sheathing. **15.** Return to Prospect and walk south to 224 North High Street, the Italianate Storr house, built in 1852 with the front section added in 1871. This is yet another variation on the popular Italianate style. **16.** Proceed east to Marshall. At 303 is the Queen Anne–Eastlake house built in 1887 by William E. Bosley. It has decorated gables and stained glass, but its most prominent feature is the wraparound Eastlake porch with pedimented entrance. **17.** The Wright house at 335 North Marshall is a tiny Greek Revival structure built in 1857. It has a wide front porch and eyebrow windows. **18.** Proceed south on Marshall to 222 North Marshall, the house built in 1850 by John H. Montgomery. The entrance and the long first-floor windows are Greek Revival, and the bracketed eaves are Italianate. **19.** Next door is a later Queen Anne-style house, built in 1894 by Irving Udell. The house has a prominent front bay topped by a gable with a fanlight, a roofed entry, and numerous gables. **20.** Return to Prospect and walk east to the William Elston house at 619. This ornate Italianate house was built in 1871. In addition to the usual bracketed eaves and hooded windows, it has a pedimented entrance and second-floor porches as well as a columned first-floor porch. It originally had a central tower with a mansard roof.

CAPITOL HILL SECTION

Take South Marshall Street across Rice Creek. Marshall expected to be the state capital, and this tour covers the area designated "Capitol Hill." As you cross Rice Creek, notice on your left Ketchum Park, the site of the first Marshall settlement, named for Sidney Ketchum, who founded the town in 1831. **1.** Continue south on Marshall to the middle of the block. On your right you will see 612, the "Governor's

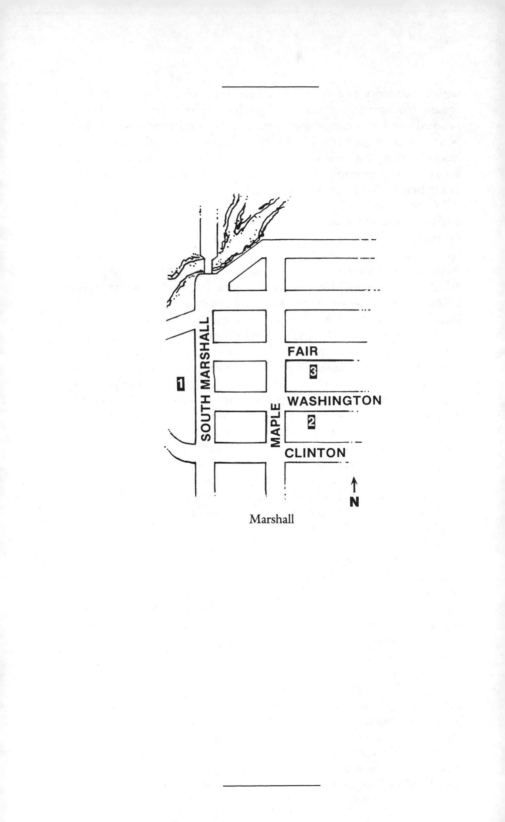

Marshall

Mansion," built in 1839 by James Wright Gordon. This one-and-one-half-story Greek Revival house was modeled after a house in Rochester, New York. The house has a columned porch across the front with a plain cornice and matching cornice under the second-story eaves. It is a National Register house. 2. Turn left off Marshall onto Washington, and in the second block on your right you will see another National Register building, the 1860 Capitol Hill school, designed by Detroit architect Sheldon Smith. This Gothic Revival structure has bargeboard-decorated gables combined with bracketed eaves. It is now a children's museum. 3. Return to Maple Street and turn right. In the next block you will see the Calhoun County Fairgrounds.

Festivals, Tours, and Other Places of Interest

The Marshall Historic Home Tour is held the first weekend after Labor Day; information is available from the Marshall Historical Society, P.O. Box 68 M, Marshall, MI 49068, 616–781–5163. The Annual Christmas Candlelight Walk, sponsored by the Marshall Historical Society, is held the weekend after the first Monday in December; information is available from the Marshall Historical Society, P.O. Box 68 CW, Marshall, MI 49068, 616–781–5163. A mini-tour of Marshall is available all summer beginning June 30, on Saturdays, Sundays, and Mondays, 2:00 P.M.; information is available from the Marshall Historical Society, P.O. Box 68 M, Marshall, MI 49068, 616–781–5163. A new walking-tour brochure with a short description and a map showing the location of all the buildings on the house tours is available, as is a walking tour of Oakridge Cemetery. The Chamber of Commerce, the Visitors' Center at the Marshall Town Hall, and the Historical Society at Honolulu House carry these brochures. The Governor's Mansion, open Sunday, 2:00 P.M.–4:00 P.M., July and August, 612 South Marshall Avenue, Marshall, MI 49068, 616–781–5163. Honolulu house, open for daily tours noon–5:00 P.M., from the third weekend in May until October 31, 107 North Kalamazoo, Marshall, MI 49068, 616–781–8544.

Historical Information

Nineteenth Century Homes of Marshall, Michigan (1971) by Mabel C. Skjelver. Marshall Historical Society, P.O. Box 68 M, Marshall, MI 49068, 616–781–5163. Marshall Area Chamber of Commerce, 308 East Michigan Avenue, Marshall, MI 49068, 616–781–5163. Visitor Information Center, City Hall, at the Fountain Circle, Marshall, MI 49068.

Lodging

Howard's Motel, Michigan Avenue west of Interstate 69, 616–781–4203.

Imperial Motel, Michigan Avenue west of Interstate 69, 616–781–2841.

Marshall Heights Motel, exit 110 off Interstate 94, 616–781–2841.

McCarthy's Bear Creek Inn, exit 36 off Interstate 69, 616–781–8383.

National House Inn, Fountain Circle, 616–781–7374.

Restaurants

Big Boy, 1205 West Michigan Avenue, 616–781–5124.

Coffee Pot, 228 West Michigan Avenue, 616–781–7477.

Cornwell's Turkey House, exit 42 off Interstate 69, 616–781–4293, handicapped accessible.

Countryside Inn, 1967 East Michigan Avenue, 616–965–1247, handicapped accessible.

Haufman House of Pizza, 124 Redfield Plaza, 616–781–4494.

Ken's Cafe, 129 West Michigan Avenue, 616–781–9577.

La Verne and Shirley's, 1225 South Kalamazoo Avenue, 616–781–3056.

Mancino's Restaurant, 113 East Michigan Avenue, 616–781–0018.

Schulers, 115 South Eagle Street, 616–781–0600, handicapped accessible.

Stagecoach Inn, 201 West Michigan Avenue, 616–781–3056.

Yesteryear's Restaurant, 116 West Michigan Avenue, 616–781–5119, handicapped accessible.

X:4
Kalamazoo
KALAMAZOO COUNTY
Michigan

KALAMAZOO presents an idyllic picture. Clean quiet streets in almost perfectly preserved neighborhoods, houses that have been lovingly tended for generations, and pleasing vistas of towering trees hanging over cupolas and architectural whimsies of the 1850s give the city an air of calm well-being. The Flowerfest in Bronson Park grew out of the thriving business in budding plants developed by the early Dutch settlers who first grew celery and then turned to other plants when their industry moved to California. The hodgepodge of industry, including celery, mint, stoves, plows, pills, and paper, paid for the city's cultural and economic growth.

The Upjohn family, which founded its drug company in 1886, is the most visible of the old continuing influences. Two fine mansions are palpable reminders of the Upjohn legacy. Kalamazoo's history is also enriched by the fact that Edna Ferber was born and brought up here.

Directions
A weekend trip to western Michigan could include Kalamazoo and Marshall. From Chicago take Interstate 94 northeast to Kalamazoo. Exit 76 north on Westnedge (Business 131) to West South Street.

ARCHITECTURAL TOURS
Two areas are compact enough to park and walk, and each can be done in an hour or less.

BRONSON PARK AND SOUTH STREET
Bronson Park is the center of Kalamazoo. The South Street area was platted in 1841 as the city's first suburb. Parking is available at Michigan Avenue and Park Street. 1. Flower-filled Bronson Park, with its unique· children's fountain, is a good place to start. (A less

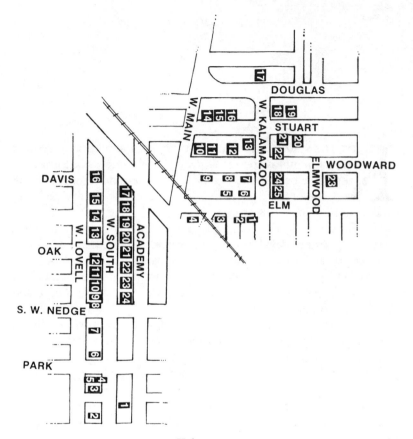

Kalamazoo

cheerful 1939 fountain depicts the forced removal of the Indians.) 2. William S. Lawrence built 219 West South Street in 1889–90. This Queen Anne sandstone house features a carved entrance door, prominent turret, and delicately leaded windows. 3. The adjacent Art Deco City Hall at 241 West South Street is in sharp contrast. Built in 1931, it was designed by the Chicago architectural firm of Weary and Alford. The facade has floral and geometric designs, as well as those depicting Kalamazoo's history. 4. Still another contrast is the grand Gothic Revival First Presbyterian Church at 321 West South Street, built by Philadelphia architect Charles Z. Klauder. The highly decorated entrance includes a large rose window. 5. The striking Victorian or Venetian Gothic Ladies' Library Association building at 333 South Park was built in 1878. 6. The Queen Anne house at 447 West South Street was built in 1878 by David Lilienfield. The windows have ornate hoods; the front porch and the front gable have fancy carpenter's lacework. 7. The 1920s Marlborough building at 471 West South Street exhibits Mission-style architecture. 8. Donald O. Boudeman built the Colonial Revival house at 515 West South Street in 1905. An elaborate two-story central portico is the most prominent feature of this house. 9. Frank B. Lay's Tudor house at 523 West South Street was built in 1908–9. 10. Edwin Carder built the Italianate house at 527 West South Street in 1866. The massive portico of the house, changing the style to Colonial Revival, was added in 1909. 11. The simple Greek Revival house at 605 West South Street was built by John Hogeboom in 1847. 12. The Tudor Revival house at 611 West South Street was built by Abraham Lincoln Blumenberg in 1904. 13. The Greek Revival house at 711 West South Street was built in 1852. 14. In 1855 Josiah Hawes built the house at 713–17 West South Street in the Greek Revival style. In 1871 the Italianate features were added. 15. In 1867 Jane VandeWalker built the Italianate house next door. Its pediment entry has matching gable bargeboard and fancy front-window hoods. 16. The Queen Anne house at 821 West South Street was built by George C. Stockbridge in 1885. 17. On the north side of South Street is a simple Italianate house at 724–26 West South. Built in 1858 in the Greek Revival style by Carlos Baldwin, it was remodeled in 1877 in the then-popular Italianate style. 18. The elaborate Italianate house at 718 West South Street was built in 1870 for Allen Potter. Note its highly decorated entrance portico and the original wrought-iron fence. 19. Lewis H. Kirby built the Tudor Revival house at 708 West South Street in 1911. 20. The house at 620 West South Street was built in 1873 as an Italianate structure. The fancy Queen Anne porch was a later addition. 21. The Italianate house at 610 West South Street was built by John M. Edwards. The house has a wide front porch with spindle trim. 22. The Gothic Revival house at 604 West

South Street was built by William J. DeYoe in 1853–54. **23.** The handsome William Wood house at 530 West South Street was built in 1877–78. The central tower is its most distinguishing feature. **24.** The house next door was built by James F. Gilmore. This Tudor-style house was erected in 1908.

STUART AREA DISTRICT

This district was Kalamazoo's first streetcar suburb. A walk through the district is a journey back to the late nineteenth and early twentieth centuries. **1.** Just south of West Kalamazoo is 310 Elm, the Italianate house built by Alfred Mills in the late 1880s. Brackets decorate the roof corners and a wide pedimented porch stretches across the front. **2.** On the same side of the street is 302, the Gothic Revival Amariah T. Prouty house. This early Stuart-area house was built in 1852. **3.** The simple Italianate Moore house at 224 Elm Street was built in 1883. The only decorative details are the window hoods. **4.** Edward B. Vincent built 222 Elm in 1893. This Queen Anne house boasts a wraparound front porch, tower, and gable. **5.** Across the street at 213 Elm stands the amazing Queen Anne house built in 1880 by Delos Chappell. A highly decorated porch stretches across the front, and the large two-story front bay is topped by a gable with a Gothic window and balcony. **6.** Go north to 303 Elm, the elaborate Beebe-Hatfield house built in 1867. Its most prominent feature is a large, enclosed, highly decorated cupola. **7.** Proceed one block west on Kalamazoo and turn left, or south, on Woodward to 324. This Queen Anne house was built by Edgar A. Crane. The house has a wide front porch, bay windows, and a high front gable. **8.** Grant Tuttle erected 226 Woodward in 1885. This modest Queen Anne house has a recessed corner window with filigreed hood and a Stick-style front porch. **9.** The simple Queen Anne house at 214 West Woodward was built by William Parson in 1880. All the gables originally had decorative carpenter's lace. **10.** Across the street at 211 Woodward is the house built in 1864 by William A. Johnson. The stately Italianate house has a cupola, an ornate entrance, and bay windows. **11.** A bit north is a simpler version of the Italianate style, built in 1873 by Charles Ashby. **12.** The house at 315 Woodward has been altered by additions and the colossal portico. It was the home of Julius Caesar Burrows. **13.** Walk one block west and turn left onto Stuart Street. The Queen Anne Taylor-Hatfield-Sutherland house is at 316–18. In the best Queen Anne fashion, it has a three-story tower with pyramid roof, numerous bay windows, decorated gables, and a wide front veranda. **14.** On the west side of the street is 229 Stuart, the Bartlett-Upjohn house. The complex house with large central tower has just been renovated. **15.** Isaiah Flagg's house at 305 Stuart is Second Empire style. Of particular interest are the shingle siding and the elaborate roof brackets. **16.** Another Second Empire house is 321 Stuart, the Davidson-McKee house, erected in 1867. This stylish house with its twin side porches has been carefully restored. **17.** At the west end of Kalamazoo is 331 Douglas, the elegant James A. Kent house built in 1865. The pagoda roof line and the window hoods make this a unique Italianate house. **18.** Retrace your steps eastward along Kalamazoo Street. Turn left, or north, at Stuart to 405, the James Balch house, built in 1889. **19.** The Charles E. Stuart Italianate house at 427 Stuart Avenue was built between 1854 and 1858. This simple but elegant house does not depend upon exterior design but on its lines for distinction. A large cupola graces its roof. **20.** On the east side of the street is 436 Stuart, the George Rickman house. The house has a decorated tower and a gable. **21.** The Queen Anne French-Allen house at 418 Stuart was built in 1895. It has a wide front porch, corner tower, and bay window. **22.** At 409 Woodward Avenue, one block east, is the Pond-Upjohn house. Built in 1882, it sports a porch with a decorated pediment and bay window. **23.** Go north to Elmwood Street and turn right, or east, to 832. This early Greek Revival house was probably built in the 1830s or 1840s and moved to this site in the 1870s. The exterior, including the portico and the grilles over the eyebrow windows, appears to be original. **24.** Return to Kalamazoo Avenue and look at 808, the Queen Anne Charles C. Capen house. Built in 1885, the house has a myraid of details, including a two-story entrance, a variety of wood surfaces, and prominent white horizontal and vertical banding. **25.** At the northwest corner of Elm and Kalamazoo is the J.J. Griffith house, built in 1870. It is mainly Italianate with a Second Empire mansard roof on its tower.

Festivals, Tours, and Other Places of Interest

In July there is a historic-homes tour including interiors as well as exteriors. For information contact Jean Bright, 436 Stuart Avenue, Kalamazoo, MI 49007, 616–344–0958, or the Kalamazoo Public Museum, 3155 Rose Street, Kalamazoo, MI 49007, 616–345–7092.

Historical Information

Kalamazoo Historical Commission, 241 West South Street, Kalamazoo, MI 49007. Kalamazoo Commission for Historic Preservation, 241 West South Street, Kalamazoo, MI 49007. Kalamazoo County Historical Society, 616–345–7092. Stuart Area Restoration Association, 616–344–7432. The Vine Neighborhood Association, 616–349–4517. City of Kalamazoo, Office of Public Services, 241 West South Street, Kalamazoo, MI 49007, 616–385–8026. Willis F. Dunbar, *Kalamazoo and How It Grew*, Western Michigan University

Press, 1959. Brendan Henehan, Gary Ciadella, and Jean Stevens, *Walking Through Time: A Pictorial Guide to Kalamazoo*, Kalamazoo Historical Commission, 1981. Peter Schmitt and Balthazar Korab, *Kalamazoo: Nineteenth Century Homes in a Midwestern Village*, Kalamazoo City Historical Commission, 1976. Kalamazoo County Chamber of Commerce, 128 North Kalamazoo Mall, Kalamazoo, MI 49007, 616–381–4003.

Lodging

Hall House, 106 Thompson, 616–343–2500.

Howard Johnson's Motor Lodge, 1900 East Kilgore Road, 616–382–2303.

Kalamazoo Center Hilton Inn, 100 West Michigan Avenue, 616–381–2130.

Kalamazoo House, 447 West South Street, 616–343–5426.

Kalamazoo Travelodge, 1211 South Westnedge, 616–381–5000.

Knights Inn, 3704 Van Rick Drive, 616–344–9255.

La Quinta Motor Inn, 3750 Easy, 616–388–3551.

Stuart Avenue Inn, Bill and Andy Casteel, 405 Stuart Avenue, 616–342–0230.

Restaurants

Carlos Murphy's Cafe, 5650 West Main, 616–343–0330.

Chaps on Main, 105 East Michigan Avenue, 616–343–3922.

Dimitri's, 116 Portage Road, 616–381–2700.

Dionysis, 141 East Michigan Avenue, 616–343–7474.

Dragon Inn, 232 South Burdick, 616–345–2716.

Flame Restaurant, 224 West Michigan, 616–349–8216.

Gilmore's Greenhouse Buffet, 143 South Kalamazoo Mall, 616–345–3541.

Greenery Coffee Shop, 100 West Michigan, 616–381–2130.

Jacobson's, 359 South Kalamazoo Mall, 616–349–6661.

Le Metropol, 100 West Michigan, 616–381–2130.

T.E. Murch's Cafe Bakery and Country Market, 100 West Michigan Avenue, 616–382–4117.

Oakley's Restaurant, 161 East Michigan, 616–349–6436.

University Cafeteria, Western Michigan University, 616–383–0001.

Waldo's Campus Tavern, 1408 West Michigan Avenue, 616–349–8674.

Glossary

Architectural Styles

Art Deco, 1925–1940
Art Deco buildings have a vertical, linear, hard-edged quality. The facades are frequently ornamented by geometric relief around the doors and windows.

Bungalow, 1890–1940
A Bungalow is usually a one- or one-and-one-half-story house made of shingles or stucco, with a sloping roof.

Chicago School, late nineteenth and early twentieth century
This American style took advantage of engineering innovations. Buildings tend to be taller and also to have larger and more windows. Two new window types were developed: the bay, which marched up the facade; and the Chicago window, which was a large fixed pane flanked by two smaller casements. Both let in more light and air.

Federal, 1780–1820
This is a simple, geometrical style derived from England; it features smooth brick or clapboard facades and large windows, including fanlights and flanking entrance side lights. It was used for both residential and commercial buildings.

French Second Empire, 1860–1890
This style was imported from Napoleon III's Parisian public works, which included the Paris Opera and the Louvre's annex. Its primary feature is a roof with two slopes, frequently punctuated by ornately decorated dormer windows and a projecting central pavilion that extends above the roof. The lower floors usually have hooded windows resembling the Italianate style. Both commercial and residential structures were built in this style.

Georgian, 1700–1776
This American adaptation of the popular British style is characterized by symmetry, geometric proportions, hipped roofs, sash win-

dows, and axial entrances. Although its use generally ended with the American Revolution, it was revived in the last decade of the nineteenth and the first decade of the twentieth century. The midwestern buildings date from that period, when it was used for residential, commercial, and public buildings.

Gothic Revival, 1830–1860

A European transplant, this style was adapted for both cottages and mansions, public buildings and churches. Cottages and houses had steeply pitched roofs frequently decorated with bargeboard or carpenter's lace, pointed and hooded windows, and intricately decorated porches. The castle mansion, made of stone, had a large carriage entry portico, battlements, towers, and a variety of windows, some of which were stained glass. Public buildings ranged from the castle to the more restrained church buildings. All featured pointed windows; churches had towers and in some instances flying buttresses.

Greek Revival, 1820–1860

An adaptation of the classic Greek temple, this style was used both for public buildings and houses. In the former the colossal columned portico and pediment are prominent; in the latter the columns are usually one story high, supporting a simple cornice. Rectangular glass transoms and side lights surround the front entrance door.

Italianate, 1840–1880

This style was widely used for both residential and commercial buildings. The houses are two- or three-story and the commercial buildings reach to four. The dominant features are a flat to gently sloping roof with a large overhang supported by heavy brackets and hooded windows. Houses feature a prominent entrance porch or a wide veranda across the front of the building.

Neoclassic, 1900–1920

The style was principally used for massive public buildings such as railway stations and government offices. Its facade was supported by colossal Greek columns, pedimented porticoes, and parapets. When used for houses, the proportions were more restrained, with columns supporting a pedimented porch. Such residences are usually described as Greek, Roman, or Classical Revival.

Prairie, 1900–1920

This purely American style was the creation of Chicago architect Frank Lloyd Wright. Inspired by the midwestern prairies, it usually features a central portion higher than the flanking wings, but both have gently sloping roofs with generous overhang which gives the building the appearance of hugging the ground. The terraces, balconies, and windows carry out the horizontal line; the windows may go around corners and have delicate metal tracery. Most structures in this style were houses, but there are some commercial examples.

Queen Anne, 1880–1900

This exuberant display of a variety of architectural forms was most popular in the late nineteenth century. Any combination was possible, and many were employed. A typical house included not only a variety of materials such as stone, brick, and various shingle types but also a variety of structural extras such as towers, turrets, pavilions, porches, balconies, bay windows, large verandas, and porte-cocheres. Numerous window styles and materials such as stained and beveled glass were used. This style was usually confined to houses and hotels, but in a very restrained version it is seen on the second story of commercial buildings in the form of bay windows, turrets, and balconies.

Revivals, 1910–1930

In the period just before World War I and afterward there was a movement to revive earlier styles, such as Georgian and Colonial, and also to introduce old styles that were not much represented in American architecture. The exotic Egyptian, the massive rough-hewn Tudor, and a Spanish form known as Mediterranean with balconies, courtyards, and tile roofs, are examples of this period.

Richardsonian Romanesque, 1870–1900

Uniquely American and a version of the Romanesque, this style relies on mass and volume of rough stone instead of decorative embellishments. One of its features was the heavily arched and recessed entry. It was mainly used for public buildings.

Stick Style or Eastlake, 1870–1890

Frequently found in conjunction with Queen Anne, this style emphasizes intricate woodwork in porches and railings as well as balustrades and pediments. The fancy ornaments include brackets and scrolls, spindles, and lacework. Charles Locke Eastlake, a late nineteenth-century British interior designer, invented this decorative style in revolt against the predominant Gothic Revival style.

Architectural Terms

Balustrade, or baluster: a railing, found in a number of architectural styles.

Bargeboard: a board, usually ornately carved, attached to the edges of a pitched roof, sometimes referred to as carpenter's lace, found on Gothic Revival and Queen Anne buildings.

Belvedere: same as cupola, below.

Bracket: a support for the eaves, frequently decorated, a distinctive feature of the Italianate or Italian-villa style.

Columns
  Corinthian: a slender column with a highly decorated top, or capital, usually of stylized leaves.
  Doric: the simplest of the classic columns, with a heavy fluted shaft and a saucer-shaped capital, or top.
  Ionic: a classic column with two opposing scroll-like ornaments on the capital, or top.

Corbel: a supporting projection of wood or stone, sometimes decorated, found on Greek Revival and Classical Revival buildings.

Cornice: an ornamental molding projecting from the top of a building, seen on Greek Revival and Classical Revival buildings.

Cupola: a small-roofed, open or closed structure atop a roof, found on Italianate and Queen Anne houses.

Dentil: a series of small rectangular blocks arranged like a row of teeth along a cornice, found on Greek Revival and Classical Revival buildings.

Eaves: the projecting overhang on the roof's edge, features of the Italianate and Prairie styles.

Fanlight: a semicircular or fan-shaped window with radiating tracery, found over a door, window, or alone in a gable on Federal, Greek Revival, and Queen Anne houses.

Fish-scale shingles: a pattern of rounded shingles that gives the appearance of fish scales, often found on Queen Anne houses.

Frieze: an ornamented strip or band frequently found underneath the cornice or on a wall, common in Second Empire, Classical Revival, and Queen Anne houses.

Gable: a triangular area under a double-pitched roof, sometimes highly decorated, particularly on Queen Anne-style buildings.

Lintel: a horizontal supporting piece above a window or door; in Federal and Greek Revival styles it was often made of limestone and in later styles such as Italianate it might be carved.

Mullion: a vertical or horizontal strip between the panes of a window, which can be decorated; seen in Gothic and Romanesque Revival buildings.

Parapet: a solid railing or wall along the edge of a balcony or roof; this detail is found on Gothic Revival and Queen Anne-style buildings.

Pavilion: a projecting section of a building or a free-standing, open, ornamental, covered garden structure.

Pediment: a triangular gable, sometimes ornamented, over a porch, door, or window of a Classical-style building such as Greek Revival or the later Neoclassical.

Pilaster: a Classical column attached to the facade, which is not a bearing pier but only decorative; found on some Neoclassical and Italianate buildings.

Porte-Cochere: a covered entrance porch into which vehicles can be driven so passengers are sheltered from the elements; popular on late nineteenth- and early twentieth-century large houses.

Quoins: stone or brick facing used to outline the corners of a building, used on Italianate buildings.

Roofs
   Gambrel: each side has two different slopes, the lower being the steeper, the roof is cut in two vertical planes on each side; seen on Dutch Colonial Revival houses.
   Hipped: a four-sided roof, each two sides of the same pitch, found in numerous styles.
   Mansard: the characteristic French Second Empire roof, with two similar slopes on all four sides; dormer windows usually project from it.

Root cellar: a structure half below and half above ground, used to store root vegetables so that they would not freeze during the winter.

Row houses: houses with common side walls, prominent in cities and towns dating from the mid-eighteenth century; the earliest are Federal in style, but also include later versions in Italianate and Queen Anne.

Spindle: a milled piece of wood used for railings and porch trim, extensively used in the Eastlake or Stick style.

Terracotta: a brownish-orange unglazed earthenware used in the early twentieth century for architectural decorations.

Tracery: the ornamental metalwork in windows, used in Roman and Gothic Revival as well as in the Queen Anne and Prairie styles.

Transom: a rectangular window above a door or large window, popular in Greek Revival entrances.

Turret: a slender tower, often for decorative purposes only, found on Gothic Revival public buildings and Queen Anne houses.

Veranda: a porch, frequently used in Italianate and Queen Anne houses.

Windows

Bay: usually a projecting three-sided large window but can be any large window in the parlor or front room.

Bullseye: a round window that usually does not open and is used for light; seen on some Queen Anne and Classical buildings.

Dormer: a vertical window projecting from a sloping roof, common to many styles.

Eyebrow: small narrow window, frequently underneath the eaves and mainly for attic ventilation in Greek Revival and Italianate structures.

Oriel: a semicircular projecting window, sometimes highly decorated, found on Gothic Revival buildings.

Palladian: a three-part window with the middle arched and two rectangular side sections, also known as a Venetian window; popular in eighteenth-century Georgian houses and used in American homes and churches, particularly by admirers of British architect James Gibbs.

Romanesque: arched window.

Wheel: divided by spokes like a wheel; sometimes found on churches and usually in stained glass.

Authors' Note

We have utilized many more sources in this book than we have been able to list. We have not quoted from these sources but have paraphrased some of the information. We would like especially to acknowledge our debt to the National Register of Historic Places under the National Park Service for the use of the information that they collect and distribute.